Dedicated to
Fred 'The Cat' Silvester,
who caught his fair
share in his time

1926 - 2002

The authors

John Silvester has been a crime reporter
in Melbourne since 1978. He worked for
The Sunday Times 'Insight' team in
London in 1990, and has co-authored
several crime books, including the
best-seller *Underbelly*. He is currently
senior crime writer for *The Age*.

Andrew Rule has been a journalist
since 1975 and has worked in
newspapers, television and radio.
He wrote *Cuckoo*, the true story of the
notorious 'Mr Stinky' case, and has
edited and published several other books,
including the original *Underbelly*. He is
a feature writer for *The Age*.

They won the prestigious Ned Kelly
Award for True Crime writing for
Underbelly 3.

TOUGH

101 Australian Gangsters

A Crime Companion
by John Silvester & Andrew Rule

Published in Australia by
Floradale Productions Pty Ltd and Sly Ink Pty Ltd
November 2002
Reprinted March 2003
Reprinted November 2003
Reprinted June 2004
Reprinted August 2005

Distributed wholesale by
Gary Allen Pty Ltd,
9 Cooper Street,
Smithfield, NSW
Telephone 02-9725 2933

Tough
101 Australian Gangsters
A Crime Companion

ISBN – 0957912129

Cover design, typesetting and layout
by Write Impression Publishing

TOUGH:

hardened, incorrigible ...

vigorous, severe, violent ...

rough, disorderly, rowdyish

– Macquarie
Dictionary

- C O N F I D E N T I A L -

(1)

CIB   HOMICIDE   SQUAD.
12th November 1979.

<u>Particulars as known regarding the death of
Raymond Patrick BENNETT @ CHUCK who was shot
at the City Magistrate's Court on 12th Nov. 1979.</u>

(This document typed at 3pm on 12/11/79)

<u>BRIEF PARTICULARS</u> : The deceased appeared before the Melbourne
Magistrate's Court at 10am on Monday, 12th November 1979 where
he was facing committal proceedings on two counts of armed
robbery.   His case was referred from the main court to the
10th Court which is on the first floor. Whilst being escorted
to this court at about 10.20am he was confronted by an armed
man who fired three shots at him. The deceased, after receiving
a gunshot wound to his chest and hand ran down a flight of stairs
into the courtyard where he collapsed into the arms of two
uniformed policemen. He was assisted to a corridor which is
near the entrance to the main court where he received medical
treatment before being transferred by ambulance to St Vincents
Hospital where he died about an hour later.

<u>ESCORTING MEMBERS</u> : Senior Detective Peter John MUGAVIN 17772
                     Senior Detective Philip Joseph GLARE 17101.
                     Both members are from the Consorting Squad.
                     MUGAVIN was holding deceased when he was
shot. GLARE was in the immediate vicinity. Both these members
made an effort to intercept the offender who threatened them with
a .38 revolver.

<u>OFFENDER</u> :   Escaped immediately after the shooting by
going down a back stairway which leads through the Magistrate's
Car Park, from where he entered the rear of the Police Garage
which houses some police vehicles. A galvinised iron sheet had

(2)

Contents

Contents

CHAPTER 1

The Dirty Dozen

Raymond William 'Gunner' Kelly

'The New South Wales Police Force (is) one of the finest in the world.' – Former NSW Premier Neville 'Nifty' Wran.

NEW South Wales detectives have always been amongst the best in the business – but the problem was that many of them were in the business for themselves.

A culture grew where corruption was ignored, tolerated and, ultimately, encouraged. Some detectives refused to apply for promotion outside the crime department. They couldn't afford the pay cut if they moved and lost their stake of the bribery fund.

So-called 'honest' police were discouraged from joining the crime department. Applicants were grilled as to whether they would 'verbal', 'load' and 'brick' suspects. If they answered 'no' they were rejected as boy scouts. Some corrupt detectives were brave, cunning and ruthless and good at getting results fast. They could gather – or plant – evidence to convict suspects. They were at their best during dangerous manhunts and would risk their lives to protect the public.

But at the same time, they saw nothing wrong in taking bribes – rationalising corruption by claiming they were actually controlling illegal networks that could never be stopped. And, besides, they thought, why shouldn't they get paid extra to make up for the dangerous work they did?

Abortionists paid, as did casino owners, SP bookmakers and sly-groggers. Police controlled the industries, ensuring smooth operations and minimising underworld violence. It was virtual franchising of crime.

Politicians, some of whom were also being paid, remained silent. Corrupt police are pliable. They won't create waves. Honest police are dangerous. The press was too busy chasing today's bread and butter cops and robbers crime stories to worry about exposing serious corruption. To attack police was to risk losing contacts and stories. The expression 'Don't shit in your own nest' covered crime reporters' general reluctance to investigate police behaviour.

Corruption was not peculiar to NSW. Police in Victoria were on the take as well. There was a time when sergeants at all major suburban stations would leave their office every Saturday afternoon to collect from SP bookmakers.

In the 1950s the newly appointed Chief Commissioner, Major General Selwyn Porter – an outsider who had not grown up in the police culture – set up a small squad of seven police, called the special duties gaming branch.

They would expose widespread corruption in the Post Master General's Department, the police force and other government agencies. The squad was led by a senior detective plucked from the obscurity of the Richmond station. His name was Sinclair

Imrie Miller – but everyone knew him as Mick. One of his men, Fred Silvester, a former English bobby with an interest in fishing and a flair for breaking into SP strongholds, found the national list of SP bookmakers held by a Melbourne betting odds agent.

Porter sent him to the NSW Commissioner Colin Delaney with a three-page report naming all Sydney's major illegal bookmakers. Delaney sat smoking as he read the basic preamble – then stopped when he saw the names, immediately buzzing for his senior men to attend a crisis conference.

Delaney appeared outraged and demanded action. It was a Friday and raids were planned for the next day. Silvester offered to attend but Delaney said he would be taken to observe activities at Randwick races.

But there were no raids. And all the identified phones were silent on race day. The massive illegal Sydney bookmaking ring had been tipped off and closed down for the day.

It was a lesson Silvester and Miller would never forget. Miller would become Chief Commissioner in Victoria and Silvester the head of the Australian Bureau of Criminal Intelligence. Both maintained a healthy distrust of NSW police.

Later, Victorian intelligence experts slipped into Sydney on an unauthorised operation to observe NSW Deputy Commissioner, Bill Allen, on his regular collection run. It ended with NSW police stealing their Victorian counterparts' expensive bugging devices. Nothing could be done because the Melbourne police had no right to conduct the operation.

Like their Sydney counterparts, Melbourne detectives were accepting bribes from abortionists in the 1960s and early 1970s. Three members of the homicide squad were jailed and after two judicial inquiries into the force during the 1970s, Miller was appointed Chief Commissioner. Victorian corruption was largely ignored by the mainstream media. Only journalists like Evan Whitton, then of *Truth*, was prepared to listen to whistle-blowers such as Dr Bertram Wainer.

While there was still corruption in Victoria there was a different culture in New South Wales. In Victoria, a detective who was thought to be dishonest was not trusted by his colleagues. In NSW any detective in the serious crime squads who would not take money was seen as dangerous and a potential loose cannon.

In the 1970s and 1980s, NSW was the 'green light' state. Corrupt police organised armed robberies, drug importations and murders. Major gangsters were given 'get out of jail free' cards. Some parked in police car parks. They drank together in illegal casinos. The coppers claimed they needed underworld contact. In reality they were business partners.

Police no longer turned a blind eye. They effectively ran the show. The were feral and in the 1980s they were so out of control they were alleged to have tried to kill one of their own, an undercover officer called Mick Drury, because he wouldn't take a bribe to throw a case.

They had become gangsters with badges. The three most notorious were Ray Kelly, Fred Krahe and Roger Rogerson.

Ray 'Gunner' Kelly was a great detective – when he wasn't working for the other side. He caught escapees Darcy Dugan and Ronald Ryan – the last man hanged in Australia – and the notorious gunman 'Chow' Hayes. And Kelly made sure the Sydney press was there to capture the moments.

Kelly was tall, well-dressed and well groomed. His nickname 'Gunner' came after he was involved in two shoot-outs, the first in 1932. He was on patrol on a pushbike when he saw three men in a suspected stolen car. They reversed over his bike and tried to run over the young policeman. He jumped on the running board and grabbed the wheel, crashing the car. As the gang tried to run him over again, he fired five shots, wounding two and killing the third. He was a hero.

Almost 21 years later he tried to stop another stolen car. This time he didn't take any chances. As he pulled up alongside, he fired, hitting and killing the driver.

Kelly knew the power of contacts. He had the best network of criminal informers in the country, was well known by politicians and courted by journalists.

He joined the police force in 1929, looking for security after the depression, and excitement after working on a cattle station. He was 23, older than most recruits and smarter than most of his superiors.

For years he could do no wrong ... at least publicly. He was alleged to have been heavily involved in the abortion rackets of the 1950s and early 1960s and to have run many of the corrupt syndicates controlled by NSW detectives.

Respected investigative author David Hickie, in his well-researched book, *The Prince and the Premier*, quoted a contemporary: 'When Askin got in, Kelly was running everything – every known racket of the period was worked by Kelly. He was an extraordinary combination of genius and evil – a brilliant detective, but he always reminded me of a snake, a python.'

Hickie quoted an unnamed detective as saying, 'Kelly was fearless and genuinely liked by many of his fellow officers but he was also known as a crook.'

One man who worked with Kelly told the authors, 'He was a natural leader of men, brave and led from the front. He would brief men and then asked if they knew their job; if they didn't he would tear strips off them.'

'The men always looked to Kelly, even if there were higher-ranking officers in charge.' Because Kelly was a constant source of stories the media would never bite the hand that fed it scoops. The press watchdog rolled over to have its belly tickled in exchange for tidbits from 'Gunner'.

Kelly was involved in most major manhunts in NSW for 20 years. He was a fitness fanatic as well as being tough, and had tremendous stamina. According to Hickie, Kelly was known as 'Headline' by the more cynical journalists of his time. In 1966, nearly 900 people paid £5 a head to attend Kelly's retirement dinner at the Chevron Hotel.

Guest included politicians, gangsters, police and journalists. Percy Galea, who ran Sydney's illegal gambling network and had paid politicians and police for years, was there. Kelly referred to him on the night as 'my old mate'.

Speeches were to be kept to a minimum. Only the Premier, Sir Robert Askin, and the guest of honour were due to speak. Askin had every reason to thank Kelly. He had helped the career politician become a very wealthy man. But right to the end the compliant press competed for Kelly's attention.

Noel Leighton-Bailey, a veteran crime reporter from the Sydney *Sun*, grabbed the microphone and tried to give a speech. His rival of 25 years, 'Bondi Bill' Jenkins, was outraged and took to the stage. In his biography, *As Crime Goes By*, Jenkins, who described Kelly 'as a good contact of mine,' attacked his long-time rival.

' "Listen you bastard," I roared, "you don't speak for me." '

'Bailey and I shaped up. Detectives and other guests who knew how we felt towards one another began shouting encouragement to the one they favoured.

'I am proud to have known Fred Krahe and Ray Kelly – they were tough men for tough times.'

Frederick Claude 'Froggy' Krahe

FREDDIE Krahe was a Sydney police legend, and that says it all. Only a certain calibre of man got talked about in the New South Wales CIB, and Freddie was one.

He was a crook – perhaps a brave one, but a crook nonetheless. Krahe became one of Australia's best-known detectives, largely because competitive and compliant Sydney crime reporters of the past spared no adjectives in praising the man they should have exposed.

'Bondi' Bill Jenkins, long-serving *Mirror* crime reporter, gushed: 'Two of my best police contacts, whom I gladly call called friends, were detectives who, in later years, especially after their deaths, undeservedly became infamous as "rogue coppers". They were Ray 'Gunner' Kelly and Fred Krahe – the greatest detectives I met in my long and personal association with the CIB. The underworld hated Fred Krahe. He was feared and despised, but I found him to be a most effective and fearless detective …

'Fred Krahe was accused of every dastardly deed from murder to taking bribes. This was not the Fred Krahe I knew for so many years. He was a big, rugged-faced man – a terrific drinker who always wore a hat. When his face became stern, it was almost frightening and he had a very intense manner whenever he'd tell you anything.

'I knew Krahe as a most capable and diligent detective.'

But an investigative journalist from a younger generation, David Hickie, described Krahe as 'King of the crooked police during the Askin era, he organised the abortion rackets, armed hold-ups, the framing of criminals and bribery payments among prostitutes and police and he maintained a reputation feared in the Sydney underworld'.

A policeman who watched him first hand told the authors, 'Freddie Krahe was a great strategist, a brilliant man and totally corrupt. He was a heavy drinker, I saw him drunk at 5.30 in the morning and then give perfect evidence at 9.30 in the witness box. He could put together an airtight brief. They were all frightened of him.'

In the 1960s, a well-known conman was charged in Melbourne with forgery, serious fraud and car theft. The man was also wanted over serious charges in Sydney and Fred 'Froggy' Krahe flew to Melbourne to discuss the case.

Krahe offered the Melbourne detective a 'sling' to give weak evidence in the case. When the offer was refused, he simply shrugged his massive shoulders and said 'No skin off my nose', then headed home. It said much for Krahe's influence that he felt he could offer a bribe with impunity in another state to a policeman he did not know.

While he could not nobble the case in Melbourne, in Sydney the fix was in. The NSW charges against the man were dropped without explanation. Krahe almost certainly told the offender he had also fixed the Melbourne matter and was paid accordingly.

During the Melbourne trial the defence called the investigating officer, expecting him to give corrupt evidence. The detective was asked, 'Is it not true that you would not expect the defendant to offend again?'

The detective unloaded, telling the court the man was a career conman and thief who had ruined lives through his dishonesty. He was found guilty, but, surprisingly, given a suspended sentence. Kelly and Krahe backed another corrupt officer, Don Ferguson, to be their man in the senior ranks of the CIB. As long as he was there, the two would be protected.

But, in 1970, Ferguson started to unravel. He wanted to move to another senior position in the force. Kelly and Krahe, who were not used to hearing the word 'No', went to visit their man. He was allegedly told, sternly, to pull his head in. He went one step further and put a bullet in it: a week after the meeting he shot himself in the head and died. Hickie reported Krahe as saying, 'The stupid bastard, he didn't have to do it.'

One of the prostitutes who regularly paid Krahe and his syndicate was Shirley Briffman. She paid $100 a week to be protected from underworld standover men and to be free of police prosecutions. When she was charged in 1971 with employing a 14-year-old prostitute she felt betrayed and swore out statements making serious allegations against 34 police.

She alleged Krahe had destroyed police files, organised robberies and sent police to false jobs to distract them from crimes about to be committed.

Briffman fled from Sydney but she didn't go far enough. She was found dead in a Brisbane flat in 1972. One strong rumour was that the overdose she suffered was courtesy of drugs pumped down a rubber tube into her throat. The tube was supposed to have been held by Freddie Krahe.

Even in Sydney, where allegations of corruption were usually met with silence, Krahe had been seen to go too far. Shortly after Briffman's death he was found medically unfit with thrombosis of the leg.

He worked for a Sydney newspaper – finally officially placed on the pay-roll after years of 'favours' – before becoming a private investigator employed by a property developer planning to destroy historic houses in the Kings Cross region.

One of the main opponents to the proposals was Juanita Neilsen, who produced a local newspaper called *Now*.

Neilsen went missing on July 4, 1975. Her body has never been found.

Krahe was employed by the sinister Nugan Hand Bank and was later charged with conspiracy to defraud the organisation. He was acquitted and died in 1981 from cirrhosis of the liver. According to Bill Jenkins, his long-time contact and loyal friend, Krahe died 'a broken man'.

Roger Caleb Rogerson

HE could be Australia's best-known policeman. He was a hero – dashing and brave – yet in the end he was found to be just another crook.

Roger Caleb Rogerson, son of a British dock worker, joined the NSW police force as a cadet in 1958. From early in his career he was identified as having the qualities to become an elite investigator.

For decades the NSW police force promoted a star system where top investigators ended up dealing with high-profile cases. The competitive media quickly learned the police who were fast-tracked to the 'A' team – detectives like the big-drinking Fred 'Froggy' Krahe and quick-shooting Ray 'Gunner' Kelly, who made his namesake, Ned, look like a choirboy when it came to crime.

NSW politicians, who have rarely understood the idea of an independent police force, also liked to associate with hard detectives – hoping the tough law and order image would reflect favourably with voters.

This led to an unholy co-operative of senior police wanting results, reporters wanting headlines and politicians wanting votes, who encouraged the 'stars' without demanding account-ability. That was the environment in which Rogerson arrived and thrived.

He was ruthless but no brainless thug and was a charismatic

leader, often taking responsibility above his rank. A former colleague told the authors he was a proficient touch typist, competent shorthand writer, excellent joke teller and good piano player. And a good learner. 'He went under the wing of Freddie Krahe and learnt all the tricks from him,' he said.

'He was never controlled and was able to run his own race. Maybe if someone pulled him up early in his career it would have been different. But there was no-one to pull him up. They were all corrupt.'

Rogerson was on first-name terms with the worst criminals in Australia. He drank with standover men and killers like Neddy Smith and Chris Flannery. He said he cultivated them to gather information. Some thought he was too close, but no-one would express any misgivings. Roger got results and few were prepared to question his methods.

One of his first mentors was the colourful Superintendent Don Ferguson. In February, 1970, Ferguson was found shot dead in the police headquarters toilets. The official version was suicide although there were always stories his death was related to pressure over corruption.

Rogerson moved to the armed hold-up squad in 1974. Two years later, he was on duty when police shot dead a bank robber and murderer called Philip Western at Avoca Beach.

In 1977, Rogerson shot dead a man trying to hold up a bank courier carrying $60,000. In August, 1979, he was present at Rose Bay when police shot dead armed robber Gordon Thomas.

Rogerson won the Peter Mitchell Award for the most outstanding police performance of 1980.

The following year Rogerson's reputation began to be tarnished. He was again involved in a fatal shooting, but this one was always dogged by controversy.

It happened in June that year. He was with three other police who went to arrest a known heroin dealer, Warren Lanfranchi. Lanfranchi's girlfriend, Sallie-Anne Huckstepp, said he was unarmed and carrying $10,000 when he left to meet Rogerson. The money was never found.

According to the police version of events Lanfranchi drew a gun and Rogerson had no choice but to fire two shots – one fatal. Rogerson would later say he fired in quick sequence but two women who heard the shots estimated the gap was around 10 seconds.

Police said Lanfranchi pointed a gun at Rogerson. The weapon was almost 90 years old and defective. Why an experienced criminal such as Lanfranchi would carry such a useless weapon, let alone point it at a man he knew had killed before, has never been explained.

A coroner's jury found that Rogerson shot Lanfranchi while endeavouring to make an arrest, but declined to find it was in self-defence or in the course of his duty. It was the first time there were doubts about Rogerson – at least publicly.

Huckstepp would lobby for years over the death of her boyfriend, claiming it was murder. She was found dead in a lake at Centennial Park, Sydney, in February, 1986. She had been strangled and held underwater in the shallows.

In September, 1983, according to undercover policeman Mick Drury, Rogerson approached him with a bribe over a Melbourne drug case. Drury declined the offer. In June, 1984, Drury was shot and almost killed as he stood in the kitchen of his home. He was marked for death because he had not taken the bribe. It was repeatedly claimed in a series of court cases that Rogerson was present when Christopher Dale Flannery, a known hitman, accepted the contract to murder Drury.

The drug dealer who would later admit he offered the bribe, Alan Williams, gave evidence that Rogerson was paid 'most' of the $50,000 payment for the hit. It was a defining moment. Rogerson was a hero to the NSW crime department and he was given a standing ovation at a police dinner – even after he was implicated in the murder plot.

But his power base was eroding. Even the NSW police force could not accept a man alleged to have tried to kill a colleague for cash.

On the orders of new Commissioner, John Avery, Rogerson was made the top target by anti-corruption police and in November, 1994, he was transferred back into uniform.

In mid-1985 he was photographed closing bank accounts and receiving cheques totalling $111,116.68. Not bad savings on a copper's wage in the 1980s. Police later found that Rogerson, a doctor called Nick Paltos and businessman Maurie Nowytarger had drawn up a fake contract to justify the money. The cover story was that the money was from the sale of a vintage Bentley. It was to be the vital crack in Rogerson's protective shield.

While police and Royal Commissions would never nail Rogerson over attempting to bribe and then kill Drury, he was to be snared over the bank money.

In September, 1987, Rogerson was charged with conspiracy to pervert the course of justice.

The prosecution said the men created a fake story to defeat the police inquiry into the accounts, by claiming $60,000 came from the Bentley sale and the rest from gambling wins. The prosecution said the money came from illegal sources, possibly drug dealing by Rogerson.

At their trial, a protected witness, known as 'Miss X' said she gave Rogerson a bag containing 'bundles of money' at Sydney Airport in exchange for a bag containing about one kilogram of white powder.

She said the transaction was on behalf of the notorious Melbourne gangster Dennis Allen.

Ironically, the same witness had not been used in a Melbourne police corruption case because her statements could not be corroborated. But in Sydney she was exactly what was needed.

Rogerson was found guilty and sentenced to a maximum of eight years and a minimum of six; Nowytarger to six years with a minimum of four; Paltos was given a minimum of 2½ years in addition to the cannabis sentence he was already serving.

But Rogerson was never one to go quietly.

He was released in December, 1990, after the Court of Criminal Appeal quashed the convictions – but the Crown then appealed to the High Court.

In 1992, the High Court overturned the acquittals for Rogerson and Paltos and sent the case back to the Appeal Court. The court upheld the original convictions although Rogerson's sentence was dropped to a minimum of three years and nine months.

Before being sent back to jail Rogerson made a statement that unwittingly reflected how he helped betray law and order in NSW. 'I have never had any faith in the justice system and this is a good example of it.'

James William 'Bill' Duff

BILLY Duff was good company. As a homicide squad detective he was known for his contacts on both sides of the law.

Duff regularly drank with Sydney crime boss Lennie McPherson and Melbourne-born hitman Christopher Dale Flannery. He said he used them to gather information but many suspected it was a two-way street.

Duff joined the police force in 1965 and made his name in the homicide squad. His best friend was police hero-turned-crook Roger Rogerson.

Duff was one of the 'old school' (read crooked) detectives. But he was clever and considered good at his job. He solved murders and his superiors weren't prepared to ask too many questions because they were frightened of the answers.

When he was seen socialising with gangsters, it was always written off as an intelligence gathering exercise.

In November, 1985, the Police Tribunal was told that Duff had conspired to import heroin from New Guinea.

In his book, *Can of Worms*, journalist Evan Whitton reports that a serving policeman from the NSW Bureau of Criminal Intelligence gave damning evidence at the tribunal against Duff.

Detective Sergeant John McNamara testified Duff had approached him and said: 'Peter Johnstone (is) getting ready to fly some smack down from New Guinea shortly ... Roger and I have worked it out. If we don't do it, some other c... will ... The first flight ... he is only going to bring down one kilo ... The next one after that will be eight and the third will be 40. The one thing we want to cover is whether BCI (Bureau of Criminal Intelligence) is doing anything on Johnstone. If you hear anything on your side, it would be worth five grand to let us know.'

'Neddy (Smith) is going to get rid of all the gear ... I've invested $15,000 in this caper. If it comes off, we'll all be walking round with pocketfuls of money. I won't forget you. There will be a big drink (bribe) in it for you.'

Duff was sacked the following year although he was not criminally charged with the offence.

He became a publican but, without the protection of the badge he was just another crook. He was a dinosaur who couldn't see the Ice Age was coming. He was eventually jailed in 1997 for heroin trafficking. He was pulled over by police in January, 1994, after he was seen leaving a panel-beating shop known to be the front for a suspected drug trafficker.

They found $17,380 in cash and 57 grams of top quality rock heroin. The drugs were worth $40,000.

Duff tried to cut a deal by giving evidence to the NSW Crime Commission. But the master deal-maker had nothing left to offer. He was sentenced to 18 months jail.

Judge Hosking said Duff was an intelligent man who had turned to crime.

'It is a matter of grave concern that a person who was once an elite detective and a respected member of the community could so spectacularly fall from grace – but that is what happened here.'

Terence Murray Lewis

TERENCE Murray Lewis was the highest-ranking police officer in Australia to do jail time – even though he always maintained he was innocent. No-one believed him.

Lewis was born at Ipswich in 1928, and was only 12 when he started work as a shop assistant at Pikes' Menswear in Brisbane. It was good practice for fitting up people when he joined the police force eight years later.

He was soon promoted to work as a detective in the consorting squad, and later the company squad, from 1950 to 1963.

In 1959, Lewis and another officer, Glen Patrick Hallahan, were awarded the George Medal for Bravery for arresting an armed German seaman.

In 1963, Lewis was promoted to officer in charge of the Juvenile Aid Bureau and in 1968 he won a Churchill

Fellowship to study international police recruiting and training. Lewis had been identified as an officer likely to make a mark. He was intelligent, had experience at the sharp end of policing and, more importantly for politicians – was seen as the type who would 'play the game'. A man with flexible principles who would never rock the boat as long as he had a first-class ticket.

But when an outsider, Ray Whitrod, was appointed as a commissioner Lewis's career stalled. The scrupulously honest Whitrod didn't like Lewis's reputation. He suspected that if Lewis made a mark, it would be a black one.

In 1973, Whitrod posted Lewis to Charleville in the state's central west. It was the furthest post the commissioner could find to keep his suspect officer from his Brisbane network. He gave only one reason for moving the influential Lewis – it was 'for the good of the force'.

From his country posting Lewis started to lobby – not senior police, but politicians. It was to be a career-long trait to ignore the separation of power and seek political support by becoming a compliant cop.

Senior politicians hate independent police who can create controversies by standing up for what is right.

Former Queensland Premier Sir Joh Bjelke-Petersen grew fond of the yes man in the blue uniform after their first meeting at the Charleville airstrip in May, 1976.

The cunning young inspector grabbed his moment. He told the Premier how he could revolutionise the Queensland Police if given the opportunity. With typical cunning he slipped into conversation that Whitrod was an ally of Bjelke-Petersen's biggest enemy – Gough Whitlam.

Bjelke-Petersen promoted Lewis over 122 equal or senior officers to the plum job of assistant commissioner.

It made the job as commissioner untenable for the honest Whitrod. He resigned in disgust and Lewis slipped into his job on November 22, 1976. He was 48. As police commissioner, Lewis became part of Bjelke-Petersen's 'kitchen cabinet'. Fellow commissioners around Australia saw him as a stooge and a joke. What they didn't know was that this stooge was running the Joke.

His brother commissioners saw him as a buffoon but that didn't stop them voting him in as the chairman overseeing the national Australian Bureau of Criminal Intelligence – not once, but twice. This meant he had access to all the information on national crime targets and put him in an ideal position to offer protection.

Lewis and several other police were accused of receiving corrupt payments for protecting SP bookmakers, illegal casinos and prostitution. He was known as 'Bribe Shark', 'Big Daddy' and the 'Big Wheel' of police slings.

In 1982, the grateful Queensland Government decided to reward its pet policeman with a knighthood, but Buckingham Palace rejected the nomination.

In August, 1983, Lewis told 56 police at the Police Academy that Premier Bjelke-Petersen had offered 'invaluable support' to the police. He said: 'The people of Queensland and the police force owe the Premier a very deep gratitude. The free enterprise policy of the Bjelke-Petersen Government has been responsible for Queensland's tremendous growth.'

It was a disgraceful breach of protocol for a senior policeman effectively to enter party politics. Worse, his statement was made in the climate of a Queensland election campaign.

Four years later, the palace finally accepted the Queensland request and Lewis was knighted – a decision the Queen's advisers no doubt later regretted.

The claims of corruption continued and the government had

to act after exposure by journalists Phil Dickie in *The Courier-Mail* and Chris Masters on the ABC's *Four Corners*. Acting Premier Bill Gunn announced a commission of inquiry into corruption in Queensland. Lewis angrily denied corruption allegations. He was a dark and stormy knight.

The 18-month inquiry, headed by Brisbane lawyer Tony Fitzgerald, QC, exposed four government ministers, a Supreme Court judge and several influential police.

Lewis was sunk by his own hand. He kept meticulous diaries – a bad move for a crook. The diaries were a bizarre cocktail of official entries, references to his health, travel observations and codes for his corrupt payments.

His one-time mate and bagman, Jack Reginald Herbert, rolled over to the commission and said Lewis had received more than $600,000 in bribes. Herbert said that he once apologised when handing Lewis a smaller than expected bribe and the commissioner responded with a quote that was to become famous – 'Little fish are sweet'.

Sir Terence's diaries showed he was apparently one of the world's most astute punters. In a 10-month streak he placed bets on 135 horses for 42 wins and 92 placegetters, which meant that only one horse had let him down.

When a former assistant commissioner, Graeme Parker, admitted corruption in 1987, Lewis signed over his share of his mansion in the Brisbane suburb of Paddington to his wife. He knew it was the beginning of the end.

In 1990, Lewis sold his home for more than $600,000 to fund his defence. He moved into a unit. Later he would have to accept even smaller lodgings in jail. In August, 1991, he was convicted and jailed for 14 years on 15 counts of corruption. He received a tax bill of $1 million in 1992 and lost his knighthood and his $1 million superannuation. The Big Shark was finally hooked.

Colin James Creed

FOR years, Colin James Creed was Australia's most famous policeman – not because he was a hero, but because he was a crook.

He was known nationally as the 'Rogue Cop' – the man who used his police training to outwit his former colleagues. He was the gamekeeper turned poacher who knew the insider's tricks.

Creed was a detective who turned into a rapist and robber. He was Australia's most wanted man in the early 1980s. He avoided arrest for more than 20 months – despite being effectively caught by police three times.

Creed was the dux of his South Australian class when he was an 18-year-old police cadet, and seemed destined for a distinguished career. But there was always something about the heavy-set, intelligent and brooding Creed that made his colleagues suspicious. He enjoyed women's company, but then could turn nasty for no obvious reason.

Some fellow police found him threatening, but most found him self-obsessed and boring.

But he didn't lack courage. His police record shows he was commended for bravery when he took a pistol from an offender who had already fired at fellow officers.

The ugly side of Creed didn't start to reveal itself until 1974, when an Adelaide woman went to the Hindmarsh police station to report she had been raped at knife-point and then rolled up in a sheet.

She was horrified when she saw that the man who had attacked her was one of the police at the station. Creed had been to her house four months earlier to investigate a burglary.

He was charged with rape but was acquitted and senior police had no choice but to reinstate him to operational duties.

In May, 1981, Creed was a suspect for rape and armed robbery. He was interviewed and released while police waited for the result of forensic tests. This time he didn't stay to fight. He ran. He travelled through Queensland, NSW, Victoria, South Australia and Western Australia, pulling armed robberies in Melbourne, Sydney and Adelaide.

While on the run, Creed slipped back to his home and secretly cleaned out his liquor bar.

Even while a wanted man, Creed tried to follow police protocol. He took time out to write a formal letter of resignation to the South Australian Commissioner. It was accepted.

He was described as a master of disguises but his greatest asset was that he was a loner. There was no-one close enough to betray him.

He kept moving and refused to panic when he looked to be in impossible situations.

Twice in Melbourne he was stopped by police but released when they didn't recognise him as Australia's most wanted man. In late November, 1981, he was questioned by police at Flinders Street railway station after a report that Creed was seen in the area. He was interviewed but convinced police he wasn't their man.

Less than a month later, police found him sitting in a car, drinking a bottle of bourbon outside a block of flats in Coburg. This time he told police he was waiting for a married woman and although he did not have his driver's licence, he promised to produce it within 24 hours.

In January, 1982, he was questioned by armed robbery police for three hours about why he was passing dye-stained money in a Brisbane hotel. He said he was a public servant named Brian Peter Walters. They could not shake his story.

Creed was so relaxed and believable police did not take him

into custody even though his fingers were still covered with green from the bank security dye bomb. The next day they returned to the suspect's hotel room … but 'Brian Walters' was gone. A fingerprint check showed the suspect was Creed.

Police around the country became extremely Creed conscious. Even his wife, a South Australian police officer, was part of the hunt.

Police in Melbourne thought they were close when they followed a solid man with a similar moustache from a seedy Melbourne nightclub to *The Age* newspaper building long after midnight. It was only after closely observing the suspect's peculiar behaviour that they realised it was rogue crime reporter, Lindsay Murdoch, who later became a distinguished foreign correspondent based in Asia.

In an odd twist, Murdoch, man of a thousand faces, had been earlier mistaken on a bayside beach as legendary football figure Ron Barassi, and on another occasion as international golfer Bob Shearer.

Ultimately, it would not be manhunts or taskforces that would catch Creed, but an old colleague on holiday. Senior Constable Ian Goldsmith recognised Creed, wearing a suit and carrying a briefcase, strolling along a Perth street on September 6, 1983. They were not friends although they had been police cadets together 17 years earlier.

Goldsmith, who was holidaying with his wife and four children, followed Creed into an ABC Shop while his wife called the police.

Creed left and walked down an escalator. Goldsmith walked up and said, 'It's been a long time, Colin, hasn't it?'

Creed had run out of tricks. He simply replied, 'Yes'. He was then grabbed by local police. Goldsmith was paid a $30,000 reward for his part in the capture.

Creed was sentenced to 21 years jail for two rapes and two bank armed robberies in Adelaide. He was sentenced to nine years concurrent for six Melbourne armed robberies. He was also charged with the murder of a woman, but the charges were withdrawn.

He served 12 years. 'I'm sorry for anyone that I hurt,' he said on his release. 'I regret everything that happened, I regret the people that were hurt but there's nothing I can do to undo all that. I've done my time. I want to put it behind me and get on with life.'

Barry Moyse

BARRY MOYSE was rising fast. The head of the South Australian drug squad, he had a national profile because he was heavily involved in Operation NOAH, a hotline for people to inform on drug dealers.

Moyse was a detective chief inspector and former president of the SA Police Association. His name was pencilled in for future promotion. He was well known and well liked by colleagues around Australia.

None of them knew he was bent.

It was the secret life of Moyse. In public, he was seen on television asking people to dob in drug dealers – at the same time he was secretly organising his own drug syndicate.

He was a regular speaker at local schools telling children of the evils of drugs – but he had seen first hand what sort of money dealers were making, and he wanted some of it. A family man in his early 40s, he was tired of paying off a mortgage.

He met a heroin dealer during a raid on an Adelaide flat and thought he could recruit him to work for Moyse Inc. According to the dealer, who later became a star National Crime Authority witness, Moyse would provide him with seized and recycled drugs every two weeks and they would share the profits.

The dealer said Moyse was keen on cash and said he needed $20,000 to pay off his mortgage. The dealer then knew he had his inside man and greed would keep him hooked. He asked Moyse why they should settle for $20,000 when they could get $250,000.

In one deal Moyse and the dealer split a tidy $72,000 profit.

Moyse was running red hot. In some cases he didn't even bother to take the drugs from police and court exhibit bags before handing them over to his man.

He provided seized marijuana seeds and a police copy of a CSIRO copy of a manual on how to grow cannabis efficiently.

No scriptwriter would dare make up such a character. The public face of the anti-drugs campaign visited the spot selected for a multi-million-dollar cannabis plantation in his unmarked police car. He later used the same car to transport back bales of the finished product. Moyse was so confident that he didn't bother to clean the boot to remove marijuana traces from his police car.

The once-struggling detective inspector was starting to be flushed with funds. He bought a second car, and took the family on an overseas holiday. The house he had once struggled to pay off was renovated.

For an experienced detective, he was stupid and lazy. He left some of the confiscated drugs he intended to sell inside his office. When the National Crime Authority raided his office, investigators found drugs that records showed should have been destroyed, including bags of amphetamines, cannabis and heroin. He was to plead guilty to 17 charges for the sale, supply and possession of heroin, amphetamines, cannabis and cannabis resin, which had been confiscated previously by police, between August, 1986, and May, 1987. In August, 1988, Moyse was sentenced to 27 years jail after pleading guilty to 17 charges of taking part in the supply and sale of heroin and cannabis resin.

Five months later, he won an appeal against the prison term, which was reduced to 21 years with a non-parole period of 16 years.

When he was released after serving 10 years, Moyse served his final month of his sentence on home detention in Port Lincoln.

He worked as a part-time cleaner and umpired in the local cricket competition at weekends.

Paul William Higgins

PAUL Higgins was one of the hard men of the Victoria Police. He was awarded 11 commendations while in the force, a record that still stands.

A champion schoolboy athlete who joined 'The Job' in 1965, he was brought up in an era when many police believed the ends justified the means – that if the law had to be bent to convict a criminal, then so be it. But there were those who believed he bent the rules to line his own pocket and, eventually, they moved against him. Senior Sergeant Paul Higgins was convicted by a County Court jury in March, 1993, of being bent – an allegation he still denies.

He was alleged to have accepted bribes of between $3000 a week and $3000 a month from a then well-known massage parlour boss, Geoffrey Lamb, between 1978 and 1982.

The investigation into Higgins and the subsequent criminal trial was the longest and most expensive corruption investigation in Australia's history, estimated to have cost $30 million.

Higgins always stood out, excelling in football and cricket as a boarder at Assumption College, Kilmore. He was a team-mate of VFL captains Peter Crimmins and Francis Bourke. He played two games of VFL football for South Melbourne and kicked one goal before his football career was cut short by a back injury.

He turned to boxing and became the heavyweight champion of the Victoria Police, beating many larger men, some of them rather flat-footed, and trained at Ambrose Palmer's gym with top-class fighters like Johnny Famechon and Paul Ferreri.

As a policeman, Higgins transferred to South Melbourne, before it became a trendy suburb. There, he had to deal with some of Australia's toughest criminals, the men from the Painters and Dockers Union.

He served with the bureau of criminal intelligence, the armed robbery squad and the consorting squad, a squad that was disbanded because of allegations of corruption.

For years the consorting squad was a law unto itself. Its duties included monitoring Victoria's heaviest criminal crews to gather intelligence and stop crime. It was also the heavy squad, used to chase escapees and crush criminal conspiracies. Members of the consorting squad were supposed to know the main criminal players throughout Australia.

Part of the squad's duties was to attend thoroughbred, harness and greyhound meetings because of the well-known fact that criminals congregated around race tracks. On-duty members of the squad would pick up cash envelopes from the racing clubs, purportedly for acting as race day security. Squad members said the cash was put into a slush fund used for entertaining interstate police when they were in Melbourne.

Higgins would later say the practice was approved by a senior officer who was to end up one of the highest ranking in

Victoria. Every Melbourne Cup carnival, pickpockets would converge on Melbourne, as would interstate detectives. The interstate detectives saw it as a paid holiday and a time to go wild. It was the consorters' job to entertain them when they were in Melbourne. During the Spring Carnival they were known as the 'Ghurkhas' because, the joke went, they took no prisoners.

In the 1970s, Melbourne police used illegal phone taps to gather information. They would fabricate informers to cover where the information came from. The police force would pay money from an informers' fund for the information to these non-existent sources. The detectives would simply pocket the money.

Detectives from the heavy squads had access to unregistered firearms (known as 'throwaways'), explosives and drugs that could be planted on criminals when they did not have the evidence to legitimately convict them.

At one time the consorters felt a well-known criminal who was talking to the media was getting 'ahead of himself'. They drove to his inner-suburban house and used seized explosives to blow up his front entrance. Their target left the area and decided to take a lower public profile for a while.

For years, Higgins had to live with the allegations he was bent. In the late 1960s he was romantically linked to a Melbourne dancer with a questionable reputation. Higgins had been selected to be part of the UN police contingent to go to Cyprus. Senior police told him to dump his girlfriend and scrubbed his name from the Cyprus group.

In the 1970s, Higgins, still single and living with his parents, liked to dress and live well. When most police his age were struggling with mortgages, Higgins always seemed to have cash in his pocket. In 1980 he owned a grey Condor, a kit car that looked like a new Ferrari. It was powered by a Ford Escort 1600 motor and didn't have a luxury car price-tag but, sitting next to the secondhand Commodores his colleagues drove, it looked good. Which didn't look good to those who suspected Higgins of corruption.

In 1979, he was charged with a minor internal disciplinary offence and transferred back to uniform. He had been set up because his command wanted him out. A senior officer in the crime department stayed back at work when Higgins was on afternoon shift. Higgins was working alone and the senior officer tried and failed to contact him on the radio.

The reason was not explained in Higgins' official diary and he was charged with not keeping his diary up to date.

Some thought Higgins would never work as a detective again. But in 1982 he used the internal appeal process to apply for a job in the crime department. Despite evidence by senior officers that they had no confidence in Higgins he won the appeal and returned to the CIB.

In 1983, police launched a taskforce, code-named Achilles, to investigate police corruption in the massage parlour industry. Higgins was one of the main targets. The taskforce was run by John Frame, later to be a deputy commissioner, Bob Falconer, who became WA Chief Commissioner, and Bernice Masterson, who became the first female Assistant Commissioner in Victoria. They were unable to gather sufficient evidence to lay charges but they were later to be in positions of authority that allowed them to support a second investigation using unprecedented resources.

In May, 1986, a police taskforce, code-named Cobra, was set up within the elite police anti-corruption branch, the Internal Security Unit, to investigate Higgins and another policeman with a colourful past, Brian Murphy. Cobra investigators flew around Australia interviewing 805 people, including former police, murderers, prostitutes and drug dealers, in a bid to gather evidence against Higgins. They ended with a witness list of 170.

Higgins, then a uniformed senior sergeant at Prahran, was arrested and charged in April, 1987. Murphy was never interviewed or charged.

It took seven years to investigate, try and convict Higgins. It took six to fight World War II.

The committal hearing began in October, 1987, and dragged on until August, 1988, when it was abandoned. During the committal, massage parlour king Geoff Lamb was in the witness box for 70 days.

The Director of Public Prosecutions then presented Higgins directly for trial in the County Court.

Behind the scenes, senior police tried to broker a deal with the police association to drop the charges. If Higgins agreed to plead to a minor internal disciplinary charge and be sacked, then all criminal charges would be dropped and he could go free with his superannuation. The association agreed and Higgins looked as if he would go along with the deal but he later refused, saying he had done nothing wrong.

The transcript from the aborted committal hearing ran to 7000 pages. The County Court transcript ran to 32,000 pages.

The trial went from November 1, 1991, until December 11, 1992. The court sat for 410 days, including 135 days of legal argument before the first evidence was presented before the jury.

The prosecution's final address to the jury went from December 16, 1991, until January 26, 1992, including a Christmas break. The defence summing up went from January 27 until February 17. The judge's charge to the jury went for one month.

Legal fees were staggering. The prosecutor in the case, Robert Redlich, QC, was paid $2,817,010 from 1990 to 1994 for the Higgins case alone.

The Police Association Legal Defence fund nearly went broke after funding Higgins to $1.8 million. The association refused to continue funding him after three emotional meetings involving the rank and file.

Higgins says he owed Legal Aid $990,000 and lost $300,000 in superannuation.

Higgins was sentenced to seven years jail with a minimum of five and was released in February, 1998. He has always maintained his innocence.

Higgins, a fitness fanatic, had to survive five years in jail with many of the men he had locked up. Armed robbers Peter Gibb and Archie Butterly tried him on early but when he wouldn't back down the situation settled. Higgins began a tertiary degree on sports science while in jail and worked out in the gym every day. His development was such that he was often tested for steroid abuse. The tests came back negative.

Many of his former colleagues dumped Higgins and refused to visit him in jail. Some were concerned that once he was convicted the former tough copper would 'roll over'. They thought he would tell all he knew about police corruption and illegal behaviour in exchange for time off his sentence. But Higgins remained silent.

When he got out he was invited to the farewell for an old friend in the job. One of the organisers had to ring him and say if he turned up the senior officers would not. Higgins now has little to do with his former squad mates and earns a living in the fitness industry. He remains bitter that he was targeted, charged and convicted.

Denis Tanner

DENIS Tanner wasn't the smartest policeman to scrape through the Police Academy, but some reckoned he was one of the toughest. As a detective, recalls a former colleague, 'he was a real tough bastard who loved to lock up crooks. I never saw him flinch once. Some coppers talk tough but lack a bit when it's really willing. Denis was not like that. He was hard as nails.'

Tanner joined the Victoria Police Force on October 22, 1973, and graduated on March 15, 1974, in 22nd position of 24 recruits. He started in the records section at Russell Street, then worked at South Melbourne, Shepparton and St Kilda before transferring to the CIB in March, 1979.

He was promoted to senior detective and worked in some of the heavy squads, including the major crime squad.

In September, 1988, the position of detective sergeant at Benalla came up. Tanner got the job. Another policeman appealed against the decision but the Police Service Board dismissed it and, on December 7, Tanner transferred to Benalla.

Tanner had grown up in the area and to return was completing the circle. His wife, a policewoman, resigned her position at Altona when she could not get a country posting with him.

While Tanner was settling in, Ron Iddles, another hard-nosed detective with a reputation for not taking a backward step, was stewing. Universally respected, Iddles was angry because a drug operation he had run, Operation Mint, had been 'sold out'. Iddles was determined to find who had betrayed him and his colleagues for a bribe rumoured to be $28,000. It could have cost an undercover policeman his life.

It was an open secret in police circles that drug squad investigations were being leaked to criminals. There was a traitor in the camp.

Iddles believed that a member of a squad stationed in the same building as the drug squad had got wind of the operation and told Tanner, who used a former policeman as a go-between to warn the targets.

It was a scandal waiting to break. Iddles was determined it would not be swept under the carpet.

Tanner and Iddles had been in the same academy class, graduating the same day. They did detective training school together, Iddles finishing dux of the course and Tanner struggling to pass.

In April, 1990, two senior officers, Detective Superintendent Neil Comrie, later to be chief commissioner, and veteran corruption investigator Chief Inspector Tony Warren, of the internal investigations department, were ordered to find the drug squad leak.

Tanner knew he was in the frame when the detective suspected of tipping him off was interviewed as a suspect. The Police Service Board was later to find the detective had 'unexplained knowledge of some aspects of Operation Mint'.

The detective was interviewed on October 18, 1989. He resigned six weeks later.

On January 16, 1990, the then Deputy Commissioner (administration), Brendan Crimmins, dropped a bombshell. He wrote to Tanner and effectively accused him of being a crook.

'An investigation has been conducted into the corrupt leak of information from the drug squad, in respect to an operation into the large scale manufacture and trafficking of amphetamines,' he wrote.

'The maintenance of efficiency of the force requires the regional commander always has confidence in his personnel and that I, too, have the same confidence in them. As the result of this investigation, these degrees of confidence are not present and in the interests of the maintenance of the efficiency of the force, you are appointed to Force Reserve as of 17th January, 1990 under the provisions of Regulations 901, Police Regulations, 1979.'

Denis Tanner was a fighter. He appealed to the Police Service Board, where the case ran for 20 days before County Court Judge Walsh, former police commander Eric Sutton and veteran policeman Fred Leslie in 1990.

Reputations were made and lost at the bitterly-fought hearing. Police turned on police, officers who had been friends for years gave sworn evidence that reflected alarmingly different recollections. Not everybody who gave evidence was impressed with the board's performance.

The board issued subpoenas to people it believed could shed light on the mystery but they could not be found. Tanner insisted he had been condemned on the basis of guilt by association and malicious gossip.

'As a general proposition, rumour and innuendo about crime and personalities are rife within the police force. I have found frequently that names are mentioned, quite inaccurately as it later turns out, but nevertheless this misinformation circulates on the grapevine,' Tanner stated.

'Sometimes this is the result of malice, other times it is inadvertent, while at other times it can be the result of misguided enthusiasm. Facts and personalities change as the story does the rounds. It is an inherent part of the job that police will pry into the business of other people and this flows on to the individual lives of police.

'I believe now that at least one reason why my name has arisen in respect of this matter is because some persons know or learnt that I am … a good friend of (suspect detective) and wrongly speculated that I must have been connected with "selling out" of the alleged drug squad job. 'The "selling out" of Operation Mint became a talking point, especially in CIB circles.'

Eleven serving and former police, from the rank of constable to chief inspector, told the board that Tanner was a 'trusted and valuable member of the CIB'. Statements of support were given by five serving and former police.

Locals prepared to vouch for Tanner included a butcher, a councillor, a supermarket manager, a school principal, a farmer, a publican and a car dealer. The baker and candlestick maker were unavailable. His record sheet was filled with praise from senior officers. He was described as well-conducted, efficient, reliable and enthusiastic.

On May 4, 1978, he had been praised in the following terms: 'Commended with three others for dedication to duty, courage and persistence displayed, with scant regard for his personal safety, in the apprehension and subsequent conviction of a desperate criminal who exercised every violent means at his disposal endeavouring to effect his escape.'

Two months after transferring to Benalla in December, 1988, Tanner hurt his knee on duty after a 'violent struggle' with a prisoner in the cells. He was off work for 40 days from April 17 to June 11, 1989, suffering from stress and anxiety 'due to a variety of factors perceived by him, not the least being that he heard the allegations that he was suspected of serious corruption'.

He had been disciplined twice in his career for inappropriate actions. In the early 1970s, he was counselled for not following procedures and, at Benalla CIB, for using inappropriate language.

He was in the process of buying a house in Benalla for $147,000. In October 1989, he was 'very belatedly' interviewed by investigators over the drug squad leak. Tanner knew from the tone of the interview that he was under suspicion.

He rang the head of the investigation, Superintendent Comrie, to find out where he stood. The future commissioner didn't mince words, telling Tanner he was likely to be sent to the force reserve, the police equivalent of Siberia.

Tanner allowed his offer on the house to lapse but he didn't give up. Someone, somewhere, liked him.

The board warned of the dangers of mess-room gossip. It found that a corrupt approach had been made to one of the targets but found there was nothing to link Tanner to the approach. It also noted the 'convincing evidence' of Tanner's ability and value as a detective in the north-east of Victoria and his 'ability to integrate his CIB duties with his membership of the community in that area'.

The board overturned the decision of the chief commissioner to transfer Tanner to the force reserve. Ron Iddles resigned from the force in disgust. He later rejoined and was given rapid promotion to become a senior member of the homicide squad. This was ironic, given that some members of the homicide squad were to give Tanner their undivided attention from 1996 to 1998.

Tanner, known only to other police before 1996, became publicly well-known that year for all the wrong reasons: his name was linked with two mysterious deaths.

One was that of transsexual prostitute Adele Bailey, whose skeleton was found in an abandoned mineshaft near the old Tanner farm at Bonnie Doon in 1995. Bailey had vanished from St Kilda in 1978, and Tanner had been the last police officer to arrest her. The other death was the alleged suicide of Tanner's sister-in-law, Jenny Tanner, at the family's Bonnie Doon farmhouse in 1984. The young mother had been found with two bullets in her brain and bullet holes through each hand, but a coroner in 1985 had made an open finding after local police presented a brief apparently slanted towards a finding of suicide. The case stank, but only the dead woman's family and friends knew or cared, and there wasn't much they could do about it.

It wasn't until the mineshaft skeleton discovery prompted an investigation of Adele Bailey's death that fresh questions were asked about Jenny Tanner's 'suicide'. A timely leak from inside the police force meant that the media exposed the scandalous aspects of the case and suggested a cover-up had taken place. This ensured that a taskforce already set up to investigate both deaths would get the time and resources to do the job properly, instead of being dismantled after a few weeks or months.

The original inquest's open finding was set aside and after 23 sitting days scattered over more than a year, the State Coroner found that Jennifer Tanner had been shot to death by her brother-in-law, Sergeant Denis Tanner. Another coroner subsequently made an open finding into the death of Adele Bailey.

Tanner eventually resigned from the police force before he was forced out under new legislation, unofficially dubbed the 'Tanner clause', passed to give the chief commissioner the discretionary power to sack police. Tanner has since been refused a licence as a private investigator and as a taxi-driver. He is believed to be making a living doing odd jobs. He is still trying to prove his innocence.

Kevin Hicks

SOMETIMES police who go bad are high fliers. People such as former NSW detective Roger Rogerson, the sort who solve some of Australia's most baffling crimes before they are exposed as being bent. They are the type who are brave to the point of reckless and live their job before they turn.

But Kevin Hicks was not like that. As a plod, he was a plodder, and lazy with it.

Hicks was 20 years old when he left his hometown of Hamilton in the Victorian western district and went to Melbourne to join the police force.

In the sixth squad of 1974 he was middle of the road and showed no signs of being highly motivated. His first eight years on the road did nothing to suggest he would be a late bloomer or a charismatic leader.

So it was a surprise when he put in for the major crime squad in the early 1980s and an even bigger one that he was accepted. He was to become involved in hunting some of the country's most dangerous men, including Pavel Marinoff − known as 'Mad Max' − the man who shot six police in 1985-86. Hicks was seen as brave enough but by no means a star investigator.

'He was a naive country lad. He was a good bloke but not a real hard worker,' a former major crime squad detective would recall. 'He sort of just fell into the lifestyle.'

The 'lifestyle' was the squad's notorious work practices, which were diplomatically referred to as 'work hard, play hard.' At least Hicks got it half right.

With his curly hair and round face he became known as 'Koala Bear' because there were already detectives nicknamed 'Bear' and 'Polar Bear' in the squad.

A former major crime squad detective, Peter Spence, who was later to give character evidence for Hicks in court, said that after chasing some of the state's most dangerous criminals squad members would sometimes go to lunch and drink until 5am the next day.

Another colleague said Hicks eventually found work to be a tiresome distraction from drinking.

While he was the longest-serving member of the squad, he

had long since stopped being productive. He was made un-official social secretary and his full-time duties largely revolved around entertaining squad guests and 'getting on the piss'.

He became lethargic and withdrawn but he didn't seek, nor was he offered, any counselling. According to Spence, Hicks's marriage broke up because of his lifestyle. His police diary would show 'licensing duties' nearly every third day – a code for pub crawls. His arrest record was lamentable. He made only one arrest in nearly two years and, despite repeated warnings, he refused to lift his work rate.

The major crime squad was running out of control. It had a squad lunch in an outer suburban hotel that ended in chaos after a drunken detective began to head-butt members of the public in the men's toilet. There was more trouble because the detectives decided the meal should be free, despite the protests of the licensee, who had the quaint idea that customers should pay for the food they ate.

By late 1991 it was all too much, or too little.

Hicks was sacked from his beloved 'majors' and moved to the drug squad as assistant property steward in January, 1992. For an operational detective it was a massive slap in the face. He was effectively made a clerk to keep him out of mischief.

In reality, he had been handed the keys to the lolly shop.

Most detectives knew Hicksy. They all drank in the police club or the old City Court Hotel, and he was part of the furniture at both. He was seen as rock solid, quiet but staunch. Most thought he had been shafted by being moved from the 'majors' and everyone in the drug squad tried to help him recover his collapsed self-esteem.

'He was a lost soul. I thought he was like a big, dumb teddy bear,' said a detective who worked at the drug squad at the time.

'He would come downstairs with his mug of coffee and go from crew to crew for a chat. We all talked to him about our jobs because we thought he missed the action. Now we know he was selling us out.'

Promising jobs started to turn cold and some targets seemed able to anticipate police actions. There were a series of internal investigations, but the rat in the ranks was not discovered.

Meanwhile Kevin Hicks, the devastated major crime squad detective, was making a comeback of sorts. He seemed to be taking his job quite seriously. One of his most important duties was to protect drugs seized by detectives and kept as court exhibits. The drugs were kept in six old locked shipping containers at the police property at Attwood, near Melbourne Airport. The laconic Hicks threw himself into his work. He replaced the keys and locks to the Attwood storage depot and took an interest in collating the evidence.

When he arrived at the drug squad he was struggling with alimony payments, a legacy of his broken marriage three years earlier. In police circles his battered 1975 Ford station wagon was a standing joke. It often sat in the no-standing zone outside the old watch-house in Russell Street for up to a week because he could not afford to fill the tank.

But he was soon able to buy a Mitsubishi V6 four-wheel-drive and a top-class motor bike and to afford an eight-week holiday with his girlfriend to Hawaii and California. He bought into a racehorse and seemed to be doing well on the punt. Colleagues simply thought his luck had changed and he was getting his life back together.

Not for a moment did they think the quiet man was talking to the wrong people – let alone looting the containers he was paid to protect, recycling the drugs and chemicals his mates in the drug squad had already seized.

Years in the major crime squad had given Hicks an impressive network of criminal contacts. One of those was Peter Pilarinos, a dangerous criminal with ambitions to be a crime boss.

Many detectives knew the Pilarinos family well and some of the serious crime squads held their social nights at a nightclub owned by his brother. Some detectives had worked the door part-time. In early 1992, Pilarinos wanted to manufacture amphetamines.

Hicks provided the keys to the police storage area and Pilarinos was off and running. They stole the drugs and even took chemical textbooks from the lock-up to ensure they could produce speed of the highest quality.

Hicks kept Pilarinos up to date on any investigations into his group and tipped him off that police planned to put a secret video camera outside his Doncaster home.

The gang needed ketone to make a batch of amphetamines and Pilarinos ordered six litres for $12,000 from an unemployed criminal who owned a 60-square home in Yarra Glen.

When it was delivered, Hicks staged a raid using a fake firearms warrant. He gave one of the crooks present a clip over the ear and threatened to arrest all present.

The man who delivered the drugs was allowed to leave. The chemicals weren't. Hicks had just done a favour for his mate Peter Pilarinos. When Hicks was finally arrested, he told his mates in the job he would beat the charges. He told them the case was a 'souffle' and would be exposed as a crust and hot air, so most were stunned when Hicks pleaded guilty. His street-smart barrister Joe Gullaci gave every indication he intended to fight the case before walking back into the Supreme Court after a lunch break to say his client would admit his guilt.

Legal sources said some thought Pilarinos was about to plead guilty and was looking for a deal. If Pilarinos had rolled over and given evidence against Hicks, the former policeman would have been looking at 10 years inside.

In May, 2000, he was sentenced to seven and a half years jail with a minimum of five.

Gary Robert Whelan

AS a policeman, Gary Robert Whelan was never going to be a high flier but he was a goer, the sort experienced police love to have in every station and squad. He didn't complain about the hours or the possible danger. He loved the work and did what was required … no questions asked. He wanted to fit in, to belong.

Whelan joined the Victoria Police in 1977 and within four years he had moved to the busiest crime area in the state, St Kilda. It was the early 1980s and drugs were taking hold.

St Kilda, like its Sydney counterpart Kings Cross, was a place filled with huge opportunities and temptations. It was a place where police earned reputations, one way or the other.

When Whelan started at the chaotic St Kilda station he looked to those with experience to guide him. One of his sergeants was Dick McLean, an accomplished officer on the way up. Even though McLean was only four years Whelan's senior, he became a father figure to him.

In May, 1982, Whelan was called to a guest house in St Kilda over a routine complaint about the behaviour of one of the guests. It was a routine job but one that had to be answered. For the eager young police officer, it was like winning Tattslotto. In the room he found 154 grams of heroin in condoms and caps. It was 75 per cent pure, indicating this was no street dealer's stash. This was close to the source.

For the early 1980s it was a huge bust, headline material. In the so-called war against drugs this was considered a battle won. Whelan was congratulated by senior officers. It should have been his ticket onto the fast track for promotion.

The following year, Whelan got his wish and was promoted to senior detective and was transferred to the stolen motor vehicle squad.

The heroin discovered by Whelan the year before was supposed to be kept under lock and key in the drug security cabinet at the St Kilda station until the case came to court. In police, drug and criminal circles it was widely known that security at the station was a joke. Property and drugs tended to walk out the door. It was suggested, but not proven, that some junkies who provided intelligence might be rewarded with a 'taste' of seized drugs.

As Whelan was celebrating his promotion to the CIB, rumours reached senior police that all was not right at St Kilda. They decided to re-weigh the heroin from Whelan's day in the sun. It was 42.5 grams shy.

Whelan was charged with trafficking, selling and stealing heroin. The trial judge directed to acquit him of trafficking and the jury found him not guilty in 1985 of all other offences. He remained suspended until 1986 and was then found guilty before the Police Discipline Board with failing to account for property, fined $700 and demoted to constable.

Most coppers do not live down that sort of blot on their record. When Whelan returned to duty he was transferred to the Russell Street Reserve, a pool used to fill holes in the force. It was commonly considered the road to nowhere.

In 1989, Whelan was moved to the audio-visual section. His job entailed videoing crime scenes and crime re-enactments for later court cases. It was important, but hardly taxing work.

But, in 1993, there was a reorganisation in the crime department and Whelan's section came under the bureau of criminal intelligence, which dealt with organised crime. Whelan's job was to set secret cameras to help build cases against some of Australia's top gangsters.

The days where police could jump into the witness box and be instantly believed were long gone. They needed irrefutable proof such as video and audio tapes to make their cases stick. The policeman with the questionable past was back from the cold and privy to some of the force's most confidential operations.

A touch of electronic expertise and a stroke of the bureaucratic pen helped Gary Whelan re-invent himself from suspected drug seller to new-wave crime buster. He was back at the big end of town and he was ready to run red hot.

All he needed was a little nudge from his old sergeant, Dick McLean.

Dick McLean

DICK McLEAN was a cop in a hurry. He was on the promotional fast track and openly spoken of as a future commissioner. But for him, that wasn't enough: he wanted it all, and he wanted it now. Especially money.

McLean was a good policeman, so good he was appointed in 1987 to the staff of the elite Airlie Officers' College in South Yarra, where he instructed the future high-ranking members of the force on matters such as leadership and management, His lectures were polished and informative and he excelled in the field during training operations, where his practical experience could be used to the fullest. He seemed to be a born leader and a modern and progressive police officer.

McLean had proved himself in the tough areas of the force; he had been stationed at St Kilda when it was the centre of

Melbourne's drug, prostitution and street crime, and he had worked in the homicide squad. Yet he was no rough diamond. He had the personal skills and diplomacy needed to deal with every stratum of society. He was as comfortable talking to career criminals as to captains of industry. Sometimes they were one and the same.

But the policeman on the make was restless. 'He saw himself as a bloke who could cut it in the business world,' a former colleague said. 'All during his career he dabbled in business.'

McLean had a furniture factory, a financial interest in a waterbed shop and even had an international diamond importer's licence while a serving policeman.

A detective who worked with him said: 'He was generous and would always give police furniture and beds at cost. He was always being touched for a cheap deal. He was never around the office to do the mundane stuff but when there was a major job on he would be as hard working as the next bloke.'

McLean once interviewed a murder suspect for 16 hours until he cracked her story. 'Dick was a good investigator, there was no doubt about that,' a senior policeman would later recall.

From the time he joined the force in 1969, there was never any suggestion he was anything but squeaky clean. But being a good policeman and a future leader was not enough to hold McLean's interest. Business called. In December 1989, McLean, then a Chief Inspector and a 20-year veteran, left policing to make his fortune in the outside world. But he found the real world of commerce a little more difficult than he had expected.

The first sign for McLean that private enterprise was not a guaranteed road to wealth came when his waterbed business sprang a leak. He may have been lacking a little on the cash front but he certainly wasn't short of ideas. He then moved into the restaurant trade.

A former colleague said: 'There was a lovely fellow we all knew from the St Kilda days. He had a little pizza parlour in Fitzroy Street. Dick was always at him with big plans, to extend it into the next shop and turn it into a flash restaurant. Eventually he went along with Dick and they became partners. They both ended up broke.'

McLean was, a detective recalled, 'on top of everything when he was in the job, but it all went wrong when he got out'.

The financial disasters and a marriage break-up didn't destroy McLean's confidence. He was a big-picture man and he was convinced that if he persisted, his luck would turn. He moved into the electronic-security industry and, finally, his big break came in 1995.

In the global field of new technology, teenage computer experts were making fortunes overnight. McLean calculated that if he could combine his knowledge of policing and security with state-of-the-art software he would be on his way.

He got in on the ground floor of a major deal. He was going to invest in a mobile 'smart phone' designed to provide immediate access to a stream of security functions for the elderly. To be manufactured in an Ararat factory, it was going to make millions. This was too good an opportunity to ignore. McLean had the idea, he had the market, he had the contacts and he had the business plan. What he didn't have was the money.

So Dick McLean, businessman and entrepreneur, turned back to what he really knew: crime and corruption, but this time from the other side. It was time to talk to his old protege, Gary Whelan.

Domenic Gisonda was a police groupie, the sort who always buys the beers and hangs on every word of a detective's war stories. Too quick to laugh at a bad joke and too slow to go home at the end of the night, the former bouncer and painter was always present at any social event run by the St Kilda police.

'He was a smarmy user,' a St Kilda policeman said. 'He would always drop coppers' names when he got a speeding ticket or a parking ticket. Every station's got one.'

Many police were irked by his too-smooth approach but tolerated him as part of the social rat-pack. One detective with a short fuse and a quick trigger finger once took offence at Gisonda but the coat puller didn't know when to leave well enough alone. He kept coming back and asking why the policeman disliked him. The detective punched him to the ground in a car-park, then pulled out his gun and fired several shots over the bleeding victim. The drunken detective was ushered into a cab and the incident covered up, but Gisonda got the message

But McLean was one of the minority of police who liked Gisonda. 'We warned Dick about him but he wouldn't listen,' a former colleague said.

Years later, McLean would return to the go-between for help to set up a corrupt venture which would cost the former police high-flier his reputation, and ultimately, his freedom.

In April, 1995, a police taskforce from Heidelberg found a drug gang was using a Thomastown factory to grow a hydroponic crop of potent 'skunk' cannabis. Police formally requested a secret surveillance camera be set up to gather evidence.

Enter Gary Whelan, who joined the operation as the video expert. He checked the area and positioned a camera and recorder at a nearby building. The operation was expected to last three weeks.

Two days later, police from the taskforce were stunned when a local criminal was able to tell them about their investigations, including details of target premises in Preston, Coburg and Thomastown. The criminal, in the most matter-of-fact terms, was able to pinpoint the exact location of the camera and the drug factory being watched by police.

Local police found the criminal was connected to a notorious 'run-through' gang, a group that raided and ripped off drug crops. Marijuana plantations are the perfect target for such gangs because the product is easy to sell and the victims can hardly complain. The rip-offs have become so regular that some cannabis growers build man traps near their large, open air crops and police fear it is only a matter of time before a bush walker is killed when he stumbles on to a remote drug property.

Police were told that information was being passed to Gisonda by a former detective, known only as 'Dick'. Gisonda then passed it on to the rip-off gang.

The original leak was suspected of coming from the technical section. This was a potentially catastrophic blow for the police department as the section was privy to every major crime investigation under way. Modern police rely on video and audio tapes as their predecessors relied on fingerprint dust as a tool of the trade.

The lives of undercover police and informers would be put at risk if the technical section was leaking.

Internal investigators set up Operation Filter and were able to establish that there were strong links from Whelan to McLean and then to Gisonda. Police gave 'information' on a fabricated drug target to Whelan and he went straight to McLean. The investigators had found their leak.

At one point, Whelan gave McLean a status report on the hydroponic marijuana investigation. Telephone taps proved the gang planned to burgle the factory and steal the drugs before police moved in to arrest the growers.

Early on the morning of Friday, June 2, 1995, the special operations group arrested two burglars as they were attempting to break into the factory.

Soon the phones were running hot among gang members as they queried whether they had been set up. Whelan knew the truth when, three days later, an internal investigator, Colin Farnsworth, arrested him in the old Russell Street police complex. In simultaneous raids, McLean and Gisonda were arrested.

It was a textbook operation, the same text that McLean used to lecture police at the officer's course only a few years earlier.

Late in 1996, McLean, then 45, was sentenced to two years' jail with a minimum of 15 months over the attempted burglary. The man who could have been a commissioner was forced to do time with convicted public officials and child molesters.

Whelan, 41, was sentenced to three years' jail with a minimum of two years three months at the same prison. Gisonda was sentenced to 12 months' jail.

CHAPTER 2

On the Loose

Brenden James Abbott

FIVE prisoners in Brisbane's Sir David Longland Correctional Centre use diamond-edged wire to cut through cell bars and slip out into the prison.

They calmly stack chairs into a pyramid to climb over razor ribbon then sprint 100 metres, only to be stopped by the first of three 'escape-proof' reinforced wire fences.

The escape looks doomed but a security video shows the men do not appear concerned or confused. The reason becomes obvious when waiting accomplices on the outside throw bolt-cutters and a rifle over the fences.

When a guard tries to stop them, shots are fired over his head and he quickly loses interest.

The jail's state-of-the-art surveillance vehicle is then 'killed' by gunfire. The guards inside have to sit and watch as the five inmates cut through the remaining fences and escape in two waiting cars.

It would have been unbelievable if one of the men had not been Brenden James Abbott, Australia's premier escaper.

In a trademark move Abbott, known for years as the 'Postcard Bandit', couldn't resist a final barb at his captors after he had cut through theirs.

He left a prisoner request form on his empty bed, seeking – and approving – his own transfer from the jail that could not hold him. It was decorated with two faces, one smiling and one frowning. You can guess who was who.

Abbott's fellow escapees, three murderers and a rapist, were scooped up within weeks. But there was no mail on the movements of the Postcard Bandit.

He surfaced six weeks later when a Perth Commonwealth Bank branch was robbed of $450,000. Police were to find a grey wig, false moustache and blue tie in a nearby industrial bin. The items had sweat and tissue residue that proved to be a perfect DNA match with Abbott.

Eight years earlier, he escaped from Fremantle jail. Again it was no opportunistic run for freedom but a well-constructed escape by a master planner. This time he and another prisoner, Aaron Reynolds, wearing overalls they made in the jail's tailor shop, broke through a barred window, walked across the prison roof, and jumped three metres to freedom.

A third inmate was in on the plan but found the jump too daunting and stayed behind.

A few weeks later, Abbott and Reynolds robbed a TAB, and fired shots when police tried to chase. When the getaway car was found, police discovered a roll of film. The developed prints showed Reynolds counting cash outside a WA police station and the two escapees posing with shotgun shells.

When Reynolds was arrested in late 1989, police found more pictures of the escapees at various holiday spots, including

Uluru, where they were photographed with a Japanese tourist. Abbott was happy to chat to the visitor – he had completed a Japanese language course in jail.

The habit of taking cheeky photographs eventually was turned into the myth that Abbott sent holiday snaps to police to taunt them, hence the 'Postcard Bandit' name.

It was too good to be true but too good a name to lose. The title stuck even though it was based, at least partially, on a fabrication. He was also known, more accurately, as the Drop-In Bandit and Captain Speedway.

Abbott's love for speed was well-known, and even when he was on the run, he spent time restoring old Holdens. It was said he raced his V8 against Queensland police at Surfers Paradise during a sanctioned drag meet. He was pulled over three times for speeding but calmly flashed his false licence and was allowed to continue.

When he wasn't playing with cars he would travel, often watching the Australian cricket team play. Why not? He had the time and the money.

Abbott's first bank robbery was in Perth on May 29, 1987, when he and two other bandits escaped with $112,000. He was sentenced to 14 years. He was sentenced to a further four years for his part in a Fremantle Prison riot in 1988.

He was an average bank robber to begin with but he taught himself to become Australia's best, specialising in 'drop-in' jobs, where he would hide in a bank ceiling until staff arrived. He would then drop in and force them to open the main safes.

He was suspected of at least 38 bank hold-ups worth an estimated $4 million.

Abbott was the third of five children born to Thelma and Brian Abbott in the working-class Melbourne suburb of Broadmeadows.

According to his sisters, Brenden was subjected to regular beatings from his father. He was not allowed to bring friends home and was forced to become self-sufficient and cunning just to survive. They were skills that would enable him to avoid police for years while on the run.

His path to crime was the well-worn one: violent family life, poor schooling record, stints in boys' homes followed by minor crimes, thefts and bank robberies. The difference was that Abbott had a real talent for crime.

According to journalist Derek Pedley, who chronicled Abbott's life in the excellent *No Fixed Address: The Hunt For Brenden James Abbott*, the man who would become Australia's most wanted criminal was interested only in cricket and girls when at school. They were passions he would not lose when on the run.

His first conviction for break and entering came when he was 14. Abbott usually sold the stolen goods to mates in what were known as 'Brenden Sales'.

With an IQ of 140 and an ego to match his intellect, he was more efficient and harder to catch as he progressed.

Six years after his Fremantle escape, he was finally recaptured in March, 1995, on the Gold Coast.

Police found the number for a Gold Coast post office box at Abbott's brother's home. When they checked the box, they found a bill for a pager. Checking the numbers they were able to locate Abbott's girlfriend's unit. They sat off and were able to arrest the escapee without incident.

He was convicted of three Queensland bank robberies, worth $1.2 million and sentenced to 12 years' jail. The court was told he was a self-taught electronics expert and a master of disguises.

Years earlier, helpful prison staff had allowed him to enrol in an acting course where he learnt about theatrical make-up – a skill he was able to use repeatedly as he disguised himself to trick police around Australia.

The fear that he would escape again made Brisbane prison authorities shackle his hands and feet when he was taken to court. He was kept in solitary confinement for a year before being moved to the high-security Sir David Longland Correctional Centre.

Rather than becoming beaten and bitter, Abbott remained charming and optimistic. He was eventually given the trusted job as education clerk and was often placed in positions where he had access to prison phones.

He didn't waste it and almost certainly was able to contact associates to help organise the escape.

One was a young man who had spent time in jail with Abbott and hero-worshipped the bank robber. His name was Brendan Luke Berichon.

The pair rented a trendy house in Nicholson Street in the fashionable Melbourne inner suburb of Carlton early in 1998.

But they had not travelled to Melbourne to go shopping, even if they did splurge at David Jones department store. On March 13, two armed bandits stole $250,000 from Armaguard officers in Dandenong. Police suspect it was Abbott and Berichon.

Abbott may have been addicted to armed robberies but Berichon had another nasty little habit – heroin. On April 20 he went to Box Hill to score but he was disturbed by Sergeant Scott Roberts and Constable Peter Baltas, of the transit police.

Berichon and a young associate saw the police and tried to disappear into the crowd, but the officers caught up with them in nearby Surrey Drive. Constable Baltas, 26, began questioning Berichon while his partner talked to the second youth.

Berichon produced a false Queensland licence and then a

9mm automatic pistol. He fired at least eight shots at the two police, hitting Baltas in the hip and Roberts in the arm.

He escaped after forcing a woman to drive him to Carlton at gunpoint.

Police tracked him to the Nicholson Street house but were five minutes too late. Abbott and Berichon had just left. Fingerprint checks proved how close they were to Australia's most wanted escapee.

But time was running out. History shows that people who shoot police don't survive on the loose for long. Berichon, who lacked the experience and cunning of his hero, became the target of a national manhunt.

Abbott should have cut him loose, but he didn't. They headed to Darwin separately and then teamed up again.

In May, Berichon was spotted by staff at a Darwin Hotel and police sat off. The bonus was when they saw Abbott outside the same hotel. Abbott was grabbed by five tactical response group police as his clothes were drying in a laundromat. He was on his way to get a pizza at a local supermarket. Berichon was also arrested.

Abbott was sentenced to 23 years' jail and could serve more for armed robberies and escapes around Australia.

He is kept in a tiny cell 18 hours a day and is under constant electronic surveillance.

Berichon, meanwhile, was sentenced in Melbourne to 13 years for the attempted murder of Sergeant Scott Roberts and Senior Constable Peter Baltas.

Christopher Dean 'Badness' Binse

MOST gangsters end up with nicknames that fit their image, such as 'Chopper' Read, Billy 'The Texan' Longley and 'Mad Dog' Cox. But master escaper and armed robber Christopher Dean Binse didn't wait for someone to give him a moniker, he picked his own: 'Badness'.

It was perfect.

Binse has tried to escape from custody eight times. In September, 1992, he escaped from the St Vincent's Hospital security ward in Melbourne, using a smuggled gun left in the hospital. He was arrested in Sydney, then escaped soon after from the Parramatta jail as prison officers fired shots at him.

No one who knew him was surprised at any of this. At 14 he had been declared uncontrollable and put in Turana boys' home. He has rarely been out of custody since, legally at least.

Binse loved to taunt whoever chased him around the country.

After one Melbourne armed robbery, police didn't have to work hard to establish the identity of the offender. Binse took out a classified advertisement in the *Herald Sun* announcing 'Badness is back.'

He bought a Queensland country property with armed robbery money and named his spread 'Badlands'. The image was completed when he drove a car with the personalised number plates: 'Badness'.

He sent Melbourne armed robbery squad detectives Christmas cards with messages such as 'wish you were here' and one covered with dollar signs. Police said one of the greetings was signed 'Lord Badness'.

He was finally re-arrested in December, 1992, by police at a house near Daylesford. The house had also been used by notorious armed robber 'Jockey' Smith, who was shot dead when he confronted a policeman only hours before Binse was nabbed. Binse was once arrested at Melbourne Airport after committing a big armed robbery. He would never pre-book, preferring the $89 stand-by tickets. 'I don't believe in plastic money, I want the real stuff. If you hadn't caught me at the airport you would have had nothing. I know that,' he told police.

After he was arrested by Melbourne detectives he expected to be bashed but when he realised the police already had an airtight case he relaxed and explained why he loved committing armed robberies. 'For the excitement, the rush. Lifestyle, you'd have to know what it feels like. It's like you on a raid, you're in control, your blood starts rushing, you feel grouse, you're hyped up. Fuck the money. It's more than excitement, it's an addiction. I don't know what it is.

'Time's going by, quick, quick, quick and you're just thinking. What happens if you see a police car?

'Most of the time, 95 per cent, I saw a Jack (police) car drive past or saw a Jack car within 10 minutes of the job. It was my good luck sign. It's already been through, it won't come back, it's going in a different direction.'

He told the police he was religious. 'I believe in God, I used to pray every day in Sydney. You've got to have some beliefs, mate.

'If you believe He's there He may help you. I can tell you what, there were a few close calls that I had. If it was meant to be I would have been dead by now.'

He said that he planned to go overseas and grow marijuana but he needed to pull one more job. He said he spent more than $100,000 in the previous six months.

He knew he was going to jail for a long time. 'Now I've got

to do it hard. I enjoyed myself. I had a good time. I've got some good memories.'

In 1993, Binse was the leader of a plan to free up to 30 of Victoria's most dangerous prisoners inside Pentridge's then top-security H Division.

Prison officers seized Binse's diary and found the plan to free the inmates from their cells and attack – and possibly kill – Hoddle Street killer Julian Knight.

The plan was for the inmates to escape on October 26. The date was picked because it was near the anniversary of Binse's escape from Parramatta.

The escape was foiled because of a security crackdown after prison officer Les Attard was stabbed 17 times with a pair of tailor's shears on October 25.

The escape plot was discovered when prison officers found the lock on Binse's cell door had been neatly cut with a hacksaw blade. They also found a home-made prison officer's uniform in the division the following day.

The shirt was made from Binse's civilian shirt. In further searches prison officers found two jail-made daggers, six jail-made Office of Corrections shirt insignias and a hacksaw blade.

According to the diary, four inmates controlled the escape plan. They were Binse; double murderer John William Lindrea, who had previously escaped from Pentridge; Robert Chapman, who escaped from a city amusement centre while on prison day leave; and a fourth prisoner who allegedly ran much of the drug trafficking in the jail. A fifth prisoner, escape expert Paul Alexander Anderson, was used by the group as a specialist consultant.

Prison authorities believe an inmate was to overpower the single night guard, take the officer's handgun and then open all 30 cells.

According to the plan, selected inmates, including multiple killer Julian Knight, who killed seven people in a random attack in Hoddle Street on August 9, 1987, were to be attacked as part of a payback. Knight was alleged to be an informer.

The escape leaders then had two plans. The first involved getting the keys to the division, escaping from H Division into the main jail and scaling the outside wall at the back of the prison.

The second was to keep the officer as a hostage and escape as a group through the front gate.

Senior police believe many escapes from Australian jails are more organised than is publicly acknowledged. The Australian Bureau of Criminal Intelligence completed an investigation, code-named Operation GAP, which found that a nationwide network existed to help prisoners on the run. It found escapers could be provided with safe houses around Australia and fake documents from the group.

The theory seemed to be confirmed by the fact that both Binse and Jockey Smith used the same safe house in Daylesford.

While serving a 7½-year term for armed robberies, Binse became the only Victorian prisoner to be shackled in leg irons and handcuffs 23 hours a day.

In 1996, he was extradited to NSW to face charges over the 1992 armed robbery of a Commonwealth Bank, theft of more than $36,000 and escape from Long Bay.

In sentencing him to 6½ years jail the judge said: 'Change your lifestyle or you will die a violent death, or else rot in jail.'

In 2001 Binse was one of the first inmates of the $20 million high-security jail within the Goulburn Correctional Centre. Built for just 75 inmates out of the NSW prison population of 7500, it was designed for psychopaths and ingenious escapers like Binse.

But he still kept in touch. When Victor Peirce was murdered in May, 2002, Binse placed a death notice saying he was shattered. It was signed 'Badness'.

Ian John Peter 'Rabbit' Steele

IAN John Peter Steele was known as 'Rabbit' because of his running ability, but police say the nickname was apt because, like the introduced vermin, he proved impossible to kill.

Police say Steele was cruel, unstable, egotistical and had violent mood changes yet was able to live undetected for more than a year after he escaped from a Sydney prison.

The Australian Bureau of Criminal Intelligence found a loose network of prison sympathisers were able to protect Steele and move him to special safe houses whenever police were close to finding the escapee.

Steele's criminal history began when he was 13. He has convictions for armed robbery, buggery, repeated escapes and attempted escapes, thefts, assaults and arson.

Steele escaped with two other men from Darlinghurst Court, NSW, on February 17, 1983. He went to Perth, where he committed four bank robberies and kidnapped victims at gunpoint.

Back in Victoria, he forced a man to drive him around for 32 hours until he was pulled up by two police near the old City Square.

The two detectives who stopped him in Swanston Street were two of Victoria's most decorated, Jimmy Venn and Paul 'Fish' Mullett.

Steele had a sawn-off shotgun pointed at the hostage but turned it on Venn. It didn't work.

Venn fired twice through the windscreen, hitting Steele in the head and shoulder. Because of the thickness of the windscreen and of Steele's skull, he survived.

He was sentenced to 17 years with a minimum of 13 and placed in Pentridge's maximum security unit, Jika Jika, but was soon in touch with his escape network.

Steele regularly wrote to two Melbourne women who helped organise houses for escapees and others wanted by police.

On October 29, 1985, Steele was moved to Sydney's Long Bay on four armed robbery charges. But on January 17, 1986, Rabbit was again on the run.

He shaved off his beard, hid in the prison workshop, cut through bars and walked out of the prison in torrential rain, wearing a prison officer's hat.

Police believe Steele was hidden by sympathisers, including the two Melbourne women who are said to be experts at hiding hot crooks.

When on the run, he hid in a Pascoe Vale house in 1983 and later in Elsternwick, protected by three sisters with extensive criminal contacts.

One sister cared for him when he had a minor arm injury and took him to the Western General Hospital where he was treated under the name of Lindsay Jury.

Police believe Steele moved from short-term accommodation houses in the Fitzroy Street area of St Kilda in early 1986 to live with a woman in Macleod under the alias Steven Harris, which he had seen in a newspaper.

Steele began to sell cocaine and was a regular at a hotel in Heidelberg where he drank with a group from a local football club and even became involved in their card games.

After being protected by the network in Victoria for more than a year, he returned to Sydney where, after robbing a bank in early 1987, he was provided with a false passport by a well-known prisoner sympathiser. Steele, a drug addict, then went to England. Soon after his arrival, he committed at least 18 bank robberies, pretending to be a modern bushranger.

In each robbery he would wave a pistol and then hand a teller a note: 'Your money or your life! Ben Hall.'

One English tabloid newspaper with little knowledge of Australian crime history and no regard for the truth insisted on changing the name from Ben Hall to Ned Kelly.

Steele was also charged and convicted of killing his girlfriend, New Zealander Carol Messenbird, 26, whose body was found in Bedfordshire in October, 1988. He has been unable to escape from his British prison.

Russell 'Mad Dog' Cox

MORE a cool cat than a mad dog, armed robber and gunman Russell Cox was to spend 11 years on the run after escaping from the maximum security Katingal Division in NSW's Long Bay Jail.

When he escaped at 8.30pm on November 3, 1977, police expected he would be back in custody within a few days. But it turned out he would not be found until cornered in a Melbourne shopping centre car park in 1988.

Cox was serving life for the attempted murder of a prison officer in an earlier escape when he broke out of the supposedly escape proof Katingal, later closed on humanitarian grounds.

Born Melville Schnitzerling in Brisbane on September 15, 1949, the child who became known as Russell Cox was a premature baby nicknamed 'Tim' by his family.

As a boy, he was in and out of youth training centres before finally being sent to an adult jail in 1966 for stealing a car in Seymour. In 1972, he started to use the name Russell Cox and began his long career as an armed robber. Cox managed to stay on the run for more than a decade because he was smart enough not to play the tough guy. For a violent criminal, Cox could appear remarkably calm. He became an expert at appearing ordinary to avoid attention.

He would always rent moderate, furnished homes near the beach which he would share with his de facto wife Eva Dean and their black labrador Devil.

Cox's brother was a champion surfer who retired in the United States, and athleticism and self-discipline ran in the family. Cox loved the beach and regularly ran 15 kilometres a day. But he didn't drop his guard. He always had a sub-machine gun under the front seat of his car and had a handgun concealed on his body even when running.

Dean, the sister-in-law of murdered painter and docker, Ray Bennett, was a qualified nursing aide and used her training to help save his life when he was shot in the thigh.

The chatty Dean and quiet Cox were seen as ideal tenants and usually provided glowing references when renting a house.

Both were health conscious. She was a vegetarian and he rarely ate red meat. She used herbal toothpaste and was a regular at health food shops.

Cox was not a heavy drinker, preferring German beers or a glass of wine with his favourite Japanese food.

Police say Cox tapped a phone line into a police station so that he was up to date on the search for him.

While on the run, the couple were still able to travel overseas to Japan and the Philippines several times using false passports.

During one raid where police narrowly missed the pair, they found theatre books which had chapters on make-up. They believed he used actor's make-up and wigs to continually change his appearance.

Cox preferred heavy, military-style weapons and kept bullet proof vests and gas masks.

He often used the alias, 'Mr Walker', the same name used by his favourite comic hero, The Phantom. Even Devil had an alias and was known as 'Butch' when they were on the run.

According to standover man turned author, Mark 'Chopper' Read, Cox won $15,000 on Tattslotto while on the run. 'I've shot people for less,' Read said.

He said Cox turned to crime when he won a raffle for a new bike when he was 10 years old but because he wasn't present at the draw it was raffled again. 'He stole a brand new bike and told everyone he had won it in a raffle,' Read said.

Read said Cox was famous in the underworld for his cool head.

'He was pulled over for licence checks and breath tests and was never fazed. Once, when there were police screaming all over the place, he just drove off. The police didn't notice the dog running after the car. Russell just opened the door of the car and Devil jumped in, barking out the back window at the police, who were blissfully unaware.'

Cox was charged and acquitted of the murder of painter and docker Ian Revell Carroll, who was shot dead at a Mt Martha house on January 3, 1983. Cox had lived at the house for the previous six months.

When police went to the murder scene they found elaborate armed robbery kits, including plans, security guard uniforms, magnetic signs to be placed on vehicles, bandages and medicines.

Cox could be extremely violent when cornered but would always try to avoid a confrontation. Once, when over-charged at a Japanese restaurant, he queried the bill but backed down rather than cause an argument.

He was given the name 'Mad Dog', not by police or associates but by a sly and prematurely balding crime reporter. The nickname stuck. The reporter's hair didn't.

Cox was arrested with another notorious escapee, Raymond John Denning, in the car park of the Doncaster Shoppingtown complex in Melbourne's eastern suburbs on July 22, 1988.

Police shot holes in the pair's car, but Cox took his arrest with typical calm. He even posed with his arresting officers for a 'team' shot in the armed robbery squad office before being sent back to jail.

Raymond John Denning

AT his peak, Raymond John Denning was an outlaw folk hero. They even wrote songs about the dashing and defiant NSW armed robber. His prison diaries were published and he appeared on *Sixty Minutes*.

But, in the end, Denning died a rat – a drugged one, at that – in a shabby house in Paddington. Far from a hero, he was a man who had turned on his own and was forced to live between two worlds.

In the 1980s Denning was seen as being close to a martyr by some socialists, criminologists and columnists. Violent, vicious and treacherous, Denning did do society a favour by helping to expose the corruption and endemic violence of the NSW jail system of the 1970s and 1980s.

Denning had been born into crime. His father was in jail when he saw his mother commit suicide by setting herself alight with kerosene. He was just 10 years old. 'I went to my mother's room and she was burning on the bed. I got a saucepan full of water and threw it over her but it was no good. She died a day or two later,' he wrote later.

In 1973, he was sentenced to a maximum of 13 years and six months for a series of violent crimes, including assault and robbery. On September 14 the following year, he attacked prison officer Willy Faber during an escape bid from Parramatta jail. He used a claw hammer to bash the warder, yelling, 'Take that, you bastard.'

He was to escape three times and was at large for 18 months in 1980-1981. He sent audio tapes to national radio stations, appeared on *Sixty Minutes* and left a letter for police at CIB headquarters. But Denning was not motivated by a selfless desire to expose the system's flaws. He was interested only in himself.

He broke out of Goulburn jail on July 15, 1988, and almost immediately took part in an armed robbery in Brisbane.

He had been out of jail only about a week when he made the almost fatal mistake of heading south. This meant he became a target (literally) of the Victorian armed robbery squad, which had learnt Denning and Russell 'Mad Dog' Cox were planning another hold-up.

They wanted to hit a Brambles Security van at the Doncaster Shoppingtown, but the armed robbery squad was alert to the plan. Denning was overpowered but Cox tried to escape, driving a Ford Fairmont with Queensland plates. Police fired several solid shotgun shells into the car. Cox had the choice of handcuffs or body bags. He chose the handcuffs

Once in custody, Denning decided he had been an outlaw long enough and offered to change sides. He gave evidence that helped clear career criminal Graeme Jensen of the armed robbery of a Brunswick supermarket where security guard Domenic Hefti was shot dead. It was a little too late for Jensen. He had already been shot dead by over-enthusiastic police, thus precipitating the revenge murders of two innocent young constables at Walsh Street, South Yarra. Denning gave evidence implicating Tim Anderson in the Hilton bombing in 1977 that killed two council workers and a policeman in Sydney.

Denning claimed that Anderson admitted his guilt to him during their 50 to 60 conversations in jail from 1979 to 1984. Anderson was charged and later acquitted.

In 1991, Denning pleaded in court that he should be freed. 'I realised that I would spend the rest of my life in prison unless I took positive steps to remedy my misdeeds ... I began to see my actions from society's point of view, having abandoned my self-centred approach to life.'

In 1993, Denning was released into witness protection to give evidence against Cox over Queensland armed robberies but was thrown out of the scheme when the charges were dropped.

On June 11, 1993, Denning had one of his few wins as a free man. The master criminal who used to steal small fortunes from banks was delighted to win $110 from the Keno machines at the Mt Pritchard and District Community 'Mounties' Club.

A few hours later he was dead in his Paddington home – courtesy of a self-inflicted accidental heroin overdose. He had been out of jail for two months.

In jail he had told fellow inmates he was tired of the diluted heroin smuggled into prisons. He wanted a stronger dose on the outside. 'When I get out, I'm going to have a shot I'll remember for the rest of my life,' he is alleged to have said.

He got what he wanted.

John Reginald Killick

FOR the helicopter pilot, it was just another routine charter flight, this time over the yet-to-be-completed Olympic stadium at Homebush in Sydney.

Routine, that is, until the passenger, a fine-boned woman in her early 40s, pulled out a handgun and ordered him to land at Silverwater Prison in the west of the city.

It was just after 9.30am on March 25, 1999, when the pilot, Tom Joyce, suddenly found himself an unwilling accomplice in an audacious prison escape.

Joyce would later say that the woman asked to fly over the prison to 'have a look'.

'For a little while she was looking very intently down into the jail and then she asked if we could go any lower.'

He told her they couldn't and then he saw her pick up her bag. 'I think my initial reaction was that she was going to take a camera out. When I looked down she was fumbling in the purse and then as I looked back she quickly pulled a pistol out. She pointed it at my head and said, "This is a hijack".'

Joyce said he planned to fight back and tried to activate the helicopter's emergency transponder, but the woman hit his arm with her pistol. She disabled the transponder and pulled off his headset, destroying any radio contact. He was on his own.

'I think I said to her "What do you want me to do?" and she said "We have to land in there and pick somebody up", pointing to the jail.'

The helicopter landed in the prison's sports yard, where maximum security prisoners were exercising.

One of them was John Reginald Killick, 57, who was about to be moved to court for an armed robbery hearing. He ran to the small, two-seater helicopter and jumped on one of the

helicopter's skids. He said to Joyce, 'G'day mate, I'm a lifer.'
He then gave him a choice. 'You can make a lot of money out
of *Sixty Minutes* or you could be dead.'

Killick might have known about escapes but he didn't know
about aerodynamics. Joyce's small helicopter was not designed
to carry an armed robber on one side and would have over-
balanced. The pilot persuaded him to get in. 'I think I said
"Don't worry, mate, I'll get you out of here".'

The woman was Russian-born librarian Lucy Dudko, the
daughter of a helicopter pilot. She handed Killick a rifle, which
he aimed through the window.

Prison guards fired four shots from the watch-towers as other
maximum security inmates tried to clamber on board. As he
took off, Joyce heard cheering from the inmates. The helicopter
was on the ground for only about 30 seconds.

Killick and Dudko threatened to shoot Joyce when they
thought he was slowing down. It wasn't forward thinking. A
dead pilot tends to make landings difficult.

But Joyce, a stuntman, skydiver, a winner of the television
show *Who Dares Wins* and a pilot involved in rescuing sailors
in the Sydney-Hobart yacht race, remained calm. He told them,
'For goodness sake, let me fly the helicopter.'

Police tried to follow the machine before it landed on an oval
near the M2 motorway in Sydney's north-west. Killick and
Dudko used radio wire and cables to tie up the pilot, then ran.

It was like a Hollywood script. The pair ran to the road and
forced a passing car to stop. Killick aimed his gun at the driver,
who was forced to take them to the affluent suburb of Neutral
Bay.

With police helicopters above them, they forced the driver
from the vehicle, sped on and then dumped the car. Police lost
them in a side street.

They were recaptured 46 days later when police found them in cabin 14 of the Bass Hill Caravan Park. They had paid $62 and signed in as Mr and Mrs M. G. Brown.

Days earlier, they had abducted a man in Melbourne and forced him at gunpoint to drive them back to NSW.

The climax was befitting the escape. Armed police spread out around the cabin and filled the pre-dawn darkness with two powerful spotlights. Then, using the mandatory bull-horn, they called on the residents of cabin 14 to come out with their hands up. It was over in minutes.

Killick was jailed for a minimum of 15 years for the escape and a series of armed robberies. He had pleaded guilty to the escape, assaulting the helicopter pilot, detaining a person for advantage and stealing a car and mobile phone.

He also pleaded guilty to the armed robberies of the Mittagong Commonwealth Bank of $32,500 in October, 1998 and the Bowral National Bank of $23,800 in January, 1999.

He had fired three shots at an off-duty policeman during the Bowral robbery.

Killick knew what to expect. He had been jailed previously for armed robberies in 1966, 1972, 1981 and 1985.

Now he is one of the few gunmen who can brag that he committed armed robberies in four decades. Judge Barry Mahoney said Killick was a manipulator and a confidence man who was a long way from rehabilitation.

The helicopter escape wasn't the first time Killick had used a woman to help him escape. In 1984, he ran from Brisbane's Princess Alexandra Hospital with the help of a woman while in the custody of two warders.

When Lucy Dudko was asked why she had done it, she told the NSW District Court: 'First of all, I love him. Second, I loved him'.

She said Killick had protected her from her allegedly violent former husband and they had been lovers for 12 months before he was jailed. She wasn't prepared to wait and agreed to his plan to help him break out.

The judge must not have been a romantic. She jailed Dudko for a maximum 10 years with her earliest release date given as May 8, 2006.

'She was determined on one thing and one thing alone and that was to rescue her lover,' Judge Morgan said.

Dudko said 'thank you' to the judge and smiled to her legal team before being led away.

The couple have applied for permission to marry inside jail.

CHAPTER 3

Live by the Sword

ALEX Tsakmakis was a Melbourne businessman who wanted to get rid of his competition – literally. In the mid 1970s, he started to bomb, burn and terrorise any opposition he could find to his car ramp business. Police don't know how many people he killed before he himself was murdered.

The smart money suggests he killed up to eight people although he was convicted on 'only' two counts.

In 1978 he took a professional runner, Bruce Lindsay Walker, for a trip on the Bay. Only one of them came back.

He bound Walker's hands and feet with chicken wire and then tossed him over the side. Walker was alive when he went under but he wasn't when they found him washed up at Point Lonsdale. Police believe he was killed over a minor dispute involving a payment for a 1935 Plymouth.

While on bail for murder, Tsakmakis robbed a Hawthorn Tattslotto agency on June 29, 1979. He forced Ivy and George

Kartsounis to lie on the floor. He shot Kartsounis twice in the head and his wife three times. Amazingly, they survived. Police say Tsakmakis pulled the job for legal fees for his murder trial.

The way the couple were placed on the ground and shot was eerily similar to the murders of three jewellers, Paul Pace, Robert Waterman and Keith Hyman, at the Manchester Unity building on St Patrick's Day, 1978.

It is alleged that the robbery was supposed to be a sham to defraud insurance, and that no-one was supposed to get hurt. But Tsakmakis changed the rules at the last second and shot the jewellers dead. He was never much good at sharing. The diamonds were never recovered.

Police believed he killed prostitute Margaret Clayton, who was found shot dead in a North Fitzroy massage parlour in June, 1979. He was also a suspect in the murder of Willie Koeppen, who disappeared from the Cuckoo Restaurant in Olinda on February 26, 1976. His body has never been found.

Tsakmakis was also listed as a suspect in the murder of National Gallery curator Brian Finemore, who was found in his East Melbourne flat on October 24, 1975, 80 minutes before he was due to show Princess Margaret through the gallery.

When Tsakmakis was sent to prison he was immediately put in maximum security, where he used his money to bribe fellow prisoners. He wanted to run the jail and used the same tactics he had used to try and run business on the outside – money and violence. He would read the *Australian Financial Review* every day in jail – he had it specially brought in – while planning murders inside and outside prison.

Fellow top security prisoner Mark Read said: 'He was just a total ruthless, crazy bastard who always wanted to kill. In jail his main topics of conversation were money, cards and revenge. He was always talking of the murders he hoped to commit.'

In 1984, prisoners in the Jika Jika Division were, unwisely, shown a movie that included a rape scene. Convicted double murderer Barry Robert Quinn baited Tsakmakis, referring to an incident in which his girlfriend had been molested during a secret police operation that had gone wrong, involving a prisoner who promised detectives to get evidence to implicate Tsakmakis in the Manchester Unity murders.

The police helped him get early release. But his way of gathering evidence was something out of *A Clockwork Orange* – he raped Tsakmakis's girlfriend.

Quinn goaded the brooding killer during the movie and also later that night. He should have known it was a bad idea to tease a psychopath. Next day, in the prisoner's hobby area, Tsakmakis threw inflammable modelling glue over Quinn, then set him on fire by flicking matches at him.

Quinn died in agony and Tsakmakis was sentenced to a further 10 years. A death notice in the paper said, 'Barry, we always stuck together – Alex.' But on July 26, 1988, what went around came around ... in this case, two barbell weights wrapped in a pillow case, swung by Russell Street Bomber Craig Minogue. He hit Tsakmakis three times in the skull and stabbed him in the neck for good measure. He died 45 minutes later. Few mourned him.

Bora Altintas

BORA Altintas sounds like the name of a new European car. It isn't. He was a South Australian drug dealer known as the 'Adelaide Assassin' – not because of his ability with a gun, but his talent with his fists.

Altintas was light-middleweight boxing champion of the state. He was also a gangster, and a bad one. In 1989, he was sentenced to 11 years, four months' jail for heroin trafficking, armed robbery and assault.

He served only five years before he was released. After his release he turned to professional boxing and won the state title, but he had his critics. In December, 1996, Altintas was shot repeatedly at close range with a shotgun as he sat in his car in Adelaide after leaving a coffee shop.

Two masked men in a white Holden blocked a carpark exit before shooting Altintas in his small Hyundai. He was the target of a well-planned hit but his boxing instincts helped him survive. When he saw the gunmen, he curled into a ball to make himself a smaller target. The dashboard of his car helped protect him from some of the seven blasts.

The two gunmen escaped and have never been found. Surgeons thought they would have to amputate the boxer's right arm but they managed to save it, although they could not remove more than 120 pellets from his body.

After he recovered, Altintas told his parole officer he was considering moving to Melbourne for safety reasons but police later found he also had business motives.

In 1997, Altintas was found to be part of a Victorian-based drug syndicate with links in four states. He was to be snared in an undercover police operation designed to catch the leaders of the cocaine and heroin ring.

The Melbourne leaders of the group gave an undercover policeman, posing as a drug courier, five small packages containing a total of four ounces of heroin to deliver to Altintas.

The courier and the former boxer met in the bar at the Adelaide Hilton on November 1, 1997. Altintas said he was having trouble raising the money and had only $7000. He was given one ounce then and the other three on credit later.

Altintas was later arrested in the final sweep. But the Adelaide Assassin had even more problems than the Victorian drug squad. While on bail he was again shot repeatedly by two men as he walked down an Adelaide street in September, 1998. This time he didn't survive. Like most boxers, he didn't know when to retire and had one fight too many.

James Edward 'Jockey' Smith

HE WAS a notorious bank robber and escapee but James Edward Smith will always be remembered by the nickname he grew to hate ... Jockey.

Born in 1942 in the middle of the war, Smith was the second of eight children. He was raised in Victoria's Colac district and, as a teenager, became an apprentice jockey. It was a lot of hard work and, like a lot of apprentices, he got too heavy to get many race rides. His supporters say he turned to crime after an unscrupulous owner cheated him out of promised payment for exercising his horses. His critics say that even as a teenager he had more larceny in him than Long Bay jail. But it could not be disputed that Smith always showed that he loved horses and racing.

By the age of 19 he was serving his first stint inside for breaking into shops. It was the start of a long criminal career.

He was soon to team up with a petty criminal who would learn the hard way that crime doesn't pay. His name was Ronald Ryan – the man who later became the last man hanged in Australia.

Smith and Ryan tried to burgle a shop and it was Smith who tried to shoot his way to freedom but, according to police, his old pistol jammed and he was caught.

In 1973, it was again a faulty firearm that stopped him from becoming a killer. This time St Kilda policeman Russell Cook was searching a car when Smith came from behind and tried to shoot him. Again the gun failed to discharge.

Smith moved to Sydney for a change of luck but was soon charged with armed robbery offences. In what was to become part of a pattern for nearly 20 years, when he was in trouble he ran. This time he skipped bail but was re-arrested nearly two months later, sunbaking on a Melbourne beach.

Taken to Pentridge, he was there less than 48 hours before he used a visitor's pass to walk out of Victoria's then maximum-security prison. Most escapees take a low profile but Smith found that living a semi-normal life gave him the ideal camouflage. He wanted to be a racehorse trainer so he borrowed a couple of handy names from the top men in the field – Tommy Smith and Bart Cummings.

It wasn't original, but it worked. Somehow he forged a new identity and became a country horse trainer, 'Tom Cummings'. For three years he lived in Nowra, racing his horses at country meetings and occasionally venturing to Sydney. He should have stuck to the bush.

In 1976, he shot Constable Jerry Ambrose in Sydney to avoid arrest. In 1977 police alleged he broke into bookmaker Lloyd Tidmarsh's home and, during the robbery, shot him dead.

He was later arrested in a phone box in Nowra. Again, according to police, he tried to shoot the arresting officer, this time Detective Bob Godden. Smith stuck the revolver in the policeman's midriff but the quick-thinking policeman managed to stick his thumb between the breech and the hammer.

He was originally sentenced to life for the murder of Tidmarsh and shooting at Constable Ambrose but the convictions were thrown out on appeal when it was alleged police fabricated his confessions. He was sentenced to 14 years for trying to kill Godden. He was better off in jail. Someone knew his movements and was waiting when he got out. The day after he was released in February, 1992, he was walking with his wife at Bondi when he was shot in the chest, stomach and leg with shotgun blasts. He was close to death but, after a month in hospital, Jockey was back in the race.

According to Mark Brandon Read, Smith was one of the best bank robbers in the country and should have been wealthy. But 'he had a reputation as a tightwad ... a man who could have a hundred grand under the bed and go out and pinch a rubbish bin rather than pay cash for it.'

Which is perhaps why, at a time when he was making good money from selling cannabis and amphetamines, Smith courted trouble by shoplifting a steam iron, kitchen knives and a plastic tray from a Grace Brothers shop in November, 1992.

He was caught. To escape he first threatened the store detective with a gun, then forced a terrified couple to drive him away from the Erina shopping centre. Police lost track of him for a few days.

Meanwhile, members of the Melbourne armed robbery squad had their own problems. Career armed robber Christopher Dean Binse was running red hot.

He had escaped from the Parramatta jail on October 24 and, a month later, had robbed the Commonwealth Bank in Doncaster of $160,000.

Detective Sergeant Steve (Larry) Curnow learned that Binse and two others, including a big name from Sydney, planned to rob an Armaguard truck in Melbourne.

The squad launched a top priority operation, code-named Farnsy. They found Binse was hiding on a farm near Daylesford. Listening devices picked up that one of the men at the farm was known as Tom. They didn't know at the time that

Tom was Tom Cummings, alias Jockey Smith. Just after 8pm on December 5, 1992, Tom drove from the farm in a white Ford panel van. Police decided to let him go. They knew he would be back and their main target, Binse, was still inside.

Local policeman Senior Constable Ian Harris was on a routine afternoon shift and was unaware of the armed robbery squad operation in his area when he spotted the van on the Midlands Highway.

He saw the driver was travelling at 80kmh, 20 below the speed limit. He checked on the radio for the 'usuals.' He was told the car had been reported stolen.

He followed the van until it turned into the driveway of the Farmers Arms Hotel in Creswick. Drinkers in the bar stood to watch the show.

Jockey got out of the van and approached the policeman, still sitting in the marked car. After a brief discussion, Harris asked the driver for proof of ownership. Smith went back, grabbed the car manual and used it to conceal a five-shot handgun. In the left pocket of his jeans was a can of mace.

Harris got out of his car and Smith shoved the revolver in the policeman's stomach. He ordered the policeman to hand over his gun but the policeman kept it just out of the reach of the smaller man.

Smith fired a shot into the ground and said, 'I'll give you 10 seconds to get your gun out of your pocket and get on the bonnet or I'll blow you away.'

Harris called on the drinkers to ring the police. He knew back-up was only minutes away. But would it be too late? He was not to know that just up the road half the armed robbery squad and special operations group were watching a quiet farmhouse while he was fighting for his life.

A local called Darren Neil had spent a thirsty day exploring mine shafts and, after a few drinks at a mate's place, decided to get some stubbies at the Farmers Arms. When he saw the police car he decided to keep driving. No need to risk his licence for a couple of beers. Then he looked in his rear view mirror and saw a man pointing a gun at the policeman, who was trying to back away.

Later, Neil could not explain his reaction. He told his two young sons, who were in the front seat with him, 'We better go back.' He got out of his car, walked over to the gunman and pushed him in the chest. Smith responded by firing a warning shot into the ground. Neil then knew this was no game.

He ran back to his car, drove to the entrance of the pub, pushed his kids to safety and then drove back at the gunman. Smith fired another shot and then pointed his gun at Neil.

It was the split second Harris needed. He grabbed his service revolver and fired three times, hitting Smith in the chest and stomach.

The shots were fatal. Jockey fell at the last.

Barry Robert Quinn

BARRY Robert Quinn was a guru-like criminal who inspired killings without actually committing them. He was convicted of a double murder although he didn't fire the shots. Five other people connected to him were all to die although he did not raise a hand to kill them.

Quinn modelled himself on the evil American multiple-murderer, Charles Manson, taking on a similar appearance and trying to behave in the same way. Like Manson, he surrounded himself with associates who would kill for him. Although Quinn was convicted of the murder of two men during an armed robbery on the Car-O-Tel motel in St Kilda in 1974, police believe his accomplice was the killer. Quinn escaped from the Fairfield Infectious Diseases Hospital in 1978 where he was being treated for suspected hepatitis. In the 69 days he was at large, five people associated with him were murdered. They were Eve Karlson, Wayne Smith, Sheryle Anne Gardner, her nine-year-old son Danny William Mitchell and Lisa Maude Brearley.

Eve Karlson, one of Quinn's girlfriends, was shot dead at a Warburton campsite by his jealous lover, Sheryle Gardner, in 1979. Although Eve was his real love, Quinn did nothing to stop the killing. He had the name Eve tattooed over his arms, legs and body. Fellow inmate Mark Brandon 'Chopper' Read said Quinn was not respected in the underworld: 'His was cowardly violence of a mindless nature directed against the weak without courage, style or flair.'

Quinn was later killed in the Pentridge prison maximum security unit, Jika Jika, by fellow inmate Alex Tsakmakis, who burned him alive on July 5, 1984. Quinn had baited Tsakmakis the previous night about the rape of his girlfriend. Tsakmakis remained silent but next day he poured modelling glue over Quinn and flicked matches at him until he burst into flames.

When Quinn was taken to hospital, nurses and doctors tried to comfort the badly-burnt man, assuring him he would survive – but a veteran Homicide Squad detective, Jimmy Fry, pushed through and told him he was about to die. He looked up and said, 'Yeah, I know. So what's the drama.'

Quinn confirmed what police had long suspected. He had not pulled the trigger at the Car-O-Tel. His partner had used a .410 shotgun to shoot Drago Pucar, 34, and Josip Slokar, 33, during an armed robbery that netted only $100. But he refused to name Tsakmakis as the man who had covered him in glue and set him on fire. By refusing to break the underworld code, he showed more dash as he died than he ever had alive.

'Mad Charlie' Hegyalji

'MAD Charlie' Hegyalji was always security conscious – men in the illegal amphetamine industry usually are. He filled books with the registration numbers of vehicles he believed might be following him, was always discreet on the telephone and chose a house that he believed offered him the greatest protection.

His comfortable brick home in Caulfield South was shielded from the traffic noises of busy Bambra Road by 10 mature cypress trees that had merged to make a six-metre high hedge so thick it had been pruned to allow pedestrians access to the footpath.

There was a 1.5-metre horizontal planked wooden fence that acted as another buffer to noise and, more importantly for Hegyalji, as a screen to block possible police surveillance.

Near the front door a small white surveillance camera was trained down the six-metre garden path. From inside the house anyone entering or leaving the property could be safely observed on a video screen.

'Mad Charlie' lived in the house relatively secure in the knowledge he had done all he could to protect himself and his business from untimely interruptions by police or competitors.

In the end, it wasn't enough. Charlie was killed by a lone gunman who used the criminal's own security fetish against him. The killer crouched under the first cypress tree inside the fence line and waited until Hegyalji came home just before 1am on November, 23, 1998, confident he could not be seen from the street.

Hegyalji was picked up by an associate about 6pm and they drank at the London Tavern, in Caulfield, the Grosvenor Hotel in Balaclava and Newmarket Hotel, in St Kilda. They met up with two other men for their night of drinking.

To an outsider, it would seem like an old-fashioned pub-crawl, but people like Hegyalji are always on the move, conducting business in pubs and clubs, and avoiding set routines that make them easy to track.

Charlie and one of the men went back to a unit in St Kilda, off Inkerman Street, just after midnight. Hegyalji rang a Yellow Cab from his friend's unit to take the short trip home around 12.40am.

When the cabbie rang the doorbell, Charlie got up to go, leaving half a stubby behind. A few minutes later, instead of being dropped off outside his house he ordered the taxi to stop about a block away from home.

It was another security habit Charlie developed. If someone was waiting for him, he could sneak up unheard. It was 12.50 am.

Hegyalji opened the wooden gate and took two steps along the stone path inside when the killer, armed with a handgun, opened fire. One shot missed but before Charlie could react he was shot several times in the head.

Neighbours heard the shots and called the police but Charlie's obsession with privacy concealed his body from police torches and the patrol car drove off.

It would have made no difference. He had died instantly and the killer, believed to be a tall man with swept back hair, was gone in seconds, running past nearby Freeman Street.

About seven hours later Hegyalji's de facto wife, Ellie, was about to make breakfast for their two children when she glanced up at the security screen focused on the front path and saw the body.

The security camera remained operational and should have provided the biggest clue in the case. But, for all his security precautions, Charlie had grown lazy. There was no tape in the machine.

The front sensor light had also malfunctioned and Charlie had not bothered to get it fixed.

It is almost certain the killer knew he would not be filmed or illuminated. He had been a guest in the house or had been told by someone who had.

Either way, it was an inside job.

When Hegyalji, then aged 13, arrived at Station Pier as a European refugee, he said to his mother in Hungarian: 'Where is the Statue of Liberty?'

He may have wanted to be an American gangster but he soon learned the ways of the underworld Down Under.

Hegyalji became a violent young standover man involved in rapes and robberies on massage parlours. In the 1970s, he began to call himself 'The Don' and modelled himself on the image of the US crime figures he revered from afar. But, by the 1980s, he found there was more money to be made by being involved in the amphetamine trade than robbing fellow criminals.

In the 1980s, a bright chemistry student, Paul Lester, quit university once he knew enough to produce the best amphetamines in Australia. He was a sought-after speed cook more interested in his hobby of tinkering with electronics than making money from illegal drugs.

But Charlie was the sort who wouldn't take no for an answer. He abducted Lester at gunpoint from a Rosebud street, then drove him blindfolded to a Gippsland property, where he forced him to produce amphetamines.

In another cook in Carlton, the process didn't work according to plan and Hegyalji poured the sludgy and volatile substance out on a tarpaulin, allowing the sun to evaporate the liquid, leaving the amphetamine powder. He called it sun-dried speed. Just the thing for inner-suburban dinner parties.

Police who dealt with Hegyalji said he was funny and, when

it suited him, charming. 'He was always jovial but he was always trying to run you. He would ask more questions than he answered,' one said. According to one detective, Hegyalji bought a book on police informing from the United States in the hope he would be able to keep the upper hand when being interviewed. 'He was prepared to inform but only out of self interest. He would give information to expose his enemies and to keep himself out of jail.'

There was no sign of him ever working for wages and he saw no pressing need to collect unemployment benefits. But if his quick wit failed he had alternatives. When police raided a Narre Warren farmhouse in 1995 as part of an amphetamines investigation, they found a hidden armoury behind a false bedroom wall.

It included almost 20 pistols, machine guns and shotguns, six cans of mace, false drivers' licences and silencers. They also found a computer printout from a national security firm that listed alarm systems used through Melbourne. A pink highlighter had been used to identify the systems used in police stations. Hegyalji's fingerprints were found on the list.

Hegyalji was called 'Mad Charlie' after he bit off the nose of an enemy when he was still a teenager. But when another criminal was given the nickname 'Machinegun Charlie' he became jealous and tried to persuade people to give him the more glamorous title. But to everyone he was still Mad Charlie.

In 1989, Hegyalji was shot in the stomach outside a house in South Caulfield and he later shot a man in the carpark of a St Kilda hotel as a payback. In 1997, he was involved in a gun battle with another criminal associate outside a panel beaters in Prahran. Both men were unhurt.

Hegyalji was charged with attempted murder and kept in custody for just over a year until he was released in July, 1998.

The charges were dropped because, as in so many cases involving the underworld, witnesses refused to testify.

Charlie went back to his old patch of St Kilda and Caulfield expecting business to return to normal but, according to police, the void had been filled by others. The people who had been left to run his business were not keen to relinquish control.

He had to flex his muscles and, when he was drinking, loved to wave his handgun around in hotels, playing up to his gangster image.

But Hegyalji was forced to stop carrying his revolver with him at all times because he was increasingly being stopped and searched by police.

In the drug business it can be as dangerous to be owed money as to be in debt. Charlie was owed more than $100,000 when he was killed but there was no chance of his heirs collecting the money. The debt died with him, not being a financial arrangement that can be listed on legal documents.

In the world Mad Charlie inhabited all his adult life, business deals were never committed to paper and, in the end, contracts can only be enforced with a gun.

Phillip 'The Iceman' Wilson

PHILLIP Grant Wilson didn't get the funeral of his dreams. The big man with a neo-Nazi background had once written in a diary that he wanted his coffin carried on a horse-drawn gun carriage through the streets of Melbourne.

Wilson, known in the underworld as 'The Iceman', said he wanted to die with honour and go to Valhalla, the mythical Norse heaven for heroes.

But there was no more honour in Wilson's death than in his life. He was blasted twice in the back with a shotgun outside a

South Yarra chiropractic clinic in August, 1987. His killer has never been found.

Wilson, 34, was two metres tall and a moderately successful businessman who owned a small engineering firm. Then he fell in love with being a gangster and became a standover man and the organiser of armed robberies.

Most criminals learn their trade through the teenage years and develop rat-cunning to survive as they graduate from youth training centres to prison farms and maximum security jails. Tricks are passed on by word of mouth. Wilson didn't know that intellect without instinct would never be enough.

His best friend, Tommy Messenger, was killed during a police raid in Wantirna in January, 1985. Messenger fired shots at police, hitting one in the bullet-proof vest, before he was shot dead.

Both Messenger and Wilson were connected to a neo-Nazi group based in Melbourne. Wilson vowed revenge. Police discovered he planned to buy a light plane, kidnap the SOG member who shot Messenger and throw him to his death.

Wilson and his crew of followers, standover men and manipulators, bought a run-down Melbourne hotel where they would recruit drug addicts to commit frauds and armed robberies and act as heroin couriers.

Two of their recruits were Lina Galea and Ricky Parr. But Wilson turned on them when he concluded they had cost him $150,000 from a drug deal.

He lured the two to a country property on the pretence of a picnic. Galea, 30, was still recovering from a car accident and needed crutches to walk but managed to hobble to the picnic rug set out on the paddock about 65 kilometres from Melbourne.

Police were told that during the picnic, Wilson shot Parr in the head from behind. The terrified Galea, hobbling on her crutches tried to escape. Wilson followed, laughing and goading her before shooting her dead. Their bodies have never been found. Wilson denied any involvement. 'I have no idea what happened to them. They're just not around any more,' he told one of the authors.

He also denied he was an underworld enforcer and a closet Nazi, although he did have business cards made out in the name of his alter ego, Philipe Von Hessler.

He did not see this as a problem. 'I've got a pretty good personality … no bloody personality defects. I don't need to bash people to prove myself. I'm not a bad sort of guy. I don't need to hurt people. I never have. I don't hate anyone. I've got a forgiving nature.'

But 'forgiving' wasn't the word for his attitude towards a member of the armed robbery squad who, he claimed, had knocked him down during a raid and stuffed a shotgun in his mouth saying, 'How do you like this, big fella?'

The Iceman hadn't responded on that occasion. The policeman, known as 'Blue Eyes', always denied the allegation. Wilson said he had not killed anyone 'in peacetime' and claimed he had been a mercenary in Rhodesia. This claim is unverified, but he was a student of warfare and an explosives expert. He used his knowledge to plan armed robberies and other crimes.

Using handpicked recruits, Wilson planned his raids to the finest detail. Because of his height, which would make him easily identifiable, the General had to be satisfied with sending others to battle.

He planned the jobs, recruited his teams, selected the targets, organised the cars, guns and disguises. He also facilitated the laundering of the money.

But, for all his planning, he did not learn the lessons of history. Even Hitler was attacked by those closest to him, narrowly escaping being blown up by his own staff. Wilson forgot to protect his broad back and did not see the killer waiting for him in the shadows of an inner-suburban carpark.

The policeman known as 'Blue Eyes' would have been considered a suspect in the case – if he had not been at the police club with 200 colleagues on the night.

Roger Caleb Rogerson
… just another crook.

South Australian drug squad boss Barry Moyse … gamekeeper turned poacher.

A dark and stormy knight … Terry Lewis.

Denis Tanner
... accused
of murder.

Rogue
detective
Colin
Creed.

George David Freeman and Lennie 'Mr Big' McPherson at the
funeral of underworld figure Paddles Anderson.

The Queen with NSW Premier and crime boss Sir Robert Askin. He didn't snatch her purse.

Lennie McPherson (left) with Nick Giordano and Chicago crime boss Joe Testa (right) on a roo shoot. Testa was later murdered in the US.

Abraham Gilbert Saffron, 'Mr Sin'.

Arthur Stanley 'Neddy' Smith. (right)

Giuseppe Arena, 'The Friendly Godfather' … money launderer, but something didn't wash. Now dead.

Robert 'Aussie Bob' Trimbole. Left in a plane, came back in a box.

Grave matters … Gianfranco Tizzoni and Liborio Benvenuto.

ALLA CARA MEMORIA DI
LIBORIO BENVENUTO
NATO. 15. 12. 1927 A BRUZZANO ZEFFIRIO (RC)
DECEDUTO 10. 6. 1988 A MELBOURNE

LASCIA NEL PROFONDO DOLORE
LA MOGLIE, FIGLI, NIPOTI
E FAMIGLIA

R. I. P.

Mr Cool and
The Songbird
… paid killer
James Frederick
Bazley (right)
and the man who
paid the bills,
Frank Tizzoni.

Like father, like son … Vincenzo and Alfonse Muratore. Both in the market. Both shot dead in Hampton, 28 years apart.

Jimmy
Siu
.....how
do you
do?

Laurie 'Last Resort' Connell. Dead set crook. Now just dead.

What a joke … corporate crook Alan Bond with his lawyer, Andrew Fraser, who did time for cocaine.

Christopher Skase. Bad suit … bad lungs … bad luck.

CHAPTER 4

Crime Legends

EVEN though Bobby Lee was looking down the barrel of a gun, he thought he had a good chance of surviving. The tough boxer turned gangster had fought his way out of tight corners before. Lee was sitting in Sydney's Ziegfeld Club and was sure the man standing over him wouldn't fire in front of witnesses. Not one or two who might be persuaded to look the other way, but 80 patrons, staff and entertainers.

It was a fatal miscalculation.

The man with the gun was John Frederick 'Chow' Hayes. It was May 29, 1951. Hayes believed Lee had killed Hayes's nephew, Danny Simmons, and he was there to even the score.

In his life story, *Chow Hayes, Gunman*, written by the crusading Sydney journalist David Hickie, Hayes said he walked into the nightclub in King Street, at 11.30pm, with a fellow gangster, Joey Hollebone.

In Hickie's book, the exchange is recorded like this: 'Lee

said: "You wouldn't do it in here, with the lights shining and all the people around." So with that I pulled out the .45 from my belt and held it just above the table ... And I said: "I'll fucking give it to you here, don't worry about that!"

'But he said: "No you won't. There are too many witnesses."

'Then I said: "Are you going to come outside?" But he replied: "You get fucked!" So then I just said: "Well, here's yours!" And I fired and hit him twice in the chest.

'He fell over and out the back of the chair. Then I stood up and walked around the table, because he'd fallen out of sight. When I arrived above his slumped body, I pumped another slug into his side and two more into his back. I fired three more times – and by this point the band had stopped playing and people were running everywhere, screaming at the tops of their voices.'

At which point Hayes and Hollebone calmly walked out of the club. But Hayes had a problem. Witnesses. Eighty of them. He was sentenced to death in 1952, had the sentence commuted and served 15 years.

Hayes admitted in the book that he was stone cold guilty, but wouldn't have been convicted if NSW police hadn't massaged the evidence. He claimed that the notorious detective Ray 'Gunner' Kelly produced a fake confession – an old-fashioned 'verbal'. 'Kelly was a better liar than I was', Hayes conceded of his old enemy.

Hayes's police record stretched 32 years from 1928 to 1970. He first got into trouble with the law when he was 11 and spent his adult life working as a thief and standover man.

Not that it did him a lot of good. He spent a total of 28 years in jail. For all that, he was one of the few to survive in his era. He told Hickie that about 50 friends and enemies of his were murdered between 1920 and 1980. He spoke willingly about his murder of Eddie Weyman. A jury acquitted him, but Hayes was later prepared to admit he was guilty. Hayes had been told that Weyman planned to kill him so he decided to get in first. It was New Year's Eve, 1945, when he fronted Weyman. 'I fired and hit him five times with the .38.'

Hayes spoke of nearly killing a criminal associate, Billy McCarthy, with a tram hook. 'He needed about 80 or 90 stitches. But he was the toughest man I ever met. I hit him everywhere I could, all over the head and arms.'

Many crims begin to mellow as they get older. Not Hayes. Prone to over-react, he gouged out fellow drinker Gerald Hutchinson's left eye with a broken beer glass in 1969 after accusing him of stealing a handful of coins used for poker machine and beer money.

He was sentenced to five years' jail. Even though he was nearly 60 when he went to Parramatta Prison he was still able to run the jail's SP network.

Twenty years later, as a frail old man, Chow Hayes said he didn't regret his life. Although he had made a fortune running protection rackets it had all slipped away and he was nearly broke. He paid $24 a week to rent a flat for the elderly although he still had enough cash to pay for his 60-cigarettes-a-day habit and to buy about 12 'middies' of beer.

'We didn't interfere with decent people, with squareheads. I only got blokes who wanted to get me,' he told Tony Stephens of the *Sydney Morning Herald*. He said he believed in God. 'But I can't work out why He allows kids to be born blind and allows a bastard like me to live to almost 80.'

Frederick William 'The Frog' Harrison

FREDDIE 'The Frog' Harrison, was a man of many parts. Gunman, gangster and navy deserter, he was the best-known standover man in Victoria in the years after World War II.

He was charged with more than 50 offences over 15 years, including attempted murder, but most of the charges wouldn't stick and he did little jail time. He appeared to be teflon coated, although teflon hadn't yet been invented.

As with so many of his type, it wasn't the law that caught up with Freddie but the underworld, in the shape of a shotgun cartridge loaded with heavy 'number four' shot, such as is usually used for larger vermin such as foxes – and deadly at close range.

A lot of people had a lot of reasons to croak 'The Frog'. He was alleged to have killed at least two rivals and he stood over SP bookmakers and sly grog shops. He 'worked' on the docks and while he rarely raised a sweat he attended regularly to receive his pay packet.

According to the legendary crime reporter Tom Prior, Harrison loved the gangster image. A flashy dresser, usually seen in a double-breasted suit and a wide-brimmed fedora hat, he was a regular at city cinemas to watch the latest Jimmy Cagney or George Raft movie. Like Alphonse Gangitano 30 years later, Harrison tried to model himself on Hollywood's celluloid tough guys.

According to Prior, Harrison was addicted to cocaine, which made him even more unpredictable and dangerous.

In February, 1958, Harrison and two friends, Jack Twist and Harold Nugent, went pig shooting near Oxley in New South

Wales. They shot two pigs and then settled into a prolonged drinking session. Things turned nasty and so did Freddie. He pulled a shotgun and threatened to shoot Nugent, who grabbed the barrel in self-defence.

Freddie fired and Nugent lost the thumb and two fingers from his right hand. Freddie turned the gun on Twist, an accomplished boxer, who managed to wrestle the gun away from him.

Harrison drove back to Melbourne without his former friends. Twist managed to get Nugent to hospital. The injured man refused to tell police what happened. He knew other ways to even the score.

On February 6, 1958, Harrison pulled up at South Wharf in his 1953 Ford Customline to pick up his pay and return a borrowed trailer he had used for the shooting trip. As he was uncoupling the trailer, an unidentified gunman pulled out a shotgun, said the immortal words: 'This is yours, Fred' and shot Harrison in the head. The Frog had been croaked.

There were 30 men in the area. Each one was to say he saw nothing. About 12 potential witnesses declared they were in the toilet at the time of the shooting. It was a two-man toilet.

The man who was helping Freddie uncouple the trailer was covered with blood from the victim. He was to tell police that when he heard the blast he looked right and walked off. The shot had come from his left so, naturally, he didn't see who the gunman was.

Constable Reginald Wilkinson noticed a boy scurrying off near the docks with something hidden in his cardigan. He searched the teenager and found he was carrying a cardboard ammunition carton containing 12-gauge shotgun cartridges. There were 22 of them and another two in his pockets. The box originally held 25, which meant one was missing. There were no prizes for guessing that it was the one in what was left of Harrison's head, 150 metres further down the wharf.

The boy was Charles Joseph Wooton, 15, of Punt Road, Windsor. He was Harold Nugent's stepson. Years later, some police would make a career investigating Wooton, who became heavily involved in the illegal gaming industry.

Police always believed John Eric Twist was the gunman, although he was never charged. It was the underworld's worst kept secret. *Truth* newspaper famously ran the deadpan headline, 'New Twist in Harrison Slaying'.

Police told Twist he was no longer welcome in Melbourne. He moved to San Remo and became a fisherman. Freddie's murder was never solved.

William John O'Meally

WILLIAM John O'Meally had every reason to be a strong Labor man. He was on death row and likely to be hanged when Labor, under John Cain senior, swept to power.

A Liberal government would have carried out the death penalty, but the ALP opposed capital punishment. O'Meally lived to be Victoria's longest-serving inmate. He was the last man to be legally flogged in custody.

Constable George Howell was unarmed when he was shot as he attempted to arrest a man he had disturbed tampering with a car near the Crystal Palace Theatre, Caulfield, on January 30, 1952. He died two days later. The dying policeman gave detectives a deposition from the operating table, but could not identify the suspect gunman in a line-up at the hospital.

What Howell was able to say was the man who shot him used an expression which had been out of fashion for years. He called him a 'fucking walloper'.

Jack O'Connor, who would rise to be an assistant commissioner, remembered that when he was a young patrol officer he had arrested a powerful burglar after chasing him over back fences. They had fought to a standstill. Then, as the exhausted thief gave up, he had only enough energy for one last insult. He called O'Connor a 'fucking walloper'.

O'Meally always maintained he was framed. When he was convicted he said in court: 'I am innocent. I couldn't do a thing like this.'

When he heard the death sentence, he fainted and had to be carried from the courtroom. Women in the gallery wept, and his wife sobbed at the bar table. But the prisoner was given a reprieve. The newly-elected State Government commuted his death sentence to life imprisonment without remissions.

His papers were marked 'Imprisonment for the term of his natural life without any remissions whatsoever.' But few things are forever. He was eventually released on parole on US Independence Day, July 4, 1979.

Retired prison chaplain Father John Brosnan said: 'Old Bill always said he was innocent.' According to Brosnan, 'He was not the hard man of Pentridge and didn't deserve the reputation as a standover man. He did stand up to the rigours of H Division in a way that no-one else could have.'

A prison officer said: 'Bill always said he didn't do it, but that doesn't mean much. They all claim they're innocent in Pentridge.'

O'Meally, a solid 31-year-old labourer from Bonbeach, a Melbourne bayside suburb, was sentenced to death in May, 1952 – just four months after the murder.

His son had been born 23 days after his arrest. He did not see his son until the boy was 21 and a father himself.

O'Meally escaped from Pentridge in 1955 but was arrested in

the back yard of a house about 200 metres from the jail. In a second escape bid in 1957, a prison officer was shot in the thigh by a fellow escapee, Robert Henry Taylor. This time O'Meally was free for 13 minutes before being recaptured.

He received 12 lashes for the escape and wounding, the last flogging carried out under Victorian law. He was kept in solitary confinement in H Division for 14 years and in that time he did not see the sky. He was to become the longest-serving prisoner in Victorian history.

O'Meally had married for the second time in 1951. After his conviction, his young wife, Lois, tried and failed to raise £1000 for an appeal to the Privy Council.

She asked O'Meally's mother in Sydney for money but she refused, saying, 'He broke my heart years ago.'

In June 1965, his wife was granted a divorce.

O'Meally was born in November, 1920, in the rural New South Wales town of Young. He was the second of four children and was named Joseph Thompson. He was later to use eight aliases.

The family moved to Sydney when he was 11, but his parents split and the children became wards of state.

His first conviction was for travelling on a train without a ticket. The penalty: two days' hard labour at a country police station. At 15, he spent three months in prison for assaulting a police officer.

While in Pentridge, O'Meally embraced Christianity. He was the altar boy in the B-Division chapel. He also took up writing, penning dozens of poems, plays and short stories. He even wrote a script for an episode of the police drama *Homicide*, which he submitted unsuccessfully to the program's makers.

He also took to painting, or so it was alleged. According to fellow inmate Mark Brandon Read, artistic prisoners at Geelong jail painted a series of landscapes, then would call on

O'Meally to sign his name at the bottom. The paintings sold for around $1500 because of the notoriety of the 'artist'.

'Bill couldn't paint a fence,' Read said.

Almost 16 years after his release, O'Meally, an ill 75-year-old man retired in Queensland, tried to get his case re-opened.

Crucial evidence in the case was a set of car keys owned by O'Meally, which were found at the scene. He told police when he was interviewed that two other men had borrowed the keys.

O'Meally claimed four men were at the scene where Constable Howell was shot but that he wasn't one of them. He said he was at home with his wife and not involved. Defence lawyers claimed none of the men would verify the story because, as accomplices, they could have hanged for the murder.

A lawyer, based in Canberra, later said that one of the four confirmed O'Meally's story. It was only after the man died that the solicitor could come forward because of client-lawyer confidentiality.

The director of public prosecutions agreed to produce all legal transcripts from archives, including appeal documents, so that defence lawyers could review the case.

But it was flogging a dead horse. Nothing came of the move and the conviction stood.

Theodore Leslie Joseph 'Squizzy' Taylor

THEODORE Leslie Joseph Taylor was not born to crime, but he was a quick learner. Second youngest of five children of a respected coachbuilder, he was born in 1888 and lived in the Melbourne bayside suburb of Brighton.

From the age of 11 he was fascinated with violence and was

sentenced to a boys home to reform, but it was already too late. He became the leader of the gang known as the Bourke Street Rats, which specialised in bashing and robbing drunks.

Taylor loved fighting, but not for his country. While many men his age were heading for Gallipoli, he was building his influence with the young Turks of the underworld.

Like Freddie Harrison in the 1950s and Alphonse Gangitano in the 1990s, Taylor loved to look like a gangster and imitate American crime bosses.

He wore silk shirts and a coat with a velvet collar and would talk to the Press, who treated him like a celebrity rather than a killer. He wore diamonds and, befitting a Bourke Street Rat, had gold in his teeth. He was, they said, 'as flash as a rat with a gold tooth'.

In the 10 years from 1917 until his death in 1927 he was the biggest crime figure in Australia. He was only about 170 centimetres tall and had a head like a ferret, but what he lacked in size was made up for by sheer malice.

According to the police of the day, he was a murderer, thief, bootlegger, illegal bookmaker, arsonist and blackmailer – and they were his good points.

He also rigged juries, bribed police and other officials and planned armed robberies.

In 1916, Taylor was charged with the murder of taxi driver William Haines. It was alleged Taylor and another man hired the taxi to take them to Bulleen, where they planned to rob a bank employee of £400. When Haines would not go along with the plan, he was shot six times and left in his cab.

It appeared an open and shut case until witnesses lost their memories during the trial and the prosecution collapsed.

In 1923 in one bank job planned by Taylor in Glenferrie, the manager, Thomas Berriman, was shot. It took him 13 days to die.

While Taylor loved the headlines, the lucrative SP network was run by another major gangster who kept in the shadows, Harry Stokes. The money was so great that Stokes and Taylor combined to go to war against another rival, Harry Slater.

Those who whip up hysteria about 'unprecedented violence' in our capital cities have no sense of history.

In 1919, Taylor tried to negotiate peace between the two gangs but he was ambushed in his car in Fitzroy. The gunman missed Squizzy, but a man walking past was shot in the neck.

The feud lasted two years and in March, 1921, Stokes and Slater opened up against each other in the middle of the city at lunchtime. It was like a scene from an American western rather than a staid Australian city. In the gun battle, Slater was shot in the shoulder and the arm and Stokes escaped unscathed. The wounded man refused to make a statement to police and when he recovered, headed back to Sydney.

Stokes was now the king of gambling in Victoria, but he doubted the loyalty of his little deputy, Squizzy Taylor.

Taylor was also behind a daring £2000 jewellery robbery although many of the gang believed their leader kept more than his share of the cash when the gear was fenced.

In one of his robberies his team escaped with £2750. Armed with handguns, they threw pepper in the face of the two workers carrying a railways payroll. Squizzy was ahead of his time. More than 70 years later authorities were to learn the value of pepper spray as a weapon, arming police with capsicum spray.

In 1927, the underworld turned against Taylor and someone paid for Sydney hitman John (Snowy) Cutmore to come to Melbourne to kill the dapper gangster.

Squizzy decided to get in first. He followed the paid killer to a small house in Carlton. Snowy was sick with the flu and went to bed – not with a hot lemon drink but a handgun. When Squizzy burst in, gun blazing, Snowy returned the fire. Cutmore died in bed – he was shot five times. Taylor died on the way to St Vincent's Hospital. He was 39.

Ronald Joseph Ryan

THE last man hanged in Australia was born Ronald Edmond Thompson, washed his hands up to 40 times day and wore a starched shirt and tie to go bushwalking with his wife – a private schoolgirl whose wealthy father was a pillar of the Anglican church and four times mayor of Hawthorn.

Born in abject poverty, the boy became a model prisoner called Ronald Joseph Ryan, and dreamed of being somebody. A compulsive gambler, he would risk anything for the big win that never came. In the end, he gambled his liberty and lost his life.

By the time Ryan had his neck broken at Pentridge prison by a scrawny old man hiding behind welding goggles, he was the most famous criminal in Australia. All his life he had craved attention and respect but they had eluded him. He found them, too late, in the shadow of the gallows in 1967.

Before his execution, Ryan believed his sentence would be commuted. Prison psychiatrist Allen Bartholomew examined Ryan just before the murder trial and found, 'He was in fact in very good mental health and he was in good spirits – I formed the impression that he enjoyed a challenge and a fight and that he was looking forward with pleasure to being in the limelight.'

He said Ryan was troubled during the trial ... but by haemorrhoids, not the prospect of a death sentence.

Ryan confided to Bartholomew his escape masterplan. Once out of Pentridge he wanted to get to friends, rob a bank, drive to Sydney, blow a safe and move to South America.

'He told his whole story in a cheerful, breezy manner interwoven with some highly amusing anecdotes. By no stretch of the imagination could one say that he showed any remorse for his actions or apparent anxiety regarding his immediate predicament.

'He has made tentative plans for his future which appear to be that he anticipates spending five years in H Division, doing his matriculation and then proceeding to a BA in commerce and economics (this I think he could theoretically do – he has the capacity).

'Whilst he feels that any sentence in lieu would be prolonged, he is hopeful that another government might well review his case after a number of years.

'In my opinion he is a man of intelligence who shows no remorse and virtually no anxiety – he is psychopathic. I feel the future is basically unmeaningful to him, he enjoys today and enjoys being in the spotlight.'

Ryan told Bartholomew that if taken to hospital for a haemorrhoid operation he could be trusted. 'Don't worry, Doc. If I give you my word I will not escape, I won't. I am an honest crim and I won't let you or Mr Grindlay (prison governor) down.'

Bartholomew must have sensed an inner strength and accurately predicted that Ryan could face his own death without blinking. 'Should the sentence be confirmed, I would expect no difficulty in handling the prisoner.'

Ryan nursed hopes of an 11th-hour reprieve but when that forlorn chance vanished, he faced death in a way that touched all who saw it, except perhaps the hangman, a dour professional.

Ryan's last thoughts were for others. He returned to his Catholic faith, confessed his crime to a trusted few, prayed for forgiveness and faced the gallows stoically, even heroically.

There were 3000 protesters outside Pentridge late the night

before the hanging. The wild scenes were broadcast around the world. Long-time Liberal premier Henry Bolte brushed aside concerted opposition to Ryan's hanging to shore up his political authority, eroded four years earlier when another condemned man, Robert Peter Tait, avoided the noose when declared insane.

Ryan was born in 1925 and grew up scarred by the stigma of illegitimacy, bruised from the beatings by his drunken father and aware his mother prostituted herself to support him and three younger sisters.

He showed early signs of criminality. At 11, he was caught stealing a neighbour's watch and sent to the Salesian Fathers' Home at Sunbury. He made his first escape three weeks later by sneaking onto a freight train with another boy, and they were arrested after stealing jam tarts.

He always saw himself as a victim of bad luck, or injustice, never his own actions.

At the end, for once, he was right. He became the victim of a political power game. Those close to the case had no doubt he was guilty of the crime for which he was convicted – shooting prison warder George Hodson while escaping from Pentridge Prison with Peter Walker on December 19, 1965.

But there was a widespread revulsion at Bolte's refusal to commute the sentence the way that 35 earlier death sentences had been since 1955.

Peter John Walker

PETER John Walker was born just after the Blitz, near London, the middle child of a troubled and violent soldier, Robert Arthur Walker, of the Queen's Guards.

He had no chance of a normal childhood after his mother,

Alma, committed suicide by gassing herself in her bed. Walker was only seven. He was eight when he was shipped to Australia with his brothers – never to see his father again. He like, thousands of others, was one of the lost children of the British Empire. He was shunted from institution to foster home around Victoria, an ideal apprenticeship for crime and jail. As a teenager he was convicted for a string of minor offences, including stealing a car and having an unlicensed gun.

He moved to NSW but his bad habits went with him. He was soon back committing petty crimes.

According to Mike Richards' comprehensive book, *The Hanged Man*, Walker returned to Melbourne and worked as a truck driver but still managed to build up large debts through gambling.

When he was 23 he attempted to pull an armed robbery on a western suburbs bank but his ambitions exceeded his abilities. In 1965, times were different. Banks actually had staff and some of them were armed and prepared to put up a fight. There was a gun battle between Walker and the bank manager, who was supported by the branch accountant. Walker was held and arrested by police. He was sentenced to a minimum of nine years.

Walker may have been a failed armed robber but he was tough and game. Inside Pentridge he made a friend in Ronald Ryan, who was looking for a partner with some dash. They decided to escape. It would cost three men their lives.

On December 19, 1965 they went over the wall. Ryan shot dead prison officer George Hodson as the warder tried to grab Walker outside the jail.

The two escapees went to a woman's flat in Elwood to hide before committing a big armed robbery on a Hampton branch of the ANZ bank.

Within days of being on the loose they held a Christmas Eve party with a group of newfound friends but the two became increasingly nervous that they would be sold out.

One of the men present was Arthur Henderson, a local tow-truck driver.

When they ran out of beer, Henderson and Walker went to find a sly-grog shop. After buying a dozen bottles, Walker shot Henderson dead in a beachside public toilet.

Walker would later say Henderson attacked and punched him repeatedly. He claimed he was forced to shoot the tow-truck driver in the head from point-blank range.

With no witnesses, Walker would later be convicted only of manslaughter for a crime that had all the hallmarks of a cold-blooded execution.

Ryan was not so lucky and became the last man hanged in Australia. Walker served a further 19 years' including almost 10 years in the hellhole that was H Division.

He was released from prison in 1984 and avoided serious trouble for 17 years. But, at the age of 59, he was arrested again. This time for cultivating marijuana. Walker was charged on March 15, 2001, after police discovered more than 100 hydroponic marijuana plants and nearly six kilos of cannabis on his Kyneton property. The dried marijuana was worth nearly $50,000.

Walker pleaded guilty to cultivating a commercial quantity of marijuana and theft of electricity. His lawyer told the court that Walker was an asthma sufferer who smoked marijuana to assist his breathing. The court wasn't convinced.

In April, 2002, he was sentenced to a year in jail and fined $12,000.

Billy 'The Texan' Longley

IN 1971, Billy 'The Texan' Longley stood for the position of President of the Victorian branch of the Painters and Dockers union. Longley was confident he had the numbers but so did the other side. That's why the ballot box was stolen and a fire set in the office, an act Longley's supporters considered undemocratic.

When the election result was announced, Arthur Morris was the winner. It was never going to end there.

Pat Shannon, the popular secretary of the union, was gunned down in the bar of the Druids Hotel in South Melbourne on October 17, 1973.

'The Texan' was charged with the murder. Police alleged he paid another man, Kevin Taylor, $6000 for the job. Longley was to serve 13 years for the murder although he would always claim he was innocent. Many said that he would be killed in jail as a payback for Shannon. But no-one was able to get close enough to the wily Longley.

Longley was no stranger to courts. He was charged with the murder of his first wife, Patricia, in 1961, and found guilty of manslaughter. He was later acquitted on appeal. And there are a few other cases.

In the mid-1960s, five dockies were shot in one night at the Rose and Crown Hotel in Port Melbourne. Police said Billy was responsible for three of them, meaning that the other two declined to complain about their bullet wounds.

It didn't look good for the man who had gained the nickname 'The Texan' from a TV western about a man called Longley with a similar penchant for Colt .45 pistols.

This time it was his lawyer, Frank Galbally, who was firing the (legal) bullets. 'He was like an umbrella from the outrageous slings and arrows of the homicide and consorting squad for me,' Longley would say later about his favourite advocate. 'Any hurdles I had to jump I went to see him.'

Longley was acquitted of the Rose and Crown shootings, which was remarkable considering his ability as a sharpshooter, honed by shooting at bottles floating past while he was fishing on the Murray River.

Even from inside prison, while serving his time over Shannon's murder, Longley remained a powerful figure. He made a series of allegations to *The Bulletin* magazine about crime and corruption that resulted in the then Prime Minister, Malcolm Fraser, setting up the Costigan Royal Commission.

Longley told the Commission that after 1958 between 30 and 40 painters and dockers had been murdered as part of a union civil war.

Longley was released from prison in 1988. Always the ladies' man, he returned to one of his great loves – dancing. Strictly ballroom, of course. And, being a gentleman at all times, when asked if it was a gun in his pocket he was always able to answer unblushingly that it could well be. 'The Texan' would never be guilty of inappropriate behaviour on the dance floor. In business, meanwhile, at an age when many people are trying to live on a pension, Longley teamed up with another colourful Melbourne identity, former experienced detective, Brian 'The Skull' Murphy.

They formed a trouble-shooting mediation team with the catchy motto 'everything can be negotiated.'

They should know.

CHAPTER 5

Dirty White Collars

Alan Bond

HE was a little signwriter with big dreams. He was the man who unscrewed the America's Cup from the New York Yacht Club only to screw his investors and the investigators who tried to unravel the source of his fortune.

The hero as villain has been a recurring theme in Australia's history. Others have been more heroic, but few more villainous than Alan Bond. And none as rich. When it came to spending other people's money he made Ned Kelly and Ben Hall look like hayseed horse thieves.

Bond was the migrant miner's son who first thumbed his nose at the establishment and then stuck it in the trough. In 1970, he went to Newport, Rhode Island, and asked to look at their 12-metre racing yachts. He was snubbed. He told them he would be back to take their cup. He was as good as his word – this time.

Australians adored him for fighting to win the Holy Grail of yachting and then building Australia's biggest company. Three times he tried and failed to win the cup.

Then, in 1983, with the help of a winged keel and a top crew, he finally won. Sure, there was a bit of the spiv in Bondy but he did bring that cup home.

The crowds cheered and the politicians lined up for photo opportunities with the little 'Aussie' battler, even though he was born in England. 'Hawkie', the Prime Minister, praised his new best mate to the heavens and all but declared the day 'we' won the cup as a public holiday.

Bondy had made it.

The man who started as a painter borrowed the equivalent of $13,000 in 1960 for a real estate deal. He was on his way. At his peak he had a slice of Arnotts, Castlemaine Tooheys, Fourex breweries, Swan Breweries, Channel 9, West Australian Newspapers, British Satellite Broadcasting, oil company Santos, retailers Grace Brothers and Waltons, the Argyle diamond mine and a Chilean phone company.

Then he took on the man they called Tiny.

R. W. 'Tiny' Rowland, and Bondy were friends with a lot in common. Seemingly wealthy beyond imagination, they remained outsiders to the establishment.

Rowland was born Roland Walter Fuhrop in November, 1917, in an Indian detention camp, where his German father, and his Anglo-Dutch mother, were held as aliens in World War I. His family were imprisoned again in World War II. Rowland would never forgive the establishment for the way his family was treated.

Bond was like him. It seemed to him that together these two 'outsiders' could do great things. Rowland owned a company called Lonrho which had interests in 800 businesses, from newspapers, vehicle distribution, textiles, mines and hotels.

In 1973 he was described by Conservative British Prime Minister Edward Heath as the 'unpleasant and unacceptable face of capitalism'. Not everyone agreed with Lord Ted. Rowland was courted by African leaders and had close links with the British and United States intelligence services.

Bond was seen as a White Knight who would help Rowland keep control of his empire, but Bondy had his eyes on taking over Lonrho. It was like a guppy trying to swallow a shark.

A corporate predator called Asher Edelman had bought a share in Lonrho. Bond bought him out in what appeared to be a move to protect Rowland, but then kept buying, believing he would be Rowland's successor.

Rowland was outraged and began his own investigation into Bond. He published a 93-page document claiming that Bond was technically insolvent. Bond's bankers demanded their money back. It was the beginning of the end for the wide boy from Perth.

In 1989 – after the sharemarket crash – Bond Corp crashed and burned, with disclosed debts of $8.23 billion, exceeding assets by $1.36 billion. The collapse was eventually estimated to have cost around $5 billion.

But what happened to the money?

Bond was eventually charged with a host of criminal and corporate offences. At one stage he was seen walking to and from court in a way that made him look brain dead. He should have been jailed for over-acting. His defence team included colourful Melbourne legal identity Andrew Fraser, himself later jailed for cocaine trafficking. His psychologist, who gave evidence of the brilliant Bond's deteriorating mental capacity, was one Tim Watson-Munro, who later admitted to cocaine use.

Bond was to serve jail time but a team of finance experts was never to find the bulk of the money the former Australian of the

Year sent overseas as a $50 million retirement fund. One of the offences related to fraud over his purchase of the Manet painting *La Promenade*.

Bond Corp had paid $5.6 million to lease *La Promenade* to hang in Bond's Perth office from 1984 before passing up the opportunity to buy it in 1988. Which was fortunate for Bond's private company, because it was able to buy the painting for $2.46 million – when it was worth at least $14 million. And Bond was able to sell it in November, 1989, for more than $17 million.

In 1995 he was able to buy himself out of bankruptcy, paying his creditors less than half a cent in the dollar. He paid $9 million on a debt of $1.2 billion. Not bad for a brain-damaged former signwriter.

Bond was alleged to have transferred $15 million overseas in the late 1980s, when his ship started springing leaks. In the next six years, he managed to move a further $30 million over to his family and away from creditors.

In 1995 Bond's wife Eileen, their two sons and two daughters were estimated to be worth $70 million in real estate, businesses and assorted trinkets.

Bond divorced 'Big Red', his wife of 37 years, and married theatre producer Diana Bliss.

Australian Federal Police always believed the key to the Bond fortune was held by a Swiss businessman, Jurg Bollag. A Bollag company bought an English mansion and 400-hectare country property. It was later passed over to the Bonds.

Bollag generously bought $1.2 million worth of show-jumping horses for Bond's daughter Suzanne, and $700,000 worth of jewellery. Bollag also paid $350,000 towards Bond's legal costs.

Police also suspected, for some reason, that property listed as owned by Bollag in London and Colorado was being held for Bond.

In his comprehensive book, *Going for Broke*, Paul Barry wrote, 'The scandal of the Alan Bond story is that he managed to hang onto a large fortune and make a fool of the Australian judicial system.

'It is often said that Bond's $1,200 million fraud on Bell Resources was a victimless crime. But the shareholders who lost their savings would hardly agree. And at least $55 million of the money taken from Bell ended up in Bond's private company, Dallhold Investments, which then funded Bond's own lavish spending.

'One cannot be sure exactly how much Bond and his family salvaged from the $5 billion wreckage of his businesses, but even if they had escaped with only Upp Hall in Britain, it would be scandal enough.

'From 1991 to 1995, Bond swore black and blue that this $12.5 million English country mansion belonged to his Swiss associate Jurg Bollag, yet as soon as his bankruptcy was annulled, the charade was abandoned. Now the Bonds, not the Bollags, are lords of the manor, and again the legal owners.

'And Upp Hall was not the only valuable asset Bond walked away with. There are also probably tens of millions of dollars in jewellery, property and family trusts, funded by Bond's now-collapsed business empire.'

In 2000, Bond was released from jail. He appeared to have recovered from his brain damage and was laughing all the way to the Swiss bank.

And they said he wouldn't make it.

BOND BY NUMBERS

1938: Born in England.

1950: Family migrated to Western Australia.

1967: Started his first private company. Bought retail, mining and media assets.

1969: Launched his first public company, WA Land; later becomes Bond Corporation.

1978: Named Australian of the Year.

1982: Bond Corp became Western Australia's biggest company.

1983: Bond's yacht *Australia II* won the America's Cup.

1987: Bond Corp shattered by stock market crash.

1989: Bond Corp admitted debts of $8.23 billion, exceeding assets by $1.36 billion.

April 1992: Declared bankrupt.

May 1992: Convicted for dishonesty offences over the collapsed merchant bank Rothwells.
Jailed for 2½ years.

August 1992: Granted retrial.

November 1992: Acquitted.

February 1995: Released from bankruptcy.

March 1995: Sent to trial on fraud charges over the painting *La Promenade*.

August 1996: Convicted of fraud and deception in *La Promenade* deal. Jailed for three years.

December 1996: Agreed to plead guilty to two counts of fraud over Bell Resources deals.

February 1997: Sentenced to four years jail for Bell Resources fraud to be served on top of his three years for the painting fraud.

March 2000: Released from jail.

Laurie Connell

LAURIE Connell, or 'Last Resort Laurie', was the son of a bus conductor who always wanted to write his own ticket. He left school at 15 to work as an office boy and a part-time tent-boxer before becoming one of Australia's richest men – and biggest crooks.

By his early 20s he had a reputation as a sharp businessman with a flair for gathering a new generation of clients. One of his contacts was Brian Burke, the stamp-collecting journalist who turned politician and became Premier of Western Australia.

Keen to promote local entrepreneurs, Burke allowed hundreds of millions of public money to end up in Connell's bank, Rothwells. Connell spent it almost as quickly as it came in.

At one point Connell was said to have $300 million. How he was supposed to have made the money was never explained. The reality was that the money was 'borrowed' from the bank to shore up a maze of Connell's private companies. Once the money was sucked into the black hole, it was never repaid.

Connell was a huge punter who kept a $4 million float in his office and spent up to $500,000 a week on the horses. Prosecutors would later claim in the WA Supreme Court trial that Connell took about $500 million from Rothwells before the 1987 stockmarket crash. He wasn't concerned if his small investors, lured by artificially high interest rates, lost their life savings.

At his peak, Connell's spending was in the same league as a heavyweight Arab oil sheik or a corrupt African president siphoning his country's wealth into Swiss banks.

He owned a private race track and tried to effectively buy WA racing. He became the owner of the biggest stable of racehorses in Australia. One was the fancied stayer Rocket Racer.

The horse was heavily backed to win the 1987 Perth Cup at Ascot. It went to the lead so far from home that it should have fainted in the straight. Incredibly, it won by a staggering nine lengths.

It wasn't just the margin that was staggering. The horse wobbled like a drunken man and would have collapsed had it not been held upright by six attendants. It was one of the most sickening sights ever seen on an Australian racecourse, especially in a major race, and a graphic example of the corruption of West Australian racing, politics and business.

It was a time when some horses were being drugged with a chemical known as 'Elephant Juice'. When used as a sedative, the chemical was powerful enough to sedate mature elephants, but at the right dose, a tiny amount, it would make a horse run until it dropped – or died.

The distressed Rocket Racer was not drug-tested as vets fought to save his life. He was quickly removed from the racecourse. It was to have one more start but then died.

After the Perth Cup, Connell shouted the Members' Bar with French champagne and that night celebrated his win with an expensive restaurant meal – also picking up the bill for every other customer. It cost him $47,000.

The Rocket Racer scandal was not the only controversy involving Connell and horses. Another notorious incident has become known as the 'Kalgoorlie Sting' and it dogged Connell for more than a decade. No matter how much he tried, the events of 1975 showed, that under his expensive suits, he was just another crook.

On September 3, 1975, Connell hit bookies at a Kalgoorlie meeting with a series of bets on a Melbourne race.

When the race was broadcast the horse that Connell, his brother and two local police backed, the aptly named His

Worship, duly won. The race was supposedly aired live on Perth radio station but it was actually recorded and broadcast several minutes after the event was run and won. Connell and his mates were in on the giggle.

Connell was banned from racecourses for two years over the incident.

In 1987, Connell bought seven houses on the Swan River and bulldozed them, planning to build a fancy mansion. He bought a $27 million private jet, luxury cars and yachts.

In the years from 1982 to 1988, Rothwells managed to lose more than $600 million. No one can prove where it went.

Connell was a close mate of another groping Sandgroper, Alan Bond. They made up the financial rules to suit themselves. In one sweet deal the Burke Government agreed to pay Bond $42 million for five per cent of the Argyle diamond mine. The stock was worth only $28 million on the open market.

Connell acted as the Government's 'independent' adviser on the deal while he was also acting for Bond. He was paid about $3 million for pushing through the transaction.

He worked under the 'Old Mates Act' and was known to take the then Prime Minister Bob Hawke on deep sea fishing trips. The press loved him until the stockmarket crash of 1987.

It soon became obvious that investors' money had vanished. The WA taxpayers were left with a $200 million shortfall and businesses went to the wall.

It was not Connell's theft of millions, but his love of bending the rules of racing, that finally brought him down.

He was acquitted by a District Court jury of conspiracy to fix the 1983 AHA Cup in Bunbury in which jockey Danny Hobby was bribed to 'throw' the race by jumping off his mount to stage a fall.

The Bunbury Cup scandal caught up with Connell in 1994,

when he was finally found guilty of conspiring to pervert the course of justice.

A court found he had conspired to pay Hobby to stay out of Australia, beyond the reach of police investigating the 1983 race fix.

Connell declared he was broke and defended himself in a long-running fraud trial over the loss or more than $300 million.

He died of a heart attack during the trial in 1996.

He was 49. Proof that not only the good die young.

Brian Quinn

ANY builder will tell you that home renovations rarely come in on time and on budget. Owners invariably demand variations and each one adds to the bottom line.

Coles Myer boss Brian Quinn knew the variations on his sprawling Templestowe home would be costly. He had budgeted on spending $250,000 but when the bill came in at a touch over $3 million he felt sick.

Later it would be the shareholders of the giant company who would feel queasy.

Quinn, one of the most respected businessmen in Australia, decided the work was a perk of office and the company could pick up the tab.

Templestowe, in Melbourne's east, is the type of suburb where you can buy a spread and build a house that reflects your personality. New money wants room to move.

Quinn was new money and a living example of the great Australian dream. No-one gave him a leg up, he didn't inherit a fortune and didn't rely on old school friends to fast track him into a lucrative career.

He started sweeping floors in an Adelaide Coles store in 1956 before rising to run Australia's biggest retailing chain. He was paid $1.5 million a year as chief executive and was worth every cent, helping the company return healthy returns for years.

He received an Order of Australia, was on the board of the Reserve Bank and controlled a company with a turnover of $10.5 billion. He retired in 1992 with a rock-solid reputation.

Why a man of Quinn's savvy would be sucked into criminality over a home renovation has never been explained but the experienced money manager had a blind spot – he didn't seem to care what was spent on his Xanadu.

He seemed to forget that the company he worked for over 36 years was not his and the profits he made belonged to shareholders.

He had bought the house in County Terrace from the company for $440,000 in 1982. It was originally a two-bedroom home on a generous .405 hectare block.

But Quinn's wife Trenna didn't want to live in a two-bedroom home and she commissioned a series of renovations that a court would later be told 'resembled the Palace of Versailles'. The Quinns appeared to be the perfect couple. He knew how to make money and she knew how to spend it.

First came the tennis court and the spa, then a 10-square court pavilion. Most houses in the area had a two-car garage. The Quinns built one for eight. They installed a floodlit cricket pitch and a driveway with gates for $157,000.

Trenna Quinn ordered a $5,000 toilet suite, $300,000 for marble walls and floors, then $110,000 for glass for the windows.

Although they were turning over huge sums, many builders were frustrated by the constant changes. They called the changes the 'Trenna factor' and just kept loading their trucks and loading their bills. She didn't like the new first floor so she ordered it to be demolished. She ordered a state-of-the-art kitchen and then demanded it to be removed, unused, when a newer one became available.

Some people can become addicted to plastic surgery. Trenna seemed addicted to renovations.

Builders were proud of their work on the marble used in the guests' powder room but Mrs Quinn ordered it to be removed and replaced with a lighter shade. The craftsmen did what they were told and charged accordingly.

Neighbours were unimpressed. Fred Solomon told reporters, 'Soon after they moved in, the jackhammers started at six in the morning. It went on for six years.

'I'm not complaining but there were sometimes so many people working on the place there were 20 cars parked in the street.

'I once asked him why there was so much work going on and he said "I have nothing to do with it – my wife looks after it".'

It was the ultimate money pit, with $6 million poured into a house that stretched over five suburban blocks. When the house was finally sold in 1996 it raised $1.9 million.

In April, 1997, a jury of six woman and six men spent 2½ days deliberating before finding Quinn guilty of conspiring with a former Coles national maintenance manager, Graham Lanyon, between September, 1982, and October, 1988, to defraud the company of $4.6 million.

He was able to call some big names as character witnesses.

They included the then Victorian Premier Jeff Kennett, trucking magnate Lindsay Fox and ACTU secretary Bill Kelty.

Quinn was to serve more than two years' jail. While in prison he went back to his retailing roots. He was placed in charge of the canteen at the medium security jail at Castlemaine.

Quinn reportedly enjoyed working in the shop that

specialised in toiletries, cigarettes, confectionary and stationery for the 250 prisoners. He stacked shelves for the set prison wage of $5 a day.

Quinn always maintained he was innocent. When he was released after serving his two years, he released a prepared statement.

'I look back on my business career with the knowledge that I gave everything I could to Coles Myer,' he said.

'I was proud to play a part in bringing about the merger of two very different retailing cultures to form the foundation on which today's great company is built.

'My role as chairman and chief executive was all-consuming and exhausting. If there is a lesson to be learned, it is to apply as much close attention to your personal affairs as to your business affairs,' he said.

'In time, I believe other factors will emerge that will throw a different light on the circumstances for which I was put on trial.'

Quinn and his wife moved to a luxury home in Queensland after his release in October, 1999. It is believed their double-storey house in Southport did not need renovations.

Christopher Skase

FOR a kid who cheated at geography when he was at school, Christopher Skase was to go a long way – about 10,000 kilometres, in fact – to avoid serious judicial examination.

While in fourth form at Caulfield Grammar in 1964 the teenage Skase was to reveal a glimpse of the man he would become. He cheated in an exam. Three were caught, two were expelled, but Skase got away with it.

At school he was seen as bright, but lazy – as though waiting for a the right challenge to spark his passions. Much later, the lazy student would become a seven-days-a-week money-making machine. He loved the fine things of life and even his critics would say that, until it all went horribly wrong, he deserved them.

Skase often said that one of his three great talents was the ability to hold his breath under water. Ironically, it would be those lungs that would eventually save him from extradition to Australia and then, ultimately, kill him.

The Skase story really starts when, as a teenager, he left school to work as a messenger at Melbourne stockbrokers J. B. Were. He stayed with the firm for two years, learning the basics of how the markets worked.

He then took a year off – driving around Australia and taking a series of jobs to cover food, board and petrol before falling into finance journalism, a field that tends to be a closed shop and an acquired taste. Most reporters see it as the strange corner of the office where people get excited over seemingly meaning-less figures and talk of businesses no-one else understands.

But once finance reporters earn a name they can become identities – and commodities – in their own right. Some, like the knockabout and likeable Terry McCrann, and the earnest pundit Robert Gottliebsen, are among the most recognised journalists in Australia.

Skase began work at the Melbourne *Sun* and later the *Australian Financial Review*. He was good but not great, giving the impression that, for him, journalism was part of the learning curve rather than a career in its own right. Other young reporters who had given this impression as youngsters were John Cornell, later to make a fortune with his mate Paul Hogan, and Nick Columb, who became a millionaire businessman and successful racehorse owner.

Skase learned some handy lessons from being inside newspapers. He was to find how journalists worked and discovered how easy it was to manipulate the press.

Later, many of the big names of finance reporting were to pump up their man and failed to scrutinise his business activities. Perhaps it was because he was one of them – their protege. At least the geography teacher had checked his results before marking his report, but the press didn't.

Skase made fools of some of the biggest finance reporters in the country. But they would get him back. Big time.

That would be later. For a while, he was headline material. Reporters were flown to business functions and corporate openings and fed champagne and press releases while enjoying five-star entertainment.

He would throw Christmas parties for $200,000. He set up an AFL side, the Brisbane Bears, ran TV stations, built massive resorts and tried to become a Hollywood mogul.

What had been boring finance stories were catapulted onto page one. Business news was now laced with sport, gossip and showbiz. Australia had many shonky businessmen, but few as glamourous as Christopher Skase.

He bought a $4 million house in Brisbane, a $1 million holiday house at Port Douglas and an $11 million mansion in Hollywood.

He had the private jet, the luxurious yacht and the string of flash cars.

In the heady 1980s, debt was a by-product of profit. Skase was not the only man with a plan to gobble up undervalued companies using other people's money but he was one of the best known.

Using a small company, Qintex, he moved away from the staid establishment of Melbourne to Brisbane, where he became a friend of then Premier Sir Joh Bjelke-Petersen. But, unlike some entrepreneurs, Skase did more than just cannibalise existing businesses to strip their assets. He was a bricks and mortar man, building the fabulous Mirage resorts at Port Douglas and Surfers Paradise for $800 million. They exist long after Skase exited.

In 1987, aged just 37, he bought the Seven television network for $780 million. It seemed to be just the beginning but the end was closer than anyone knew, for Skase tried to swallow too much. He tried to buy the American MGM studio for $1.2 billion. Later he upped his bid to about $1.5 billion. He was being choked by ambition and debt.

It couldn't last.

When he had to come up with a mere $50 million down-payment for MGM, he couldn't raise the cash. It was the first sign that his silver spoon was wrapped in tinfoil.

It led to an investigation and the inevitable bankruptcy of Qintex. But what the corporate detectives were to find was that Skase was paying himself and his team about $40 million in management fees when there was supposedly no money to pay debt. The ship was going down but the captain had a mink life-jacket. In June, 1991, Chris and his loyal wife, Pixie, decided it was time to explore opportunities off-shore. They went to the Spanish island of Majorca.

He declared himself bankrupt with personal debts of nearly $170 million and corporate debts of $1.5 billion. He did leave some assets – $1000 in cash and $167 in the bank, plus a little office equipment.

Christopher, who was always good at figures, could see they didn't add up. He was charged with 32 offences relating to Qintex but would never stand trial. He lived in a $6 million Spanish mansion but said he was living a 'basic existence.'

The Australian government tried repeatedly to get their man back to stand trial but Spanish courts accepted he was too ill to return home.

Many believed Skase was lying when he claimed he needed a lung transplant to survive. He had been a heavy smoker and his respiratory system was collapsing.

The man who had been the darling of the media and had owned his own network was to become fodder for television current affairs programs. The very producers who had fawned over Skase now went after him. Whenever there was a lull in real news it seemed a team would be sent to 'get Skase'.

Images of him, hooked to a respirator and in a wheelchair in court were compared with him walking, swimming or playing tennis. Often bodyguards would chase the TV crews away, providing more pictures for the programs. Sometimes Skase, Pixie or those close to the family would provide suitably outraged quotes protesting their innocence.

Politicians from both sides routinely attacked him, all claiming they would eventually get him back to Australia to face justice.

But it didn't matter. The man they all thought was faking his illness died in August 2001. He was 52.

MILESTONES

1948, September 18: Born in Melbourne, son of a
well-known radio announcer, Charles Skase.

1972: Joined the *Sun News-Pictorial* and, later, the
Australian Financial Review.

1974: Formed Team Securities. Bought shares in country
radio and television operator and Qintex.

1977: Parted from Team Securities and took over Qintex.

1979: Married Pixie. Invested in the jewellery business.

1982: Skase became executive chairman of Qintex
Australia Ltd and chairman of Hardy Bros Ltd.
Qintex invests in Queensland television.

1983: Skase became chairman of United Telecasters Ltd
and of Qintex America Ltd.

1984: He became chairman of the Mirage Resorts Trust.

1987: Skase paid $780 million for the Seven network. The
share market crashes leaving him exposed.

1989: Qintex collapsed under debts of at least around
$1.5 billion.

1991: Declared bankrupt, claiming assets of only
$5000 and personal debts of $172 million.
Left the country.

1994: In February, Spanish police arrested Skase in Majorca.
A Spanish court ordered his extradition, but a
higher court upheld his appeal to remain.

1998: In July, Spain refused to renew Skase's residency visa,
giving him 15 days to leave the country,
but Skase appealed and was allowed to stay in
Spain because of ill-health.

1999: Skase family said he would have major lung surgery on
March 1, the same day he was supposed to leave Spain.
In June, he was hospitalised after a lung collapsed.

2001: Skase lodged an appeal against deportation on the
grounds that rights had been abused. The appeal was
rejected, but Spain suspended deportation proceedings
after Skase's health continued to deteriorate

2001: July 12: Doctors announced Skase has less than a
month to live.

2001: August 6: Skase died at his Majorca home.

Andrew Fraser

ANDREW Fraser is a classic example of the man with the silver spoon who destroyed himself by sticking it up his nose.

For years, Fraser was the lawyer of choice for half Melbourne's underworld. Smart, ambitious and prepared to defend anyone over anything, he was loved by crooks and hated by many coppers.

His client list was a *Who's Who* of the gutter. Killers such as Dennis Allen swore by him. Members of the homicide squad swore at him.

He was taped in jail urging one of his clients not to crack and say anything over the murder of constables Steven Tynan and Damian Eyre at Walsh Street.

He represented the well-known Moran family in Melbourne for years. He provided them with shrewd advice and they provided him with a steady income.

Fraser's first advice to his clients was to remain silent and not to co-operate. But, while he had seen many of his clients ruin their lives with drugs he wasn't smart enough to learn the lesson. He followed them down the same dead-end street.

For more than 10 years he used cocaine in his private life while still acting as a competent lawyer. Then it all began to unravel.

The former champion schoolboy athlete, who once dreamed of running at the Commonwealth Games, became a full-blown addict. By September, 1999, he was consuming at least four grams of cocaine a day, valued at $1000. He was of the work hard, play hard school but eventually found it was impossible to juggle both. Long, boozy lunches, meetings with notorious criminals and living on the edge were part of the lifestyle he claimed to love. But he wanted more and that tipped him over the edge.

Battling bankruptcy and a shrinking law practice, Fraser could not fund his insatiable appetite for cocaine without trafficking in it. He would later admit to 3AW's Neil Mitchell that 'in the last year I would have spent over a hundred grand' on the drug.

Fraser had a reputation as a street-smart and cunning lawyer. He often used underworld slang learnt from his many high-profile clients. He prided himself on his knowledge of investigative techniques and made a handsome living by advising suspects on the best way to counter police tactics.

Yet, when it came to drug dealing, Fraser was incredibly dumb. He was an easy pinch for the drug squad. Like an animal raised in captivity, the private school-educated Fraser was not equipped for life in the wild.

In a Prahran bar, Fraser slipped into the men's toilet to do a deal. He had become so complacent that, when he heard a mobile phone ring in the cubicle, he yelled out to the occupant, 'Don't you hate it when that happens?'

The man from behind the locked door just laughed. He was a drug squad detective there to observe the deal.

Fraser was taped by police in his office during a long and rambling conversation in which he advised his drug partner, Werner Paul Roberts, on how to go about importing cocaine.

'Look, I understand, mate, I've done this, I've given pertinent advice before in these situations ... '

Fraser told Roberts to call from a pay-phone when he returned from his overseas drug-buying trip, and he agreed to be the 'legal backstop' if things didn't go to plan.

They didn't go to plan. Roberts lured a former girlfriend, Carol Brand, on his overseas trip by implying he wanted to resume their relationship. What he really wanted was an innocent 'mule' to help move the drugs through Customs. They went to Europe and then Africa, where Roberts obtained souvenirs, including some wall plaques that were loaded with cocaine.

Carol Brand had no idea what was happening, but no-one would have believed that later if it hadn't been for police listening devices which recorded the couple's rather strained conversation when they got back to Australia.

After landing in Sydney, Roberts insisted on staying in a motel, hiring a car and driving back to Melbourne. Brand realised Roberts was not genuine in his romantic intentions towards her. There was none of the jubilation to be expected from a pair of smugglers who had just landed $2.7 million of cocaine. Later, after police arrested them both, and Fraser (and another conspirator), Brand's lawyer Paul Galbally used transcripts taken from listening device recordings and telephone intercepts to show that she was an innocent dupe.

Judge Leo Hart was not impressed with Fraser and Roberts' lack of gallantry, all the more so because Fraser had disgraced the legal profession.

In 2001, Judge Hart sentenced Fraser to seven years jail and branded him 'dishonourable and disgraceful', as he sentenced him on charges of drug trafficking and possession, and being knowingly concerned in the importation of 5.5 kilograms of cocaine.

'You had bound yourself by oath to uphold the law and to conduct yourself honestly,' Judge Hart said. 'To behave in the illegal, dishonourable and disgraceful way that you did ... involves a degree of public scandal, which reflects on the profession as a whole.'

Jimmy Siu

BY anybody's standards it was a lavish wedding. More than 650 guests in a five-star Melbourne hotel, the best wine and food and a bottle of cognac on each table.

The well-wishers included members of the judiciary, senior police, high-profile media identities and Melbourne business figures.

The groom was beaming and his young wife Linda, a former casino croupier, looked stunning. A Melbourne County Court judge, an old friend of the groom, delivered a warm and humorous speech on behalf of the couple.

Jimmy Siu had been married twice before, but the novelty hadn't worn off. His small chest puffed with pride as he wandered from table to table in the manner of a man comfortable in any company. His new wife changed outfits several times during the reception – a Chinese custom to indicate wealth. It was April 26, 1992.

Siu might not be a household name in Australia but in certain circles, he is a figure of influence and intrigue. He built a small business empire after arriving from Hong Kong nearly 40 years earlier as an electronics student. His first job was moving and cleaning empty beer barrels at a brewery. 'I was too weak to move the full ones,' he often joked later.

Five days after arriving in Australia he went to Melbourne University to enrol and became lost. A law lecturer took pity on him and gave him a meal. They became life-long friends. The lecturer became the judge who spoke at the third Siu wedding.

Jimmy Siu has come a long way from the days when he was an electronic equipment repairman, but he is still known as a man who can fix anything.

He progressed to be the public face of the lucrative Shark Fin chain, with a turnover once estimated at $10 million, and was spokesman for the Chinese Restaurateurs Association.

His command of English and his energy saw him become a trouble-shooter for many in the Chinese community. He was able to get things done, knowing which bureaucrat to approach and how to sort out most problems. He was used as a court interpreter and developed contacts in the Immigration Department, the Victoria and Federal police. He was also a registered financial broker.

While Siu was relaxed and confident when dealing with Melbourne's largely European decision-makers, he remained a dominant figure among Asian businessmen.

For decades, he has been of interest to the gaming squad and was known to have interests in a Chinese casino. He would book the most expensive hotel suites in Melbourne to host invitation-only card games where millions would change hands in a weekend. He agreed to stop the games after police received a legal opinion that they were illegal. Siu may not have been in Kerry Packer's league but he was on the international VIP gambling list, welcomed at Jupiter's in Queensland and several giant casinos in Las Vegas.

In 1990, the gaming squad started a protracted blitz to cripple Chinatown's illegal casino industry. There were four known clubs and police began to raid them fortnightly, seizing tables and the punters' money.

Each club contained about six tables and each table was owned by a syndicate. If the syndicate lost, they would lose the table. It had been a lucrative industry for decades.

But with the new blitz and new suburban clubs the casinos were on the verge of collapse by late 1992. According to court evidence, it was then that 'The Fixer' was called in. Siu and his friends blamed one policeman in the gaming squad for the blitz, and they were determined to remove the threat. Siu was prepared to offer big money to police to allow his favoured gambling den to continue operating. He also wanted Sergeant Ivan McKinney transferred from the squad.

When the first bribe offers were informally put on the table, the gaming squad began a nine-month operation, code-named 'Grasshopper', to trap the big money players behind the corruption scheme.

Siu had learned that when you want action, go to the boss. On this occasion the boss was McKinney's direct superior, Senior Sergeant Jeff Maher – who pretended to be a corrupt policeman.

According to the evidence, Siu's plan was simple. Maher would be paid $2000 a week to keep open the club Siu was representing and a bonus of $1000 for closing the opposition.

He even suggested that Maher raid Siu's favoured club regularly to avoid any suspicion. 'Every two months, three months you have to close the joint,' he said.

Never short of an idea, and always ready to advise someone on his side, Siu told Maher how to launder the bribe money, suggesting he set up a false off-shore loan to explain his new wealth.

Eventually, Siu and two other men were arrested and charged with attempted bribery after police gathered around $23,000 during the controlled operation. Siu pleaded guilty and several business friends, and a County Court judge, provided character evidence for the court. In 1994, he was sentenced to six months' jail but ended up serving one month.

'What I did was silly. I made a mistake. I regret what I did and I have learned my lesson,' he said.

A policeman who has known Siu for years said it was out of character for him to make a bribe offer. 'It was a real tragedy. He made the best suckling pig you've ever tasted.'

Siu continued to gamble, being prepared to risk $100,000 on one bet. He was alleged to have lost – and then won back – at least one of his restaurants. He has always been a respected guest in Australian and international casinos.

Despite his conviction, Siu was always welcome at Crown casino and was a regular in the Mahogany Room for high rollers. Siu's relationship with Crown has raised the eyebrows of more than one police officer. He could not get a job as doorman to the Mahogany Room, as he could not pass the probity test, yet he owned three restaurants in the complex.

He is a close friend of one of the senior executives of Crown, although he says he has moderated his gambling.

'I used to be a big punter, but now I am a small fish,' he explains.

He said he was not employed by the casino but would refer people to Crown. 'I get on very well with senior management there. I have a fair bit of contact with the casino people. They scratch my back and I scratch theirs.'

But if Siu wanted to keep away from any further court room dramas after his bribery case, that hope was lost on January 12, 1998, when bandits burst in to his Shark Fin headquarters in Bourke Street. Brandishing a replica handgun, they bound and gagged two female staff members and escaped with $50,000.

Police later arrested three men, including soccer star Con Boutsianis, over the robbery. But it wasn't quite what it seemed. The defence argued that the armed robbery was a front for an insurance fraud engineered by Siu. The charming restaurateur gave evidence in the Magistrate's hearing, saying he had no 'direct' knowledge of the robbery.

When asked about his bribery conviction he said he regretted what he had done but had not considered bribery a serious crime as it had been 'part of life' in China and gambling had been part of the Chinese culture for 3000 years. In March, 1999, Magistrate Barbara Cotterell said Siu's statement that he was not aware of the armed robbery plot was 'not credible.'

The charges against all three men were dismissed. The magistrate said at a subsequent costs application: 'I dismissed the charges against each of the defendants on the basis that each defendant, for his own particular reason, believed that the actions they performed or organised were carried out with the consent, or at the request of Mr Jimmy Siu.

'The lengthy cross-examination of Mr Siu revealed a web of intrigue, unsustainable denials and allegations and inexplicable actions, all held together by lies.'

The matter was not over. The Director of Public Prosecutions directly presented Con Boutsianis and James Andretti for trial. Andretti was later bashed outside a Prahran nightclub and found unfit to stand trial because of his injuries. Boutsianis was to plead guilty to one count of theft but, significantly, not to armed robbery. He maintained he was told it was an insurance scam organised by Siu.

The star striker avoided jail and was allowed to continue his soccer career. County Court Judge Leslie Ross fined him $20,000 but did not record a conviction against Boutsianis. When asked about his alleged involvement in the robbery, Siu remains, as always, charming and credible. 'I was not involved. Why would I be that silly? If I was supposed to have set it up with the other three I would have made $12,500.'

He said he had documents to prove that over two months at the time of the robbery he won $20,000 at Crown casino. 'Why would a man of my status do that for two days' takings?'

CHAPTER 6

The Great Bookie Robbery

Leslie Herbert Kane

LESLIE Herbert Kane was the toughest of three brothers who made their living scaring other gangsters. He was born in Carlton on December 1, 1945, and became a painter and docker on Melbourne's wharves from the age of 14.

He soon found that crime was easier and more lucrative than working on the waterfront.

He gave up the ship docks in port for criminal docks in court. He had appeared as the accused 27 times by his early 30s.

After the Great Bookie Robbery of April, 1976, police were not the only ones hunting the team that escaped with much more than the official $1.4 million taken from the bookmakers at the Victorian Club.

It was an ideal scenario for gang warfare. War was declared in a Richmond hotel in mid-1978, when Vincent Mikkelsen – a friend of the Bookie Robbery mastermind, Ray (Chuck) Bennett – refused a drink from Les's brother Brian Kane.

Mikkelsen committed an even graver social indiscretion by winning the fight that ensued, biting off part of Kane's ear in the process.

Musing much later about Kane's reaction to this humiliating disfigurement, veteran criminal lawyer turned judge, Joe Gullaci said: 'It's hard to be the number one standover man in town when you've got a piece bitten out of your ear.'

That mouthful of ear was eventually to give Melbourne's underworld heartburn and put the wind up the police force. But all Brian Kane knew then was that it was bad for his reputation.

Mikkelsen came to expect massive retaliation. Bennett said Mikkelsen's life should be spared and was warned: 'If you stick your head in, it will be blown off.'

From there, the story unfolds with brutal inevitability. Fearing a pre-emptive strike, Les moved his second wife, Judy, and their two children, aged three and five, from the western suburbs to a unit in Wantirna, in the far outer-eastern suburbs.

It wasn't far enough. On October 19, 1978, a Thursday night, the Kanes got home after visiting relatives. Judy turned on the light in the main bedroom and saw three men waiting. They were armed with silenced 'machine guns' that had been specially modified for the dreaded 'toecutter' Linus Driscoll.

Bennett and Mikkelsen pushed past Judy and grabbed her husband in the bathroom. Another man, identified as Laurence Prendergast, took her into another bedroom and held her, face down. She heard a cry from her husband and muffled shots.

When she was let up, she saw pools of blood in the bathroom and the body lying in the passageway near the door.

The killers threw Kane's body in the boot of his distinctive pink Ford Futura sedan and drove off. Judy Kane left with her children and returned the next day to clean the unit. According to police 'Mrs Kane found sinew-like tissue on the carpet where her husband had been laying near the front door.' Neither the corpse nor the car was ever found. Of course, the gunmen had a head start because Judy Kane observed painter and docker protocol by not speaking to police until they heard about her husband's 'disappearance' and contacted her first.

The three men were charged with the murder but, without a body, the prosecution floundered and they were acquitted. Kane's friends and family were never going to accept the decision.

Mikkelsen and Prendergast left Melbourne immediately for distant destinations. (Prendergast was later to make the mistake of returning. His body, like Les Kane's, was never found.)

Mikkelsen's brother-in-law, Norman McLeod, was shot dead outside his house in Coolaroo on July 16, 1982, in what police still believe was a case of mistaken identity.

Bennett, still to face charges on the payroll robbery, chose to stay in custody rather than apply for bail. He believed he was safer inside. He wasn't.

Raymond Patrick Bennett

RAYMOND Patrick Bennett, also known by his boyhood name of Ray Chuck, was probably the most dashing Australian crook of his generation, but a reputation like that wins enemies, and he had plenty.

To his friends, Ray Bennett was tough, loyal, and good company. He was a leader and respected by those who followed him.

Bennett was the man behind the 'Great Bookie Robbery' of April 21, 1976. That job was not planned in a Melbourne pub but half a world away.

He flew secretly to Australia for a few days while on pre-release leave from a British prison on the Isle of Wight. He was spotted by a policeman in the Melbourne suburb of Moonee Ponds. Bennett and his friend Brian O'Callaghan had led the 'Kangaroo Gang', robbing jewellery shops all over Europe.

Bennett's hand-picked team of six men robbed bookmakers on settling day at the Victorian Club, then in Queen Street. A seventh man, in Pentridge at the time, but involved in the planning, received his share.

The haul was officially declared as $1.4 million but was much greater. The bookies had allegedly not declared all bets to avoid paying gaming taxes. Some claim the final take was around $12 million, but more sensible estimates put it at less than $3 million, which was an astonishing amount of cash at a time when the average wage was about $120 a week.

The gang escaped with 118 calico bags filled with untraceable bank notes.

Bennett's time in Britain had not been wasted. He learnt commando tactics he would use in the Bookie Robbery from an English team known as 'The Wembley Gang'.

Bennett used a time and motion man to assist with the planning and even set up a secret training camp in rural Victoria for his hand-picked team. He was to armed robbers what famed Hawthorn coach John Kennedy had been to league football.

The robbery earned Bennett and his crew the unwanted attention of people who wanted to redistribute their wealth, some willing to use boltcutters and blowtorches to do so. There was even a plot by former friends to sell out the gang to the insurance underwriters saddled with the massive loss.

Police, bookmakers, and other criminals suddenly had several million reasons to resent Bennett. Tension rose between Bennett's crew and a group of painters and dockers led by the Kane brothers, Brian, Les and Ray. Certain members of the consorting squad backed the Kanes, standover men who had controlled 'ghosting' rackets on the wharves for years. The circumstantial evidence is intriguing rather than damning. One grievance the consorters had against Bennett came from the fact that they routinely provided unofficial security for bookmakers on settling days at the Victorian Club.

But, on the day the Bennett gang struck, the usual armed detectives were not there. They had been sent at the last minute on a useless errand to Frankston, a coincidence that led some to suspect Bennett had bribed a corrupt senior officer to help set up the robbery.

One slip during the robbery probably sowed the seeds of the gang's destruction. When the masked men ordered all present to lie face down, one of them said to the then well-known boxing trainer Ambrose Palmer, 'You too, Ambrose.'

The robber instantly regretted his half-friendly warning. He had once trained at Palmer's gymnasium and knew the old man would recognise his voice. Palmer forgot to mention this to police, the story goes, but accidentally let slip the robber's identity to people connected with the Kane brothers. Word got around, and members of Bennett's gang became targets for opportunists who wanted a share of the bookies' cash.

Fearing they would be attacked, Bennett's crew moved first. Les Kane, regarded as the most dangerous brother, was murdered. His body was never found. Bennett, Vincent Mikkelsen and Laurie Prendergast were later acquitted of the murder.

If Bennett wanted to disappear to evade the Kane family he had a big legal hurdle to jump. He was still facing armed robbery charges. He chose to stay in jail rather than be bailed because he knew he would be an easy target on Melbourne streets.

Bennett knew the rules of the underworld and he knew they

would be coming after him. It was only a matter of when and where. He took out a huge life insurance policy, asking if the company would pay if he happened to be 'shot walking down the street'. Months earlier, he sent his young son overseas to keep him out of danger.

Bennett had been transferred from prison to the holding cell at the Magistrates' Court for his committal hearing on armed robbery charges over a $69,000 payroll heist in Yarraville.

As Bennett and the three detectives escorting him walked through the old Melbourne Magistrates' complex, shots were fired. It was 10.17am on a Monday, six days after the 1979 Melbourne Cup.

One of the escorting police, Phil Glare, said a man walked towards Bennett, looked at him and said: 'Cop this, you motherfucker', drew a snub-nosed revolver from inside his coat and fired three shots.

Bennett turned and ran down the stairs. Glare yelled, 'He's off, grab him!' Detective John Mugavin chased Bennett, assuming the shots were blanks and that it was an escape attempt.

Glare moved towards the gunman, who pointed the pistol at him and warned: 'Don't make me do it.'

Bennett collapsed, saying: 'I've been shot in the heart.'

The gunman was able to escape through the courts and then through a pre-cut hole in a corrugated iron fence in a garage behind the building. The killer had an intimate knowledge of the area, and a planned exit route through a maze of stairs and doors. This led some scallywags to speculate that police might have been involved in the murder.

It remains unsolved.

Brian Kane

BRIAN Kane knew he would die young. There was a bullet out there with his name on it and it was only ever a matter of when and where he was going to meet it.

'He was convinced I would outlive him,' veteran prison priest Father John Brosnan said hours after he buried the man who had the reputation of being one of Australia's toughest gangsters.

In the early 1980s, Kane was in the middle of an underworld war that had already claimed three lives and was far from over.

The Kane clan of career standover men had their eyes on some of the money from the 'Great Bookie Robbery' and had identified the mastermind of the job, Ray Bennett, as a possible target.

Brian Kane made a comfortable living by frightening fellow criminals and was well-qualified to demand a share of the bookie robbery funds. He was not accustomed to taking no for an answer. For years he had collected money from illegal gambling in Chinatown and had a slice of a major two-up school.

According to fellow standover man Mark Brandon Read, 'Brian was a violent, cunning criminal who had the bulk of the criminal world and the waterfront bluffed, beaten and baffled.'

But a man like Bennett wasn't easily frightened. He was not going to plan one of Australia's biggest crimes to give up the profit to a family of sharks.

Brooding dislike had erupted into bloodshed after Kane was on the receiving end of a beating in a Richmond hotel from one of Bennett's mates. Brian Kane's brother, Les, vowed revenge and threatened to attack Bennett's family, but the man they called 'The General' decided to hit first.

Bennett and two others shot Les Kane dead in his Wantirna home in October, 1978. They were charged and acquitted of the murder.

Brian vowed to avenge his brother's death. In November, 1979, Ray Bennett was shot dead in the City Court while being escorted by police to an armed robbery committal hearing.

Brian Kane was believed to be the man who killed Bennett, although it has become part of underworld folklore that he had some police assistance along the way.

But there was one problem with the theory that Kane pulled the trigger, with or without the connivance of bent police. According to one notable underworld source, Brian Kane hated firing guns. He usually carried one and was known to have pistol-whipped a man into a coma, but he wasn't a great one for shooting. It's possible someone else did the job.

Brian Kane kept a low profile after Bennett was murdered but Ray was popular and Kane knew his cards were marked. Kane could not disappear. He was Melbourne bred and standover men can't make themselves invisible. Kane was a cool professional, so he knew it was only a matter of time.

The time was 9.30 on a Friday night in November, 1982. Brian Kane was sitting next to a pretty girl at the bar of the Quarry Hotel in Brunswick when two men wearing balaclavas walked into the hotel and opened fire with snub-nosed .38 revolvers. He was shot in the head and chest.

Rumour has it that his pistol was in the girl's handbag and he died lunging for his gun.

According to Father Brosnan, he knew he wasn't bullet proof. 'I don't think he knew he was going to die like this but he was realistic man; he knew what was possible. The best thing about him was that he wasn't a hypocrite.'

Father Brosnan taught the three Kane boys, Brian, Les and

Ray, at the St John's School 25 years earlier. 'I taught them how to fight. I didn't do a bad job, did I?'

One policeman said after Kane was murdered that he would 'be no great loss.' He was wrong. There were 169 death notices placed in *The Sun* – including a handful from star footballers – in the week after his death.

The murder was never solved. It was never going to be.

Norman Leung 'Chops' Lee

NORMAN 'Chops' Lee was one of the greatest enigmas of the Australian underworld. He was the only man to face court over the infamous Great Bookie Robbery, but he did not throw any light on the subject.

Lee's best friend was Raymond Patrick Bennett, the acknowledged mastermind behind the robbery.

Lee was alleged to have laundered $110,000 through a solicitor's trust fund, bringing $60,000 into the office in plastic bags.

The allegations were never put before a jury. Lee was released at a magistrate's committal over the Bookie Robbery because of insufficient evidence.

Lee was of the old school. Police seized an expensive safe from his business when they were looking for the money from the bookie robbery and took it by truck to the Russell Street police station. Detectives asked Lee what was in the safe. He remained silent. They asked him for the keys, and he did an impression of a deaf mute. Police called in a safe expert, who drilled out the lock, rendering it useless.

It was empty. But, on principle, Lee would not talk.

After he was acquitted, Lee went to Chinatown for a celebratory meal – and then seemed to slip under the police radar.

He owned a successful dim sim business – it was rumoured to

have been kicked off with bookie robbery money and, according to underworld legend, was said to have been used to dispose of the body of an enemy.

But, in 1992, Lee came back into the picture – big-time. An armed robbery squad special investigation, code-named Operation Thorn, was working on a team it believed was going to try to pull off a million-dollar stick-up.

They knew the two team leaders were Stephen John Asling, then 32, and Stephen Michael Barci, then 35.

Asling and Barci were close mates. So close that, in 1990, Barci was charged with using Asling's passport. The charge was later withdrawn.

Police believed the two formed the core of one of Victoria's more proficient armed robbery teams, a group that relied on inside information and was prepared to use firearms to succeed.

In May, 1990, the two planned and executed the armed robbery of a Brambles armoured van at Port Melbourne, in which a shot was fired. They also robbed a Greensborough McDonald's store of some $3000 in 1992.

In the Port Melbourne job, Asling and Barci ambushed two security guards, who were having breakfast, and forced them at gunpoint to lie in the back of their armoured truck. They were taken to a darkened warehouse in nearby Swallow Road where they were bound, hand and feet, before the gang took $426,169.81 and the crew's revolvers. One of the abducted guards was David Lapworth, who later admitted being the inside man for the robbery team. After Lapworth's arrest in April, 1992, the armed robbery squad went after Asling and Barci. They obtained warrants to bug four telephones as part of the operation.

Police said that, while conversations between the men indicated they were planning another robbery, they would never discuss the location over the phone. It was clear that three men were needed for the job. Police were convinced they knew the name of the third man and even had his phone tapped. He had been in on the Port Melbourne job and was set for the next big robbery. But, with just weeks to go, the third man pulled out. Asling and Barci needed a replacement and quick. A man who knew the stick-up business and could be trusted.

They turned a wild card, a small businessmen with a minor criminal history, Norman Leung Lee. Police concluded the team would hit the Ansett building at Melbourne airport to grab $1 million to be delivered by armoured van and then be couriered by plane.

On July 28, 1992, the three bandits arrived at the airport in a panel van. They were armed with three pistols and two rifles: a .38 revolver, a .357 magnum, a .38 pistol, a .223 self-loading rifle with 26 cartridges, and a .308 rifle. They also had three rubber masks – two Michael Jacksons and a Madonna – for disguises.

Barci and Lee carried spare ammunition. Lee had a dozen .357 rounds in his pocket. It would do him no good.

The SOG arrest team also brought along a small arsenal, including a 12-gauge pump-action Remington shotgun with pistol grip, semi-automatic pistols, knives and gas masks. No-one could accuse the 'Sons Of God' of being under-prepared.

There were three bandits and 52 police. Normie and his team were driving into an ambush, the most one-sided fight since the fall of the Alamo.

The police plan was to grab the three gunmen before the robbery but the position of the SOG van left not enough time to intercept the bandits. They would not move in during the robbery in case the gunmen took hostages.

It meant police were forced to let the robbery take its course, despite the risk the bandits could shoot Ansett staff while it was in progress.

The robbers arrived around 1.16pm and parked near the Ansett depot. The armoured van was late, arriving about 1.45pm.

Asling reversed the stolen van within 30 metres of the Armaguard vehicle. Barci and Lee jumped out of the back of the van and ran into the office.

They grabbed three large red bags containing $1,020,000.

The five-man SOG arrest team was parked in a disguised police van at least 100 metres from the Ansett depot. They had no chance of stopping the job: the bandits had committed the robbery and were back at the van by the time police arrived.

Lee threw two bags in the back of the van and Barci dragged his along the ground. 'As I dragged the bag down the steps I noticed a man in a van to my right. I fanned the gun past him and I was surprised that he grinned at me,' Barci later told police.

'When I got to the van Norm was inside the van on the rear passenger side, squatting. I then picked up the bag I was dragging with both hands and put it in the back of the van. I was pushing the bag in and Norm was pulling it. I then spun around and sat on the rear of the van on the driver's side with my legs hanging down. At the same time Norm grabbed me by the collar of my jacket to help push me in,' he said.

The SOG arrived as the two men were settling in the back of the getaway van. A witness heard the bandits scream 'Go, go, go!', but the back door catch was not closed. 'It was then that Steve hit the accelerator and Norm and I were thrown out the back of the van,' Barci said later.

'We were screaming, "Stop, stop, stop",' Barci said, as Asling tried to outrun the police. Not only had the two bandits been flung out, but one of the three cash bags went too. Suddenly, it was every man for himself.

Barci and Lee chased the van as the SOG arrest team jumped from their vehicle. According to police, Lee, armed with a .357 magnum, lowered his gun and appeared to be about to give up. He then raised the gun. 'His actions left me no choice but to fire my weapon to protect myself,' one SOG member said later.

Two SOG police fired, hitting him in the back of the head and to the left side of the chest and left wrist. He was dead by the time he hit the ground.

Another SOG member fired five shots at Barci, hitting him at least three times – twice across the back and once in the left shoulder. He has been left permanently disabled.

It was later found that Barci's gun had fired one shot, probably discharging when he fell to the ground.

Asling sped off, reaching up to 80 kmh. An SOG marksman fired one shot at the tyres, blowing out the rear passenger wheel. The van was then rammed by an SOG four-wheel-drive. Police had left little to chance. If the bandits had escaped the inner net, they would have been blocked by road graders the police had commandeered to park across the only road out.

Barci later pleaded guilty to three counts of armed robbery and was sentenced to 15 years in jail, with a minimum of 10. Asling was also sentenced to a minimum of 10 years for the three armed robberies.

Ironically, Normie Lee may have been facing a death sentence before he decided to join the crew. He was a fit-looking 44-year-old man of 73 kilograms and 171 centimetres tall who didn't know he was sick.

During the autopsy it was discovered he had a serious heart problem including a 70 per cent blockage in his left coronary artery. If he hadn't been shot, chasing the getaway van, the general shock of seeing armed police arrive at the scene could have killed him, anyway.

The man who investigated Lee back in the Bookie Robbery days – retired deputy commissioner Paul Delianis – believes he was one of the quiet achievers of the underworld.

'The question is whether he was quiet between the bookie robbery and the incident at Tullamarine or whether he was always too clever to come under notice. I think it was probably the latter,' he said. 'He moved in a circle of top crims. It would be a reasonable hypothesis that he was simply not caught.'

CHAPTER 7

All in the Family

Liborio Benvenuto

MEN with real power rarely feel the need to show off. Rupert Murdoch is said to prefer inexpensive suits made by hard-working Hong Kong tailors to Savile Row labels at 10 times the price. The most powerful media tycoon on the planet doesn't need to show people he is rich – the world already knows.

In his own humble way, Liborio Benvenuto was the Murdoch of his field. A small, dapper man known for his even temper and sense of vision, Benvenuto always claimed he made a success of his life through hard work and the support of his family.

But police always believed he was the head of a bigger family – the Calabrian Honoured Society – known in Australia as the Mafia. Benvenuto was a peacemaker who stopped a war, but he was no pacifist.

Born on December 15, 1927, in Reggio Calabria, the son of the boss of seven Italian villages, he rose to prominence in Australia following the 1963-64 'market murders', committed at the height of a struggle for control of Melbourne's Mafia, which had a stranglehold on the wholesale fruit and vegetable markets. He was related through marriage to Vincenzo Muratore, who was murdered in 1964 and his son, Alfonso Muratore, murdered in 1992.

It was during the power struggle in the markets that Australians first learned that traditional Italian organised crime had become woven into the fabric of the lucky country.

It began when Domenico Italiano, a migrant barely known outside his own closed community, died peacefully of old age in his West Melbourne home in late 1962. His funeral, held at the nearby St Mary's Star of the Sea Catholic Church, gave an insight into the power of the man.

The funeral was more befitting a head of state than a little-known migrant. Thousands of people attended the church and the grounds. The pallbearers, including Italiano's son-in-law, Michele Scriva, carried the body to its final resting place under an elaborate headstone in the Melbourne cemetery.

In hindsight, it was no surprise that Italiano was accorded such respect. He was known as 'il Papa' or 'The Pope' and was the Godfather of the Honoured Society – or, as it was known in some circles, the Black Hand.

Police already knew of its existence, with reports of mob-related extortion going back to the cane fields of Queensland as early as the 1930s. But they were unaware that the organisation had become such a power in the fruit and vegetable industry.

Calabrian migrants were helped in the industry by The Society but, in return, they were indebted, often for life.

Shortly after the death of the much loved Italiano, another old Italian died. He was Antonio Barbara, known as 'The Toad'; he had been Italiano's right-hand man and his violent streak was well known. He had served five years for killing a woman near the Queen Victoria market in 1936. The loss of both men left a void at the top of The Society and a dangerous power struggle developed.

The dead men's places were filled by Domenico Demarte, who took Italiano's position, and Vincenzo Muratore, who was the financial adviser. One man who was not happy with the succession was Vincenzo Angilletta, a gunman who had migrated to Australia in 1951. Angilletta sold fruit and vegetables, but he had bigger ideas. He wanted The Society to become the Australian version of the Sicilian-based US Mafia. He wanted extortion rackets to be broadened to include non-Italians, a move rejected by Demarte and the elders.

Angilletta responded by refusing to sell his produce to designated wholesalers but went direct to the public. He was warned but refused to conform. He was stabbed once on Society orders but still refused to return to the fold.

Demarte, Muratore and the elders decided Angilletta must die. The renegade knew he was a marked man and began to carry a small pistol for protection. It did him no good.

In the early hours of April 4, 1963, he was blasted twice with a shotgun from behind. It is considered a dishonourable way to die, not to be allowed to see the killer's face. Forensic tests found he was killed with lupara shot – the same heavy shot once used by wolf hunters in Calabria.

Angilletta's friends vowed revenge. They blamed Demarte and Muratore for the hit. On November 26, 1963, Demarte was shot at 3.30am as he left his North Melbourne home on the way to the market. He survived but immediately retired hurt from his senior position in The Honoured Society.

On January 16, 1964, Muratore was shot as he left his Hampton home about 2.30am. He was dead by the time he hit the ground. The Victorian Government asked for international help. It arrived in the shape of John T. Cusack, one of the world's most respected organised crime investigators. In 1957, Cusack had managed to document a key Mafia meeting in New York and, as a result, 60 major mob criminals were arrested.

After completing his investigations in Melbourne he submitted to the government a 17-page report that was never officially released. He made it clear that organised crime was already well entrenched in Australia.

'It is already engaged in extortion, prostitution, counterfeiting, sly grog, breaking and entering, illegal gambling and smuggling aliens and small arms. Its infiltration and effort to control the fruit and vegetable produce business has been exposed. Within the next 25 years, if unchecked, the Society is capable of diversification into all facets of organised crime and legitimate business,' he wrote.

Cusack uncovered the Society's rules. 'Aid was to be extended to a member, no matter what the circumstances; there was to be absolute obedience to officers of the Society; an offence against an individual member was an attack on the Society and must be avenged; no members could turn to a government agency for justice and the final rule, which has caused countless police investigations, was Omerta, the code of silence.'

No member was to reveal the name of other members or reveal any of the organisation's secrets. 'They realise in silence there is security while testimony against a Society member can bring death.'

Detectives solved none of the murders and, eventually, peace returned but it was Benvenuto and not the police, who stopped the murders. His lieutenant was Michele Scriva, Italiano's son-in-law and related to Benvenuto through marriage.

Scriva was born in Reggio, Calabria, on June 19, 1919, and migrated to Australia at 17. In 1945 he was the main suspect in the killing of Giuseppe 'Fat Joe' Verscace, who was stabbed in Fitzroy. Scriva and two other men, Domencio Demarte and Domenico Pezzimenti, were charged. They were acquitted but, five years later, Scriva was charged with stabbing Frederick John Duffy. Duffy had attempted to intervene in a fight and was stabbed to death. Scriva was sentenced to death but was commuted to life. He served 10 years.

The new Godfather wanted peace but you could not head the Honoured Society with a pacifist philosophy. Turning the other cheek won't stop a shotgun blast.

On May 10, 1983, Benvenuto's four-wheel-drive vehicle was blown up at the wholesale fruit and vegetable market, where he worked with the Muratore family. When asked what was behind the attack he said: 'I have no enemies, only friends at the market. I don't know why anybody would do this. I have never done anybody harm.'

A year later, two market identities were found murdered in the Murrumbidgee River in the Riverina region of New South Wales. Rocco Medici and his brother-in-law, Giuseppe Furina, both from the Melbourne suburb of East Keilor, had been tortured and their bodies dumped in the river. One of them had his ears sliced off as a warning that he heard too much. Police were told it was a payback for the attack on the Godfather.

Benvenuto died of natural causes on June 10, 1988. But on May 8, 2000, his son, Frank, was shot dead in Beaumaris. His murder remains unsolved.

Alfonse Muratore

ITALIAN names have been common in the wholesale fruit and vegetable business in Australia for decades, with the same family names cropping up in each generation. And, although the market was switched from the Queen Victoria market to the new Melbourne Wholesale Market at Footscray, the old ways of business prospered.

The market has a turnover in the multi-millions of dollars. It sells 6000 tonnes of produce a day and is reputed to be the biggest growers' market in the world.

It is a vibrant, energetic environment but for years it was underpinned by a culture of corruption built on a cash economy, a fortress mentality backed with the constant threat of violence. To survive, you had to pay, and keep paying.

A registered casual grower at the market could pay a daily fee of about $30 for a stand to sell his produce. But if he didn't pay a bribe on top of that, his stall location at the market would be changed daily so that his regular customers couldn't find him. The choice was simple, stand on your principles and watch your produce go rotten waiting for customers, or pay up and get on with business.

Some market officers had several schemes operating. One would walk into the coffee shop at the market and drop his hat on a table. Within a few minutes it was full of money.

Some of the corrupt market officers called the bribe network 'insurance money' or the 'retirement fund'. The growers in the market called it 'the club'.

Buyers paid bribes to get into the market early to pick up produce, to park their truck undercover, to keep the fruit and vegetables out of the weather, and to leave the site before the 6.30am exit time.

The sellers paid bribes to crib space for their stalls, to protect them from parking fines and to be given prime selling spots. Friday was collection day. Money was left on the seats of unlocked trucks or just collected from the stalls. It was no great secret.

Some market officers were netting $25,000 a year in tax-free bribes. One was ordered to pay $50,000 in back taxes. Three were found guilty of accepting secret commissions. One was sentenced to 16 months' jail.

The schemes were varied. It wasn't just small greengrocers who were forced to pay bribes. No-one was immune. Even Australia's biggest retailing company, Coles Myer, had to pay. This meant that in real terms, every Australian was paying a secret tax to organised crime for the staple of life. Food.

'It was all about money and power,' then National Crime Authority chief investigator Peter Fleming said. 'That is why people were prepared to kill for it and others prepared to die for it.' The schemes were varied. Growers said one corrupt official would, for a price, condemn truck-loads of perfectly good fruit as unsuitable for human consumption. It would then be secretly transported to a market merchant, who would then sell it to a supermarket chain for a huge profit.

The market is a huge, undercover city. There were more than 750 forklifts on the property and they were supposed to be left in a secure cage. There was a massive black market in the forklifts. When police raided a huge marijuana property in the Northern Territory they found expensive farm gear, including four special motorised produce trolleys reported missing from the Melbourne market.

There was also a huge trade in produce pallets, which went missing at an alarming rate.

There was a spate of robberies, mainly because the market people were resistant to change and would not deal in anything but cash. Some merchants used two sets of books. Income tax was routinely avoided.

The corruption went into the corporate world. Some merchants began demanding a tax of 20 to 50 cents for every case of produce sold. This, combined with a double invoicing scheme, was costing Coles Myer about $6 million a year.

In 1989 Alan Williams, a senior executive with the Coles Myer produce section, realised the company was paying exorbitant rates for fruit and vegetables. When a glut of cauliflowers flooded the market, the price dropped, but Coles Myer was still paying an inflated price.

Williams ordered an internal inquiry, recruiting one of his own men, John Vasilopolous, to bring prices into line. Williams tried to report his concerns to police. They failed to act.

Vasilopolous was a family man. He was hardly expected to put his life on the line over the price of onions but he was prepared to do his job. He started to send some produce back, claiming it was sub-standard. In reality, he believed the prices were too high.

Some buyers had taken bribes to look the other way. Vasilopolous would not. He was rocking a corrupt system that had been operating for at least 12 years. He was costing the Honoured Society money.

From July, 1990, he began to receive death threats but he still resisted paying inflated prices for fruit and vegetables. He was reading at home in December 19, 1990 when the doorbell rang. He called out to find out who was visiting. A male voice replied: 'Open the door, John.'

He opened the door slightly and was blasted by a man armed with a shotgun. Doctors later removed pellets from his left thigh, right leg, left side of the stomach and chest, right upper arm, left forearm and elbow. He was lucky to be alive.

He left his promising career and Coles Myer brought in produce wholesaling company Costas in a bid to insulate itself from the violence and corruption in the industry. But even then, while some of the obvious scams were closed, corruption continued. In July,

1992, two well-known market identities, Alfonse Muratore and Orlando Luciano, met Coles Myer representatives in the Parkroyal Hotel on Little Collins Street to tell them of some of the schemes that had been costing them money. Coles Myer security men checked the area, sweeping it electronically for bugs before the four-hour secret meeting.

Police believe the two men were pitching for business, claiming they could do the job cleaner and cheaper.

Muratore had been out of the markets for two years and wanted to re-establish himself. But his reputation was tainted.

He was married to Liborio Benvenuto's daughter, Angela. Shortly after his father-in-law died in 1988, Muratore left his wife for a pretty blonde woman, Karen Mansfield.

He had betrayed his wife, the Godfather's daughter, and was trying to take Society business. This was not a wise life plan, although it meant he would not have to save for his retirement. The ambitious Muratore had effectively signed his own death warrant.

About 1.30am on August 4, about two weeks after his secret meeting with Coles Myer men, he was shot dead outside his Hampton home, in a carbon copy of his father's death, nearly 30 years earlier.

Things hadn't changed. One tight-lipped witness told police, 'You can put me in jail ... they can give me the death sentence.'

While detectives have not charged anyone over the killing they believe they know the identities. One was a member of the 'Big Three', the men who have run Society business since Benvenuto died in 1988.

There was a public inquest in which alleged killers were named and motives discussed but no-one was ever going to be charged. Just as with the 1963-64 market murders. A three-year National Crime Authority investigation into Italian organised crime, code-named Cerberus, found that the 'Mafia' was different in real life than in the movies.

It found that individual corrupt cells were involved in crime but there was no one 'Mr Big'. It said individuals came together, motivated by profit and greed.

'Networks are used to facilitate organised criminal activity, particularly through the formation of temporary syndicates for the purpose of carrying out specific criminal ventures,' the report said.

'It is the family and extended family relationships that retain a significant role in Italo-Australian criminal organised crime at both the regional and national levels.'

'There is a natural reluctance to inform on a family member or ... associates who share a ... town of origin.'

The study found that the syndicates had been involved in running extortion rackets from the 1930s to the 1970s, until the drug trade took over as the major money-making business. The NCA investigation found the gangs not just involved in the cultivation and distribution of cannabis, but in importing marijuana, heroin and cocaine and the production and distribution of amphetamines.

Operation Cerberus also examined murders from 1974 to 1995 to see how many were connected to the Italian crime gangs. 'While it is apparent that some members of the Italo-Australian criminal community have utilised murder as a mean of discipline and suppression within this country, it is also apparent that the threat of such extreme violence to the innocent members of the community is minimal. In fact, considering the extent of the Italo-Australian community within Australia and the perceived extent of the criminal element of the same community, the use of murder is a relatively rare occurrence.'

This was of little solace to the family of Donald Mackay.

Robert 'Aussie Bob' Trimbole

AUSTRALIA'S most infamous drug dealer, 'Aussie Bob' Trimbole, died a free man in Spain in 1987 – 12 years after he was first identified as a major organised crime figure.

The Trimbole story remains one of the most shameful cases in Australian law enforcement. It involves cover-ups, lies, bungles and incompetence.

The former Griffith garage owner went bankrupt with debts of $10,986.63 in 1968, yet a few years later owned a restaurant, butchery, licensed grocer and a clothing shop ... not to mention police, horse trainers and jockeys.

Trimbole did not just develop unexplained business acumen late in life. He was the man who organised the murder of Griffith anti-drugs campaigner Donald Mackay, in 1977.

Mackay wrote to police in 1975 identifying Trimbole and other Calabrians as players in the local drug trade. Six of them met to decide how to deal with this whistle-blower. They knew the local police were on side, but Mackay, the owner of a local furniture store, was seen to be dangerous because he was honest, brave and outspoken, a rare treble in the small community. Ironically, it was those qualities that sentenced him to death.

The group considered trying to bribe Mackay or set him up with a woman, but concluded he was beyond corruption. They then made a decision that would impact on law enforcement for decades. They ordered that he was to be murdered. Trimbole, the most junior of the group, was instructed to get the job done.

He employed hitman James Bazley. Impressed by his work, he would later employ the same man to kill drug couriers Isabel and Douglas Wilson.

'Aussie Bob' Trimbole was in charge of the retail arm of the

Griffith cannabis production group. He had good contacts in Sydney and was able to organise distribution of the drugs.

The 1979 Woodward Royal Commission described him as, 'In all probability, the practical leader of the organisation growing illegal marijuana crops in Griffith, NSW.'

But, even though he had been publicly outed as a crime figure, Trimbole continued to associate with many respected men in NSW and Queensland. In his diary were the telephone numbers of judges, lawyers, police, jockeys and race callers.

He would regularly place cash bets at the races for more than $20,000 and police were to claim he had 13 jockeys on his payroll. His phone calls were illegally taped by Sydney police, revealing that he was involved in race fixing, distributing false passports, heroin trafficking and bribing police.

In 1980 he refused to give evidence at the Melbourne inquest on the murder of the Wilsons on the grounds he would incriminate himself.

Yet he was allowed to remain free.

In 1981, Trimbole became deeply worried that he might finally be jailed after the Stewart Royal Commission into drugs was set up.

He rang a police contact who advised him to escape overseas on May 7, 1981.

He moved to Nice in France and, although he was regularly visited by his daughter, Glenda, and son, Craig, police were apparently unable to find him.

Eventually, Trimbole was arrested in Ireland in October 1984 but, because of a procedural mistake, he could not be extradited. He was freed and moved to Alicante, Spain, where he died in May, 1987. The only way they could get Bob back to Aussie was in a coffin.

Gianfranco Tizzoni

WHEN a member of the Mafia turns informer he knows he has probably dug his own grave. Oddly enough, even before Gianfranco Tizzoni became one of the biggest informers in Australian crime history, he had his organised.

Frank Tizzoni had spent around $7000 buying his grave on the side of a hill at the Templestowe cemetery in Melbourne's north-eastern suburbs before he slipped out of the country to hide. The only thing missing was the date of death.

But it was not a Mafia hitman who killed the man they called 'Songbird'– it was just a weak heart. He was 53.

And Tizzoni didn't get to use the black marble tomb, complete with his family crest, that he had left in Templestowe. He was buried in Italy in July, 1988, close to where he lived out his life as a sick, bitter and disillusioned man, regretting his decision to expose the inner workings of the group he once referred to as 'The Family'.

At the height of his influence, Tizzoni drove a Mercedes coupe with personalised plates, owned a luxurious house in Balwyn and a farm in Koo Wee Rup. He could afford his lavish lifestyle thanks to the $2 million a year he made from marijuana.

Tizzoni migrated to Australia in 1955 and was later naturalised. He became a private investigator and worked with notorious underworld figure Tom Ericksen as a debt collector.

From 1971 he became the Melbourne distributor of cannabis for the Griffith cell of the Mafia and distributed about 200 kilograms a week. He was set for life but he fell for the trap of behaving like a Mafia Don. He didn't just want the money – he wanted 'respect'. To get it, he oversold himself.

In a bid to ingratiate himself with the influential 'Aussie' Bob

Trimbole, Tizzoni bragged that he could have people killed if necessary. Eventually, the people who had made him rich called on him to back up his claims.

In 1977, Trimbole told Tizzoni that Griffith businessman Donald Mackay was becoming troublesome and could expose the network. He had to go.

Tizzoni made contact with a Melbourne armed robber and hitman, Frederick Bazley, through a gun dealer called George Joseph. Tizzoni persuaded Bazley to take the contract and the only instruction given was that the firearm should not be the traditional Mafia weapon of choice – the shotgun.

Mackay was killed in the carpark of the Griffith Hotel. His body was never found.

Two years later, when Trimbole wanted two drug couriers murdered because they were talking to police about the Mr Asia drug syndicate, he again turned to Tizzoni.

Tizzoni employed Bazley to kill Isabel and Douglas Wilson. But the hitman was careless. The bodies were found in a shallow grave at Rye in May, 1979.

It was bad luck and a split-second decision that eventually exposed Tizzoni.

Police were following his Mercedes and another vehicle from a huge marijuana crop near Canberra in March, 1982, as they headed towards Melbourne along the Hume Highway.

Experienced investigator John Weel was instructed to follow but not intercept the two vehicles but, as they reached the outskirts of Melbourne, it was close to evening peak hour and the policeman felt he could lose the targets.

He took it upon himself to pull them over and 'found' a bale of marijuana in Tizzoni's boot.

After he was arrested, Tizzoni used a private investigator to establish if Weel could be bribed. When he realised he was caught by an honest cop, he knew the only way to avoid a long jail term was to turn informer.

It was the biggest break for police investigating Italian organised crime since the market murders of 1963-64. Police agreed to drop charges of trafficking and possessing marijuana valued at $1 million in return for his testimony.

But there was a problem. If Tizzoni was allowed to walk free he would have been murdered within weeks as it would have been obvious he had become an informer. So police invented a cover story for their supergrass. Weel pretended to be corrupt to allow Tizzoni to claim he had bought his release.

The story was so realistic that a Mafia figure paid $30,000 as his part of the bribe money for Weel. Tizzoni simply pocketed the cash – and kept talking to the police.

Tizzoni pleaded guilty in October, 1984, to conspiracy to murder Mackay and the Wilsons and was sentenced to five years' jail. He was released into witness protection after a year.

While under police protection he was taken to the Golden Age Hotel in the heart of Melbourne. He was able to sit quietly at a seat with his police minders, unrecognised even though some of Melbourne's best-known investigative reporters were at the bar drinking chardonnay.

Tizzoni was released on parole in February, 1986. Then the man who was disposable to the Mafia found he was just as disposable for the authorities who had promised him a new life.

He was ordered not to leave the country and hit with a back-tax bill of almost $1 million. But, clearly, Tizzoni hadn't told police all he knew. If he had, he would have been marked for death, but he survived.

Experienced crime reporter Keith Moor was able to find Tizzoni living under his own name in Italy. He interviewed Australia's most important informer over a quiet meal and then headed home to write the story. If one reporter could find him, then so could The Family – had they wanted to.

One of Australia's top investigators, Carl Mengler, headed the ultimately successful investigations into the Mackay and Wilson murders. He believes Tizzoni stopped short of exposing the true leaders of the Griffith Mafia.

'I think it is fair to say that Tizzoni took some secrets to the grave,' Mengler said. 'There would be some people who would breathe easier now that he has gone and those secrets have been buried with him.'

James Frederick 'Mr Cool' Bazley

JAMES Frederick Bazley is Australia's oldest-known contract killer – and the man who murdered anti-drugs campaigner Donald Mackay at Griffith in 1977.

Bazley was supposedly going to be in jail until he died but he walked out an old man, still as staunch as ever, refusing to divulge any details of what he knows.

He had a long and violent criminal record culminating with being sentenced to life for killing three people for cash, yet he looked more like a gentle grandfather than a gun for hire.

Bazley was paid just $10,000 to kill Mackay, who was shot in the car park of the Griffith Hotel on July 15, 1977. The body has never been found.

Mackay was killed because he was determined to expose the marijuana industry in the district. The heads of the Griffith syndicate, known variously as The Family or the Honoured Society, then hired Bazley to kill Mackay, a family man who owned a furniture shop in the town and was active in local politics, sporting groups and the church.

Bazley also killed drug couriers Isabel and Douglas Wilson,

whose bodies were found buried in the beach town of Rye in May, 1979.

The Wilsons were killed on the orders of the Mr Asia drug syndicate boss, Terrence John Clarke, after corrupt police told him the couple were talking to Queensland detectives.

He was paid $20,000 for the double murder. He was also told to kill the Wilsons' dog, Taj. But, as a dog lover and former poodle breeder, he refused. The dog was later found wandering in a Brunswick street.

The murder of Mackay was to become a defining moment in the exposure of organised crime in Australia because the formerly unknown Griffith businessman was to become a national martyr – a symbol of mainstream opposition to drug trafficking and the corruption it bred.

As a result of the public outcry there was a series of inquiries and royal commissions that exposed judicial, political and police corruption and resulted in the Australian Bureau of Criminal Intelligence and the National Crime Authority being set up.

Police say Bazley remains the only person alive who really knows what happened in the Griffith carpark the night Mackay disappeared.

Two of the key figures are now dead. An informer, Gianfranco Tizzoni, who acted as a middle man in hiring Bazley, died in hiding in Italy in 1988, and the notorious crime figure Bob Trimbole, who helped organise the contract killing, died in Spain in 1987.

Bazley was sentenced to life in 1986 for the murders of the Wilsons, nine years for the conspiracy to murder Mackay, and a further four years for a $270,000 armed robbery. He has always maintained he was not involved in the three murders.

Police said that when he took the contract to kill Mackay he was told the body was never to be found and a shotgun was not to be used, as it was seen as the traditional weapon of the Mafia. He used his favourite weapon – a French made .22 'Unique' pistol with a specially-fitted silencer. He broke the cardinal rule of criminality by not getting rid of the weapon afterwards, a lapse that helped convict him. And, although Mackay's body was disposed of 'professionally', Bazley got sloppy when he buried the Wilsons in a shallow grave near a house he and his wife were known to visit.

After he was convicted, Bazley was resigned to dying in jail. He told veteran crime reporter Tom Prior in 1987: 'I'm in here for keeps. The only way out is over the wall or in a pine box.'

But the Supreme Court later set his minimum sentence at 15 years, giving him some hope of freedom.

When he realised he could live long enough to be freed, he started to lobby for his release.

Bazley contacted former deputy commissioner and head of the homicide squad, Paul Delianis, and asked him to give evidence on his behalf before the Parole Board.

'I told him that would be possible if he would say what happened to Mackay's body,' Delianis said. 'That was the end of the phone call and I haven't heard from him since.'

Delianis says only Bazley can solve the mystery. 'I believe he is the only person who would know. He was a loner. Every time he worked with someone he would come unstuck. He saw killing as a business. To him, it was just a job.

'I suspect that he buried the body somewhere near Griffith and I believe he acted alone.'

Bazley, known as 'Mr Cool', is dapper, quietly-spoken, polite – and elderly. He wants to spend his final years with his wife, Lillian, and in 2000 was given day leave to prepare himself for life on the outside.

Bazley has a heart condition but has kept himself relatively fit. He acted as a 'personal trainer' for disgraced Coles Myer boss Brian Quinn when the former top businessman was serving just over two years for fraud. Bazley was old but not without influence in prison. His support, presumably paid for in some way, would make the wealthy Quinn's sentence easier to bear.

Carl Mengler, a former deputy police commissioner, who built the case against Bazley, believes the hitman should not have been freed until he confessed what he did with Mackay's body.

'He was the worst sort of murderer. He was an intelligent man who simply killed people he didn't know for money. Jim Bazley showed no mercy to his victims and has left their relatives to grieve every living day of the rest of their lives.

'He has never shown any remorse for what he has done.'

Mengler said Bazley's age should not have been be used as a reason for his release: 'He was a mature man when he accepted the contracts to kill. He has no excuses.'

Bazley was a Painters and Dockers gunman in the 1970s, and was shot twice during the notorious dockies' war. He has a 50-year history of armed robbery and violence, but prison officers say he was a model inmate and well-respected by fellow prisoners. 'He is still well connected,' one officer said.

For all his experience, Bazley was no master criminal. For a career armed robber he found ridiculous ways to get caught. In 1975, he robbed a Melbourne bank of $10,000 but was grabbed by a one-legged butcher who worked next door.

Bazley became overconfident and lazy when he murdered Isabel and Douglas Wilson. He and Lillian regularly rented a holiday house in Rye. In bushland next door he noticed a hole had been dug which was used by local children as a play pit.

But a man on his regular walk also noticed the hole, and grew curious when he saw it had been dug deeper and was next day filled with fresh soil and tea-tree. He called police and the bodies were found. The trail went directly to Bazley.

Bazley was 75 when released in late January 2001, from Loddon Prison, near the Victorian country town of Castlemaine. He politely refused media interviews and headed off with Lillian, his ever-loving wife.

Pasquale Barbaro

PASQUALE Barbaro was from Plati, Calabria. He was a poor shepherd who dreamed of a better life in Australia – but, in the end, he was the lamb who was led to the slaughter.

Barbaro arrived in Sydney aboard the *Toscana* on January 4, 1957, and moved to Melbourne, where he was employed as a cheese maker. Later, he moved to Canberra where he worked as a council gardener until he hurt his back and was granted an invalid pension. As early as 1969 he was identified in a secret police report as a Mafia figure. Investigations indicated that while he was not rich, he lived beyond the means of an invalid pensioner.

He was a respected member of a sub-section of the Italian community and treated with deference. Letters were addressed to him as 'il Principale' – the correct expression for Godfather.

Yet he didn't appear to be a powerful gangster and had only one conviction, for carrying a pistol.

For two decades Barbaro was the Mafia Governor of a large area including Canberra and, according to police, was one of six Honoured Society chiefs in Australia. Police say he was paid a financial tribute from many of the marijuana plantations harvested in the 1970s and early 1980s.

In 1982, he ordered the murder of Giuseppe Montelone, who was a senior and influential NSW marijuana producer. Montelone was murdered because he tried to freeze Barbaro out of the profits from a major cannabis plantation following a long-running dispute between the two.

As was usually the way, the victim was betrayed by someone close. But the man who set up Montelone, Bruno Morabito, was later to pay with his own life. Morabito drove Montelone to the Narrabri property where he was killed in 1982 and later told police he had been tied up by two masked men who then murdered his friend.

It was a simple execution. On his 50th birthday, Montelone was stood up against a wall and shot. Police had no doubt that Morabito lured his friend to the execution spot but could not crack his story. Detectives lacked evidence but a jury of Morabito's peers had already found him guilty and sentenced him to death.

In December, 1989, Morabito was murdered – stabbed six times and shot twice while on day leave from a Sydney prison, where he was serving eight years for drug trafficking. Meanwhile, in 1984 Barbaro had left his wife and moved to the Philippines. It was his first big mistake.

He was stripped of his powerful position in the Honoured Society in his absence. Earlier, he had been given a letter of introduction addressed to a senior minister in Manila signed by former Federal Immigration Minister Al Grassby, a regular visitor to certain Calabrian families in the Griffith area.

Barbaro married a Filipino and returned to settle in Brisbane in 1986. It was his second mistake.

In April, 1989, he was shot in both shoulders while in his bedroom. At the time, one of the authors was told that another attempt would be made on his life. 'He has dishonoured them.

Honour cannot be repaid with money or gold. It can only be paid with blood. It does not matter how long it will take. It will be done,' said a man connected with the group.

Queensland police began to work on the wounded and frightened Barbaro, trying to get the former Godfather to turn informer. He was terrified, sold his house and put the telephone in his wife's maiden name.

After a month he said he would talk – for a fee of $50,000. He became a National Crime Authority informer and later dropped his asking price to $10,000.

He would tell his new wife he was going to see doctors about his wounds when he went to talk to NCA officers. He had much to say. Three of his brothers had been connected with heavy drug trafficking in Australia.

The Woodward Royal Commission had already identified financial dealings between Pasquale Barbaro and known members of the Honoured Society. Justice Woodward found some of the transactions were clearly designed for laundering black money.

Some members of the Barbaro clan were connected with the decision to murder Griffith anti-drugs campaigner Donald Mackay.

Desperate for money, Pasquale Barbaro attempted to sue one of the authors for $200,000, even though the subsequent defamation case would expose family members as connected to drug trafficking and the Honoured Society. It was his third mistake. His days were numbered.

NCA investigators tried to persuade him to enter the witness protection program but he thought it was safer to live in the community and try to keep a low profile. It was his final – and fatal mistake. On Sunday, March 18, 1990, he walked out of his house at 5.55am, telling his wife he was heading to a local flea market to buy a lock. He drove his car down the drive of his home in the Brisbane suburb of Runcorn and then walked back to lock the garage.

Police found that the killer was waiting in a vacant block next door. He attacked Barbaro, 58, and stabbed him in both arms. Barbaro yelled out in Italian and then was shot once in the chest with a handgun.

He staggered away and the killer fired a second shot, which missed. Barbaro collapsed outside his home and died where he fell. Police believe the killer was recruited from overseas for the hit and was sent home when the job was done. It's called outsourcing.

Giuseppe Arena

IT was probably the proudest moment of Giuseppe Arena's life. On an August evening in 1987 he moved contentedly among 450 people gathered at a popular reception centre in the northern Melbourne suburb of Brunswick, graciously accepting their best wishes.

Giuseppe Arena's only daughter, his pride and joy, was being given the best traditional Italian wedding her father could provide. He had, in fact, wanted 900 guests and only strong words from his family persuaded him to halve the list.

It was a memorable night. Giuseppe, after all, was known as 'The Friendly Godfather' and was a popular and influential figure in the Italian community. As he circulated among the large crowd, they kept coming forward. Some shook his hand or patted him on the back. Some kissed him on the cheek.

The night went perfectly.

A year later Giuseppe Arena was dead. The father of three was shot from behind after taking out the rubbish at his

Bayswater home on August 1, 1988. It was a classic Italian organised-crime hit and, as such, has never been solved.

His widow, Maria, has no idea who killed her husband or why, but she now knows the quicksand-like grip of Omerta – the code of silence.

Mrs Arena says that, except for her immediate family, she has been abandoned by all of the guests who were hugging and congratulating her husband at their daughter's wedding. 'They have all dropped off like flies,' she was to say.

'Since the funeral we have not heard or seen from any of them. They were our friends. Now they are all too frightened even to pick up the phone and ring: they should be ashamed of themselves. It is as if when Joe was buried we were buried too. If that is the Calabrian way then they can have it. They used him, now they have discarded us.'

Mrs Arena knows that one of the guests, trusted to share the family's wedding celebration, may have already been considering ordering her husband's execution.

'Joe' Arena was an insurance broker who understood figures but couldn't see that the odds were lengthening against him. Arena was also a big money launderer for interests in Mildura and may have been seen as the man destined to become one of the most important members of the Honoured Society in Australia.

In late May, 1988, he was called to the death bed of Godfather, Liborio Benvenuto. Police were told the older man anointed him as his successor. Benvenuto, 62, died on June 10 of natural causes.

Within days of the death Arena's status appeared to grow. Certain members of the Italian community would go out of their way to shake his hand.

Always well-liked, Arena now had something else … respect.

Within three weeks of the Godfather's death, Arena, who was only 50, sold his insurance business for just $60,000 and gave up full-time work.

He had shares worth $113,000, four cars valued at $20,000 and jewellery worth $20,000. He was worth a total of $216,768.67 – hardly enough to retire on. Clearly he expected a substantial income stream from some other source.

But he also appeared to be a worried man. The usually outgoing salesman began to become withdrawn and suspicious.

One associate of Benvenuto was an avowed enemy of Arena and bitterly opposed his promotion within the Society.

Italian crime expert Pino Alarcchi wrote in his book, *Mafia Business*, that moves to appoint a new Godfather often end in violence.

'Attempts to impose candidates for the succession "from above" almost always undermine the group's cohesion and spark off conflicts,' he wrote.

Arena was born in Calabria on September 28, 1937, and arrived in Australia on March 12, 1951. He became a Mr Fixit for the Honoured Society. When a member from Griffith needed a Melbourne lawyer it was Joe who made the arrangements – although he later complained that the Griffith man was cheap and nasty and had not shown appreciation or offered any financial reward.

Arena was a fixer and a fixer is only as good as his contacts. He had an inside man in the Tax Department who protected him from investigations. The officer was seen at an Honoured Society wedding at a time when he was in charge of investigations into several of the group's key figures.

Arena was well-known to many police and made a habit of stopping off at the Springvale and Oakleigh police stations to drop off a slab and have a few beers. He also helped organise the finance for a business deal on behalf of the son of a prominent Melbourne lawyer.

He used his family home as a surety to get bail for an Australian man charged over a $2 million heroin deal in 1982. The man was later acquitted of the charge and was seen drinking with several members of the jury.

Arena had his own troubles with the law. He was convicted of manslaughter after he killed his wife's lover in 1976. He served two years.

It was only after Arena's death that police learned he was a major Mafia money launderer. They found he had cleaned $536,000 for Mildura crime figures.

On July 17, 1986, Joe Arena walked into the Westpac branch in St Kilda Road and produced $80,000 cash and asked for it to be lodged in his account. A week later he was back with another $88,000.

The money was later transferred to a Mildura motelier.

In one land deal designed to launder illegal funds, Arena and two others bought a block of land in Mildura for a wildly-inflated $750,000. Its true market value was $85,000.

At one point – out of office hours – $350,000 cash from the land deal was spread over the solicitor's desk to be counted and lodged in the lawyer's trust account.

Only days before he was murdered Arena returned from Mildura after laundering $18,000. But he sensed trouble – he was 'beside himself with worry.'

Police say the killer knew his movements and was waiting when Arena stepped into his backyard to bring out his rubbish bin at his home in Bona Vista Road.

He was hit from behind, the traditional method of death with dishonour for Society members.

Two of his close Mildura contacts, brothers Tony and

Victor George
Peirce ...
obviously lost
his balance
in a police
station.

Victor and Wendy Peirce in happier times. Below: Peirce (in jacket) with Jedd Houghton and Graeme Jensen casing an armed robbery target. All have been shot dead.

Dennis Bruce 'Mr Death' Allen.

Family snap … Dennis pulls a gun on mum, Kath 'Granny Evil' Pettingill.

The Peirce/Jensen robbery gang at work.

Jensen threatens a man and his child during a bank job.

Graeme Jensen … killed by police at Narre Warren when he attempted to escape. He put it in reverse. They put him in neutral.

Jason Moran (right) in his favourite court suit. Smoking is bad for your health.

Mark Moran … murdered outside his home.

Big Al Gangitano … lived like a gangster and died like one.

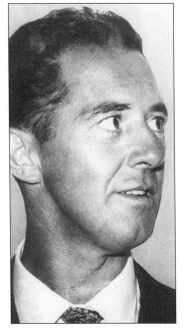

Billy 'The Texan' Longley (top left).

William John O'Meally (above) … the last man flogged (legally) in prison.

Theodore Leslie Joseph 'Squizzy' Taylor … good crook, bad chins.

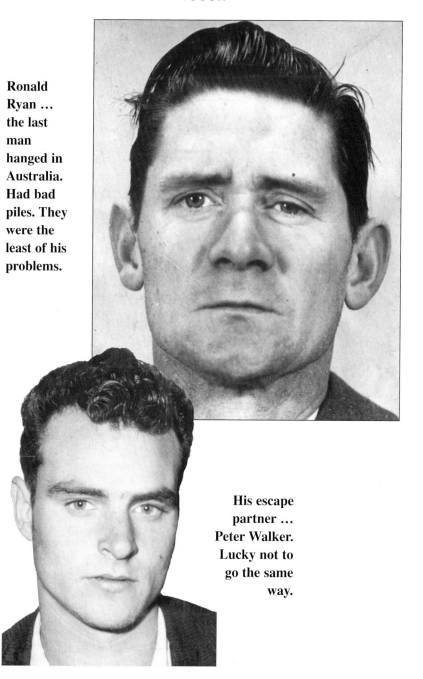

Ronald Ryan … the last man hanged in Australia. Had bad piles. They were the least of his problems.

His escape partner … Peter Walker. Lucky not to go the same way.

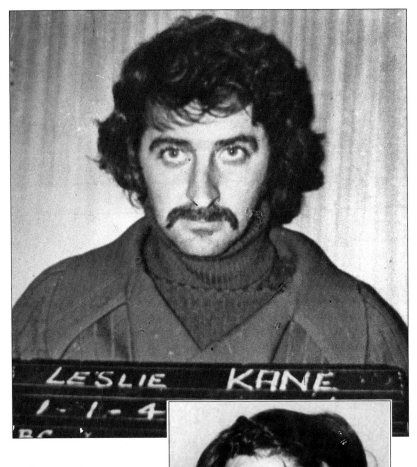

Brothers in arms …
Leslie Herbert Kane
(above). His body
was never found.

Brian Kane
(right) … shot
dead in the
Quarry Hotel.

68–150 RAYMOND P CHUCK B.23.748
P.23.10.75 H 5'10"

**Raymond Patrick
Bennett … master
crime planner.
Gunned down at
the Melbourne
Magistrates' Court.**

**Normie 'Chops'
Lee (left) … shot
during an armed
robbery at
Melbourne Airport.**

Normie Lee thought he could make a million dollars from the robbery …

... but the special operations group was waiting.

The incredible shrinking bomber ... 'Jenny' Craig Minogue with Chopper Read and (left) after the diet kicked in.

The Russell Street bombing.

Maurice John Marion as Bank Enemy No. 1 ... did he get away with murder?

James Richard, 'Birdman' Finch ... said he was innocent of the Whisky Au Go Go fire. He lied.

Pasquale Cufari, were later jailed for unrelated offences – Tony for tax fraud and Pasquale for trafficking marijuana valued at between $11 million and $18 million.

Tony Romeo

DEPENDING on who you talk to, Tony Romeo was a simple migrant farmer or a smooth Italian gangster. Either way, when he was shot dead in mid-2002, the whisper was that he was being punished for bringing dishonour to his family – or perhaps someone else's.

Everybody is wiser in hindsight. If Romeo had to do his time over again, he might well decide against returning to his hometown of Griffith after doing eight years' jail for a multi-million-dollar drug conspiracy.

What he didn't know was that the day he got out of jail in Victoria, someone stole a white Toyota Prado in Griffith. Someone, the theory goes, who was waiting patiently for him to come home. Six weeks later, on July 1, the man once seen as an heir apparent in the Calabrian crime syndicate, the Honoured Society, was shot dead while pruning a peach tree. About 30 people were working in the same orchard at the time, some close enough to hear the thud of the bullet in Romeo's chest, but no one saw anything.

Hours later, a vehicle was 'torched' near Darlington Point, about 50 kilometres away. It was the Toyota stolen six weeks before. Coincidences do happen, but police tend not to believe in them. If the Toyota had been used as a getaway car by the shooter, the hit was a long-range plan hatched months, or years, earlier.

Whether an outside shooter was paid to do it – as James Bazley was to kill anti-drugs campaigner Donald Mackay in 1977 – or whether it was local talent was a puzzle that occupied police for weeks without any sign of a breakthrough. In any case, given the code of silence known as Omerta, finding the trigger man would be unlikely to answer more intriguing questions, such as who ordered the shooting – and why?

What police do know is that the shooting fits a pattern that goes back generations in Italian organised crime, in which 'honour', family, business and affairs of the heart are mixed together, often with deadly results.

Clues to Tony Romeo's violent end could lie in facts uncovered by the remarkable feat of undercover police work that led to his arrest.

In July, 1993, a Victorian detective and a policewoman posing as an art dealer and his girlfriend arrived in Griffith. It was the first move in an audacious 'sting' that would eventually put Romeo and several others behind bars.

The detective, with his 'girlfriend', studied Tony Romeo and Rosario Trimbole close up for the first time after months on surveillance, watching them and others through a long lens and listening to tapes and wiretaps. He had pored over their photographs, form and family histories.

Romeo and Trimbole were related, like most Griffith Calabrians, who tend to inter-marry. The pair, in their late 30s, had equal standing in the Honoured Society's pecking order. They deferred to some older men in the organisation, but had power because they were more at ease in the wider world.

Romeo, relatively tall and well-dressed, stood out from Trimbole and the other Calabrians. He had married well by his standards – his wife was a Sergi, one of the district's biggest biggest and best-known Calabrian families.

The odds against the undercover police getting friendly with their targets were long, but they managed it after befriending a woman in the local RSL club who knew the Calabrians, who often gathered there to talk 'business' while pretending to gamble. The Calabrians were wary, but the 'art dealer' appealed to their greed: he told them how easy it was to conceal black money by buying art.

Soon Romeo, Trimbole and others were regular visitors to the East Melbourne flat the police had rented as cover for the undercover couple. They all ate and drank together in Lygon Street and city bars. When the undercovers visited Griffith, Romeo showed off the huge six-bedroom house he was building at a cost of $1 million, and filled their car with cases of oranges and wine.

The detective told his new friends about exploiting the art market, and showed interest in buying drugs. The Italians promised to help – and tipped him winners of fixed horse races.

But dabbling in art wasn't Tony Romeo's only weakness. He brazenly started bringing an 18-year-old waitress with him for weekends in city hotels.

But early 1994, the undercover detective became so trusted that he talked his way into a plan to import $6 million of cannabis from Papua New Guinea via a Torres Strait island. It was a good plan – but not for Romeo, Trimbole and several others arrested on June 19, 1994.

It was a humiliating and expensive blow for the Honoured Society. Two of its leaders, Romeo and Trimbole, were exposed as falling for a scheme police had known about from the start. Five of their followers had been arrested.

The committal hearing, in the new security court at Melbourne Magistrates Court, ran a long time. The evidence was damning – so damning that Romeo and Trimbole were to plead guilty at their subsequent trial, where they received 13 years' jail with a minimum of eight.

But the most damaging evidence for Tony Romeo, perhaps,

might not have been about drugs, guns or money. It was when a prosecution witness testified, in detail, about Romeo's weekends in Melbourne with the teenage waitress. While the dalliance was secret, it didn't matter. But this was in open court, in front of Romeo's wife and family. They might have forgiven his lapse, but some people in the Honoured Society can't tolerate bad manners.

The girl might not have been Romeo's only domestic problem. Rumours in Griffith suggest he had also been too close to another Calabrian's wife.

Either way, he had broken the only commandment that matters in organised crime … he had been caught. And if he were killed because of infidelity, he would not be the first Italian criminal to do so.

On August 4, 1992, Alfonso Muratore was shot dead outside his Hampton home, near where his own father had been murdered in 1964. Muratore had left his wife, Angela, the daughter of the late Liborio Benvenuto, known as 'the Godfather' of the Melbourne fruit and vegetable markets.

In late 1993, another high-ranking Honoured Society member, Rocco Barbaro, had his leg blown off with a shotgun at a Griffith property. He insisted it was an accident with his own gun, but police always wondered, in that case, why the shot came from behind?

CHAPTER 8

Colourful Sydney Identities

Abraham Gilbert Saffron

ABRAHAM Gilbert Saffron, the man who became known as Australia's 'Mr Sin', was born just after World War I ended. His first years were spent with his family in a small flat above his father's drapery shop in Sydney.

By the time he turned eight, young Abe had already learned that vice paid more than tailoring: and earned his pocket money selling cigarettes to his father's poker-playing friends.

He left school at 15 and joined the family business, 'Saffron & Son' on Pitt Street. His family wanted him to be a doctor. Had he done so, given the nature of his later business, he would have been a gynaecologist. As it turned out, he didn't need a medical degree to make money out of the naked female form.

In 1938, Saffron was charged over a minor starting price bookmaking offence. In those days he lacked the police contacts to have the charge fixed – but he was a quick learner. He soon learned that where illegal bookmaking was concerned, the only crime in Sydney was to offer police an insufficient bribe.

Two years later, in 1940, Saffron was convicted of receiving stolen car radios and received a suspended sentence. This apparent lenience might have been connected with the fact that he almost immediately joined the army ... wartime courts were known to encourage young lawbreakers to avoid jail with a sudden display of patriotism. Regardless of the reasons why he joined up, young Saffron soon decided the army wasn't for him and transferred to the merchant navy.

It might have been a shrewd decision, for he survived the war when many of his contemporaries didn't. And he learned first hand there was more money in servicing servicemen than serving the nation.

By 1947, Saffron had opened the first of his many clubs – The Roosevelt. It was later described as 'the city's most notorious and disreputable nightclub' and closed on court orders.

In one court case, Saffron was alleged to have whipped a girl at a party and was described as 'completely depraved'. Today he would have been offered his own game show and a spot on celebrity *Big Brother*.

In the Vietnam years, he was able to set up strip and vice businesses to cater for US and Australian soldiers on leave. He knew what had been known for thousands of years: sex sells.

In 1976, he was named in South Australian Parliament as 'one of the principal characters in organised crime in Australia'.

The South Australian Attorney-General, Peter Duncan, told Parliament some of Saffron's employees were linked to the disappearance and suspected murder of Sydney newspaper publisher Juanita Neilsen, who had led a crusade to clean up King's Cross. Saffron was subsequently subjected to intense investigations by the Costigan Royal Commission into organised crime. A later hearing of the Licensing Commission was told he was known as 'Mr Sin', involved in pornography, connected with massage parlours and the underworld.

He was alleged to have offered bribes to police. In Sydney, where premiers on either side of politics were routinely on the take, this was hardly headline news. It would have been had Saffron not offered bribes.

Despite an Australia-wide reputation as a crime boss he was able to visit senior police in their Sydney offices as if he were a respected business figure. Again, this wasn't considered unusual in the city that produced Sir Robert Askin, one of the rustiest of all rusty knights.

Saffron had his share of luck – good and bad. It was hard to tell whether six suspicious fires in nightclubs he owned or controlled were good or bad luck. Were they lit by jealous competitors, or were they torched for insurance?

Typically, it was not the NSW police who broke Saffron's vice-like grip on vice. In 1985, he was arrested by the National Crime Authority and charged with tax evasion involving millions of dollars. He was later jailed. Finally, Mr Sin was in the bin.

George David Freeman

ONLY in Sydney would a man like George Freeman reach the top of his chosen career.

For a quarter of a century, everyone seemed to know he was an organised crime figure – everyone, that is, except NSW's finest.

By the time he was a teenager, Freeman had started his apprenticeship in crime. His record was long but unimpressive. It included convictions for evading rail fares, stealing knives, shirts, fountain pens, a tin of biscuits and a car radio. Mr Big he wasn't, but he was learning.

In 1954, he was sentenced to three years hard labour for breaking and entering. In the early days, street police seemed to have no trouble catching him but, as his influence grew, he seemed to fall off the law enforcement radar.

He was regularly referred to as a crime boss, yet police could arrest him only for a few minor gaming offences. He was able to pay the fines out of petty cash.

Freeman made the leap from street crim to mobster when he realised that he needed contacts to survive. He built bridges with other influential criminals, including Stan 'The Man' Smith and Lennie McPherson, and he had influential friends in legitimate society.

Few gangsters could look as comfortable in the members' reserve at Randwick races with then chief magistrate, Murray Farquhar, and few gangsters counted powerful police and politicians as 'friends.'

Freeman always saw the big picture – even before he was a Mr Big. In 1965, he met suspected US Mafia figure Joe Testa and three years later he flew to Chicago to stay with his new friend.

They were to set up a construction company together but there was no evidence they were interested in the building trade. Freeman was shot in the head on Anzac Day in 1979, but survived. The man who allegedly fired the shot, John Marcus Miller, didn't. He was shot dead outside his Coogee house six weeks later.

Royal Commissioner and former NSW policeman Justice Donald Stewart found that Freeman was linked to race fixing, SP bookmaking and illicit protected casinos. Stewart also exposed Sydney's worst-kept secret – that Freeman had improper relationships with senior police, lawyers and members of the judiciary.

Illegal phone taps on Freeman's phone showed he regularly tipped Farquhar horses to back. No wonder the chief magistrate liked him. The tips were 98 per cent right. It would take someone with more character than the greedy Farquhar to resist such a temptation.

In August 1984, Freeman was charged with wounding Frank Hing, a man named in NSW Parliament as having Triad connections. But witnesses were reluctant to give evidence and the case against Freeman failed.

In the same year, Melbourne hitman Christopher Dale Flannery moved to Sydney and Freeman put him on the payroll. He reasoned it was better to have a mad dog like Flannery on his side.

Flannery went missing in May, 1985, while on his way to Freeman's home.

One theory (and there are many) was that after an underworld war, several major crime figures, including Freeman, agreed Flannery had to go if there was to be lasting peace. It was said Freeman was lured to a meeting on the promise of road-testing an Israeli Uzi machine gun.

He was supposedly grabbed from behind and garrotted near Freeman's boat house.

As author, playwright and former Pentridge prisoner Ray Mooney noted much later, 'Market forces acted to secure survival. Flannery disappeared, and it was business as usual.' Well, almost. It took a while to settle down. Although, as the astute Mooney also observed, a criminal's real status is gauged by how many people are willing to 'back up' (avenge) for him. If nothing happens within six weeks then 'it ain't gonna happen.'

Flannery had people wanting to back up for him, starting with his widow, Kath, but they weren't quite up to the task. Kath always blamed Freeman for her husband's disappearance and organised an attempt on his life.

Four people, including the son of a retired NSW judge, met in a North Fitzroy hotel where they decided to kill Freeman as he left the Maroubra surgery of Dr Nick Paltos, a known drug smuggler.

Freeman was to be shot as he pulled up at the surgery for his regular Thursday visit. A woman was to stand in a bus shelter across the road and use a walkie talkie to signal when Freeman arrived. But the plan was aborted when the two hitmen spotted men near the surgery and concluded they were Freeman's bodyguards.

They were actually federal surveillance police working on Paltos as part of a secret operation, code-named 'Lavender', an investigation into the importation of more than seven tonnes of hashish with a street value of more than $40 million. Paltos was later arrested and sentenced to 20 years.

One of the hitmen later said when Freeman arrived, 'He started pointing at us as he sat in the car.'

Freeman later wrote in his autobiography that the 'underground grapevine ran hot that night. It was no secret who let out the contract on me.'

In his book, Freeman revealed that in NSW the only way you could make crime pay was to cut the police in for a piece of the action.

'From my experience, the only real "organisation" of crime in Sydney has come from individual police. Because when it comes to criminal networking, crooked cops have the game to themselves.

'The more crime you commit, the more crooked cops you

attract – they're never too far away to miss out on their part of the action.

'I've known some crooked cops, but one stood out in the pack: Sergeant Fred Krahe.

'Krahe was deadly and evil. It was a measure of the fear the man generated in both crooks and police that he was never brought to justice. Everybody was frightened of him.

'Fred Krahe, one of the real organisers of crime in Sydney, was able to pension himself out of the NSW police force so he could operate virtually untouched.

'When it came to dealing with crooks, Krahe had his own pricing scheme. After he'd arrest you, the paying began. You'd pay him to get bail, you'd pay some more later for a reduced sentence, you'd pay for remands, you'd pay for whether or not he gave verbal evidence against you, and you'd pay again if he decided not to give evidence against you at all.

'And believe me, everybody paid. It was stupid not to.

'If you didn't, you went inside and, by the time Krahe had finished giving evidence against you, the magistrate or judge was wishing he had the power to pull out your toenails as well. I've never seen a man lie like him, then or since.

'Krahe not only stood over crims once he arrested them, he had others working for him, doing everything from stealing cars to house-breakings and armed robberies.

'He had a feared reputation as a killer, and as a cop he had every reason to carry a .38 with him at all times. He boasted that he even slept with it under his pillow at night.

'Krahe was a protege of another famous, and controversial, cop: Ray Kelly. Like a lot of cops in those days, Kelly was the master of the verbal – in fact, he probably invented it.

'Kelly played the game from both sides and wasn't exactly penniless when he finally retired, a hero, in 1966. There were at least two blocks of flats and probably more – although he said he had lost heavily in a company crash in 1960. Not bad for a lowly sergeant.'

But it wasn't crooked police but a crook chest that got George in the end. Freeman had chronic asthma. The man who survived being shot in the head died from complications from an asthma attack in March, 1990.

Leonard Arthur McPherson

IT WAS a crime straight from Al Capone's scrapbook. A Mr Big becomes annoyed when a businessman unwisely moves in on a lucrative whisky contract. He pays thugs to get rid of the competition. The businessman is bashed and is lucky to escape with his life.

The Mr Big is, or was, the late Lennie McPherson, Sydney crime king.

It happened in late 1990. Big Lennie was cross because a businessman was moving in on a deal being done between a relative of McPherson and an American supplier.

The McPhersons were making nearly $10 million from selling the whisky but the Americans wanted more profit at their end of the deal and began looking around for another distributor. Enter the businessman, thinking he would fill the gap.

Lennie decided to make the competitor lose interest. His thugs attacked the man in his own home leaving him with a broken arm, a torn ear and a bruised face.

In 1991, the National Crime Authority charged McPherson with maliciously inflicting grievous bodily harm to the victim with intent to cause such harm – a charge with a maximum 25-year sentence. He was finally found guilty in 1994. He was 73.

Lennie McPherson was a living example of why the NSW criminal justice system was a joke for so long. Many police suggested McPherson was a protected species because he provided information to them. And there was little doubt some detectives and Big Lennie were often on the same side – their side.

Everyone from school children to nuns knew that McPherson was a gangster, but he remained untouchable. He was named everywhere from Royal Commissions to toilet walls as the Mr Big of Sydney, yet he was given the green light to continue.

He said he was a modest man of modest means and couldn't understand why he attracted such publicity.

He claimed he made a living through doing a few small building jobs and trading antiques – a sort of upmarket rag and bone man.

Once asked in a Royal Commission how he made his living he replied, 'I do the best I can.' It was a good answer and a good living. Lennie's best was pretty good because when he was eventually raided by the National Crime Authority on tax matters he was hit with a back tax bill of $1,065,000. He managed to pay $500,000 of it from his savings.

McPherson was not always rich and infamous. He was sentenced to jail in the late 1950s for just over three years for breaking and entering.

He lived in interesting times. In 1960, a John Joseph Unwin and another man were charged with trying to kill Big Lennie. Then McPherson was charged with the murder of George Joseph Hackett. He was also charged with trying to kill his own wife. He beat both charges. He was arrested over driving a car at Unwin with intent to murder him. Unwin refused to give evidence and McPherson escaped again.

In 1967, a gunman called Raymond Patrick 'Ducky'

O'Connor was shot dead at the Latin Quarter nightclub. Lennie and two other men were drinking at the same club. No charges were laid.

Like many gangsters, he carried a gun only in peace time. During World War II, he stayed well away from danger, leaving it to 'mugs' who went to war for a few shillings a day. Instead, he worked as a driller at the docks in Balmain.

In 1969, he was fined $100 for consorting with criminals. In the early 1970s, he was identified in the Moffitt Royal Commission as a Mr Big. A Commonwealth Police report into McPherson was tabled in evidence at the commission.

The report found that McPherson was an associate of an American organised crime figure, Joseph Dan Testa, who visited Australia in 1969 and 1971.

In 1980, the Woodward Royal Commission found that McPherson was connected with prostitution and drug rings in the Philippines.

In 1985, the Building Industry Royal Commission found that McPherson tried his hand as a standover man at construction sites. At his 1994 trial for organising the bashing described above, McPherson did everything possible to avoid jail. He claimed he was unfit to stand trial – even apparently dropping off to sleep in the witness box.

In the end it didn't work and he was sentenced to four years jail. He had to leave his heavily-fortified home in Gladesville for an even more heavily-fortified cell.

He said he would rather be dead than go to jail. In the end he got the double.

He died from a heart attack in 1996 in Cessnock jail, about 160 kilometres north of the city he had dominated for decades.

He was 75.

Arthur Stanley 'Neddy' Smith

AT any other time, Arthur Stanley Smith would have been an easy pinch. Big, brash and not particularly bright, Smith should have been no match for trained and dedicated detectives.

But the man they called 'Neddy' was born in the golden era of NSW crime. He was given the green light by crooked police. The man himself said, 'Thank Christ for corruption.'

He served nearly eight years for a violent rape but from the mid-1970s was protected by those who should have targeted him. One of his closest friends and protectors was the notorious Roger Rogerson, king of police corruption. For Neddy, it was better than a royal pardon.

In October, 1978, police raided Neddy's heavily-fortified Sydney home and found $40,000 and later recovered a safety deposit box containing jewels and $90,100 cash. The Woodward Royal Commission on drug trafficking found that Smith's drug syndicate was moving 11 kilograms of heroin a month.

Smith helped organise the fatal meeting between Rogerson and heroin dealer Warren Lanfranchi in 1981. The dealer was there to cut a deal and was said to be carrying $10,000 bribe money.

Rogerson shot Lanfranchi dead. Police claimed the criminal produced an ancient and faulty gun and threatened Rogerson, who had no choice but to shoot him – twice. The allegation that Lanfranchi was carrying $10,000 must have been false because the cash was never recovered.

Smith was the only civilian witness called who backed Rogerson's version of events. After all, they were great mates.

In 1985, Smith was deliberately hit by a car that mounted the kerb as he walked along a footpath in Waterloo. When the driver saw his victim was still alive he tried to back over him but Smith escaped with six smashed ribs and a fractured leg.

Smith became the operational arm for NSW detectives who set up armed robberies. In less than six months Armaguard lost nearly $1.5 million in 19 robberies without one arrest.

In 1992, the Independent Commission Against Corruption began an investigation into claims that a corrupt cell of NSW detectives were organising the armed robberies.

Commissioner Ian Temby found that Smith was a pivotal figure. 'I conclude that over a period in excess of a decade, Smith was helped by various police officers, who provided him with information, looked after him when charges were laid or threatened and generally acted in contravention of their sworn duty. The evidence shows that Smith was friendly with a number of police officers and very close to a few.'

It was all there for Neddy, but he started to believe he could do anything. Drunk after a heavy day with Rogerson, he became involved in a road rage incident and stabbed a tow-truck driver, Ronald Flavell, to death in Coogee.

Even then he thought the old ways would work. He told a former policeman, 'Listen, can anything be done to pull this madness up? Money is no object.'

But no longer could he be protected.

He was found guilty of the Flavell murder and of killing brothel keeper and car salesman Harvey Jones, who had been shot dead in July, 1983.

It was alleged that in jail he bragged of killing six people, including Lanfranchi's former girlfriend Sallie-Anne Huckstepp.

Smith was charged and acquitted despite the Crown producing a secret jail tape which recorded Smith saying he had attacked Huckstepp from behind, punched her before grabbing her by the throat, lifting her up and strangling her for about six minutes. He said to a cellmate that he put a cord around her neck and garrotted her before dragging her into a pond and standing on her back in shallow water until she was dead. He said the killing was 'the most satisfying thing I ever did in my life'.

But Neddy, diagnosed with Parkinson's Disease, had nothing to celebrate over the victory. He was left to serve life in jail over his two murder convictions.

From jail he wrote his memoirs, *Neddy – The Life and Crimes of Arthur Stanley Smith,* which exposed the system in NSW. It made staggering reading.

'In Victoria, there isn't much corruption. They kill you down there. They certainly don't do too much business.

'But when I was working in NSW, just about everyone was corrupt and anything was possible. Late 1980 was the beginning of a decade of crime and corruption within the NSW police force that will never be equalled.

'There has always been crime and corruption within the NSW police force but nothing like it was then. And I was in the middle of it.

'I had police organising crimes for me to do, then keeping me informed as to how much – if any – progress was being made in the investigations. I had what is commonly known within criminal circles as the 'Green Light', which meant I could virtually do as I pleased. Nothing was barred, with one exception – I was never to shoot at any member of the police force. But apart from that, I could write my own ticket.

'I bribed hundreds of police and did as I pleased in Sydney. There was no limit to what I got away with. I could never have committed any of the major crimes I did, and got away with them, without the assistance of the NSW police force. They were the best police force that money could buy.'

Sir Robert Askin

HE was probably the most influential man in the underworld yet he never needed a gun. He was the man who could fix anything but he was never arrested.

He was the enemy of good government yet he was knighted for services to the people he betrayed.

He was Sir Robert Askin, Knight of the Realm, NSW Premier, and probably Australia's most corrupt politician.

The son of a tram driver, he was a bank clerk, soldier and bookmaker before being elected to the NSW Legislative Assembly in 1950. He was Liberal leader and Premier from 1965 until 1975.

Sydney had been a city on the take since the Rum Corps ran it, but Askin's period in power took organised crime and corruption to a new level. They became a core industry in NSW – there was no political will to combat the problem because so many politicians were either in on the 'giggle', as the police slang went, or they turned a blind eye.

For somebody of Big Bob's propensity for getting his snout in the trough, it was a heaven-sent opportunity.

It was alleged, and has never been disproven, you could buy a knighthood from Askin for $20,000 because he had the power to make recommendations to Buckingham Palace.

While Askin was weak on combating criminals, he was tough with demonstrators, once allegedly ordering police to 'drive over the bastards' during a protest against US President Lyndon Johnson in 1966.

According to respected investigative journalist and author David Hickie, Askin was paid $100,000 a year by the illegal gaming industry run by Percy 'The Prince' Galea.

One of Australia's finest journalists, Evan Whitton, quoted

former newspaper owner Max Newton as claiming he delivered $15,000 in a brown paper bag to Askin in 1970 on behalf of a Filipino investor.

'I told him who it was from and I've never seen $15,000 disappear so quickly in my life. He took the money and whipped it into the top drawer of his desk and said, "That's very kind of him; I'm deeply grateful".'

Many politicians will not confront police corruption because of the possible controversy. Askin actively embraced it, promoting the bent at the expense of the straight and becoming 'business partners' with them. Honest senior police were kept at a distance because nothing frightens a bent politician more than an honest cop.

Corruption thrived. Thieves in police uniforms were fast-tracked to positions of responsibility.

Chief Superintendent George Barnes, who was found in an illegal Chinese gambling den and widely known to be corrupt, was promoted to Assistant Commissioner by a grateful Askin only days before his (Barnes') retirement so his superannuation payout would be greater. After all, it was only taxpayers' money.

Askin also appointed Fred Hanson, a well-known crook, to be his police commissioner. Hanson was also alleged to be getting $100,000 a year from the Galea network.

In 1980, Hanson died behind the wheel of his car in his garage, dressed in pyjamas. His widow died six years later leaving an estate of $1.2 million, which was a lot of money at that time – enough to buy a dozen substantial houses. Which casts an interesting light on Askin's estate. When Askin died in September, 1981, he left $1.95 million. Three years later, his widow died, leaving $3.7 million.

Sydney has always been different from other Australian

cities, and not just because of the harbour, the bridge and the Opera House. It is a place where serious, endemic corruption rarely sparks outrage because, ultimately, high-fliers there tend to be judged by how much money they have, rather than what they do to make it.

The harbour city has developed a culture where social climbers are comfortable in the company of bent businessman and rumoured drug dealers.

Where else in the world are disgraced bookmakers who rig races splashed in the social pages?

CHAPTER 9

Melbourne Killers

Dane Sweetman

DANE Sweetman was a small-time criminal and full-time loser when he embraced the racist world of neo-Nazis while serving two years jail for armed robbery.

His love of violence was ingrained. He had been found guilty of attempted murder by age 16. But it was while in jail in the late 1980s that Sweetman found a violent cause to match his vicious nature. As far as he was concerned, he was no longer just another head case, he was a political freedom fighter.

He covered himself in tattoos, including swastikas, Nazi skinheads, KKK and Native White Protestants Supreme. From within jail, Sweetman wrote to colleagues urging them to violence and providing plans on bomb-making.

In one letter, Sweetman told a Nazi sympathiser how a group of Right-wing fanatics had a secret organisation called 'The Guard' in Pentridge prison in 1987. 'Give the dogs what they deserve, full-on racial warfare, there is no stopping us when we've started,' he wrote. From jail, Sweetman provided detailed plans for a car bomb. 'I've seen them blow the entire back end off a Commodore,' he wrote.

In his rambling jail diary, 'Dance of the Skin, Reflections of a Neo Nazi Skinhead', Sweetman gave an insight into the mind of a disturbed racist. He said that while in prison in the 1980s he developed his Manifesto for Racial Warfare. He declared he wanted to kill drug users, pushers, homosexuals, doctors, teachers, police, child molesters, priests and pornographers.

'We recruited men within the jail and even some in blue for the purpose of information. There are many screws (prison officers) who espouse our Guard philosophy, some are Klan (Ku Klux Klan).'

In his diary, Sweetman claims responsibility for a secret race war on the streets of Melbourne. He admitted a series of violent crimes, including murder, arson, stabbings, bashings and street assaults. 'The day after my release (in December, 1989) we set about and thus fire-bombed the St Kilda Road Synagogue. The Yids were furious.'

He said his group returned the following day and daubed the synagogue with racist taunts and Nazi slogans before throwing more fire bombs. 'We then made our petrol bombs right there on the street. It was a job well done.'

He said that soon after his release he began to walk around the city. 'The place was awash with yellow, black and mongrel brown faces.' He gloated over details of his gang attacking two Asian men in the city and using a razor to slash one's throat. He wrote about attacking another man because he suspected he was a homosexual. Sweetman said he brought gloves and balaclavas at a city army disposal shop for the job.

His gang wrapped the man's head in a sheet and beat his genitals with a baton and Sweetman jumped on him, breaking five of his ribs. Like many of his German Nazi heroes, he was hypocritical about homosexuality. He had already been charged with the sexual penetration of a male under 16.

As a payback against the man who informed police of an assault, Sweetman wrote, he built another bomb. 'I sat the bomb at the base of the front door, I lit the fuse and ran ...

'Later that night we drove back to the scene. The house was a scene of utter destruction, the front door was nowhere to be seen, the veranda had a huge gaping hole in it and the brickwork surrounding the door was blackened and ruined.

'The paper said no-one was hurt which was unfortunate as we wanted to see as many hurt and maimed as possible.'

He wrote with pride of kicking a young woman in the street because she had an Asian boyfriend. By the time he was 22, he had been charged with attempted murder, malicious wounding, intentionally cause serious injury, possession of a pistol, assault with a weapon, armed robbery, assault by kicking and murder.

When police arrested him as a teenager, they went to his room and found the walls covered with posters from horror movies, and kit creatures from horror movies. They also found two sawn-off shotguns and a canister of cyanide in a secret storage area.

A policeman, who wrote a report on Sweetman in the early days, stated with bureaucratic understatement: 'The defendant appears to be pre-occupied with violence.'

In 1991, on his birthday, December 19, he was sentenced to 20 years with a minimum of 15 for the murder of David Noble. He expected a longer sentence. Sweetman murdered Noble with an axe at a party to celebrate Hitler's birthday on April 20, 1990, and then cut the legs off the body before dumping the remains in the Boulevard, Kew.

He stunned the court when he produced a prison 'shiv' and slammed it into the bench, saying he had it to kill a police witness. Sweetman is due out of jail in November, 2005, but few believe he is reformed. He has a written hit list of 11 witnesses and police he intends to attack. 'Your day is coming,' he wrote. But while Sweetman has vowed war against the world, mainstream prisoners are tired of him. His predatory sexual behaviour in jail has resulted in him becoming an outcast.

On December 30, 1994, five of Australia's toughest prisoners went to see Sweetman. The committee was a murderer, a drug dealer, an armed robber and two brothers with violent records.

'They told Sweetman that he was a boy raper and a dog. They said they knew he was providing sweets and canteen goods to a group of younger prisoners in return for sexual favours,' a prison source said.

'He was told he was to be put off (murdered).'

Next day he put himself into protection in Barwon prison. But on seven occasions notes were put under his cell door telling him he would be killed. In March, 1995, he was moved to the protection unit in K Division in Pentridge. Fellow inmates included Paul Denyer, the Frankston triple murderer, multiple rapist and double killer Raymond 'Mr Stinky' Edmunds, and Hoddle street mass murderer Julian Knight.

Paul Steven Haigh

WITHIN three weeks of turning 21, Paul Steven Haigh was to graduate from violent street thug to serial killer. In the next 11 months he was to kill six people, including a nine-year-old.

The adopted boy who became a male prostitute was only 12 when first convicted. He is unlikely ever to be released and may become Australia's longest-serving prisoner.

Prison consulting psychiatrist, Dr Lester Walton, wrote of him: 'Mr Haigh presents as an articulate, pleasant, co-operative man who appears at ease with the task of psychiatric assessment. His vocabulary and content of conversation were consistent with superior intelligence.

'Mr Haigh has a somewhat grand manner but, in short, he appeared to be completely free of clinically significant psychiatric disturbance.' Or, in three words of only three letters, he was bad, not mad.

In two cases, Haigh killed during botched armed robberies.

On September 21, 1978, he tried to rob Evelyn Abrahams in the Tattersalls agency where she worked in Chapel Street, Prahran. The prim spinster, 58, was bewildered when confronted with the hyped-up Haigh. She turned her back on him and asked her boss, 'What should I do?'

Haigh didn't give her a chance, and shot her in the back of the head with his shotgun.

On December 7, 1978, he tried to rob a Caulfield pizza shop. He jumped on the counter and screamed for money, but shop owner Bruno Cingolani tried to put up a fight.

The 45-year-old father of two girls grabbed a long-bladed knife from a drawer. It was the last thing he would ever do. Haigh shot him in the stomach from point-blank range.

Even though he was dying, Cingolani continued to fight, grabbing the barrel of the gun. Haigh ran off.

On June 27, 1979, Haigh went to a flat in St Kilda to kill a woman he believed was spreading stories that he was a police informer. She was not home. Haigh was psyched to kill so he shot her boyfriend, Wayne Keith Smith, 27, instead.

'It was not hard to kill Smith. It takes no hero to murder. The most puny man in the world can pull a trigger. The obstacle is a psychological one,' he told one of the authors inside Pentridge.

'As Smith lay fearful on the bed I aimed the gun. It jammed. By the time I rectified the problem in the mechanism my aim had dropped from his head. The bullet hit his neck. He gurgled and lost consciousness.'

Sheryle Ann Gardner could have implicated Haigh in two murders so when he arrived at her St Kilda home on July 22, she knew she was in trouble.

Gardner had already been involved in one murder so she knew that Haigh might be preparing to kill her. In a horrible gamble, she called her nine-year-old son, Danny William Mitchell, back to her car in the hope that his presence would protect her. It might have worked with another type of criminal but not with Haigh.

He quietly got in the car and ordered her to drive to Ripponlea. 'It was not intended that Mitchell be killed. Unfortunately though, because his mother, Sheryle Gardner, insisted on his presence and because of circumstances, it became necessary to silence him also.

'I shot him, along with his mother, so he couldn't say, "Paul did it."

'His mother, I shot first. As Danny's back was to me, crying, I shot him too. He was not aware I had the gun trained on him.

'Gardner lived by the sword and died by it. What one sows, this they reap. Maybe one day I will meet my end in a similar fashion. If so, I have no right complaining.'

Haigh went to their funerals. He also placed a death notice for Smith and went to his funeral.

Haigh's sixth victim was his girlfriend, Lisa Maude Brearley, 19, whom he stabbed 157 times. He would later admit that of all his killings that was the one that haunted him. He said he sometimes sees her in his dreams.

Asked why he stabbed her so many times he said he lost count and felt compelled to begin again. Haigh said he was more troubled by hitting a dog than killing a person. 'I love animals dearly and though killing humans was not difficult at this point in my life, hitting the dog troubled my conscience badly.'

Despite his bent for violence Haigh admits, 'I always was, and still am, a coward.'

In 1991, he helped kill fellow prisoner Donald George Hatherley. Police said Haigh hanged Hatherley, 36, in his Pentridge cell on November 14. Haigh held on to his legs and pulled down to make sure he was dead.

Haigh said he was helping Hatherley to commit suicide but he was convicted of murder for the seventh time. Justice Coldrey said Haigh took advantage of the death wish of an unstable and vulnerable man for his own self-fulfilment.

In other words, Haigh loves to kill.

He is serving six life sentences, plus 15 years for the Hatherley murder and a further 15 for armed robberies.

Edwin John Eastwood

IT IS hard to believe, but there was a time in the early 1970s when Edwin John Eastwood was more famous in Australia as a real-life crook than his namesake, Clint 'Dirty Harry' Eastwood, was as a make-believe cop.

That's because Eastwood and another loser had played high stakes and lost by kidnapping an entire country schoolroom of children for ransom. The odd thing about Edwin Eastwood is that his start in life was probably as comfortable as the actor's.

Young Edwin did not have the usual criminal's excuse of being the product of crushing poverty, a broken home and a violent upbringing. His father was a successful engineer and the family lived in the pleasant Melbourne bayside suburb of Edithvale. Eastwood, born in 1951, showed an early interest in the sea but was rejected by the navy.

He became a plasterer and had no trouble with the law until he was nearly 21. Out of work, he and a school friend pulled three small armed robberies.

Eastwood was such a criminal mastermind that he committed the robberies on railway stations and a fast food outlet without wearing a mask.

He then watched Clint Eastwood, in *Dirty Harry*, and decided to follow the plot of kidnapping children. He must have fallen asleep during the last reel: the good guys won.

Eastwood drove around Victoria until he found a one-room school at Faraday, a blink-and-you'll-miss-it spot about 100 kilometres north of Melbourne. In October, 1972, he kidnapped six children and their young woman teacher from the school. He rang *The Sun's* chief police reporter, Wayne 'Smokey' Grant, to announce the kidnapping anonymously. He left a ransom note at the school demanding $1 million.

The teacher managed to kick her way out of the van to foil the plot and Eastwood was later sentenced to 21 years with a minimum of 15. But he escaped from Geelong Prison and, in February 1977, he tried the same trick again. This time it was the Wooreen Primary School in South Gippsland. He kidnapped nine children and seven adults. He asked for $7 million, the release of 17 convicted inmates, 100 kilograms of heroin and 100 kilograms of cocaine. He was nothing if not ambitious. He was eventually arrested and shot in the leg. When asked what would happen to the policeman who shot the kidnapper, Chief Commissioner Mick Miller said: 'More target practice.'

In 1981, Eastwood was charged with strangling standover man Glen Joseph Davies to death in Pentridge's top security Jika Jika Division. Astonishingly, he was found not guilty on the grounds of self-defence.

He was released from prison in 1990, a born-again Christian

who vowed to keep out of trouble. Within 10 weeks of his release he was back in jail – this time for planning to burgle a drug factory to provide chemicals for speed dealers. He released a book but it was withdrawn from sale when it was found that it might prejudice an upcoming murder trial.

He changed his name to David Jones and again said he was finished with crime. But he surfaced in Cairns and, in April 2001, was charged with theft, unlawful use of a motor vehicle and possessing sawn-off firearms.

For reasons never explained, he had driven a stolen car from Victoria with a plan to steal an unoccupied yacht. In the car police found flippers, a boogie board, paint, navigation maps, how-to-sail books and tools. He also had two large knives, a sawn-off shotgun and rifle, and an extendable baton. He later told police he needed the weapons to protect himself from pirates.

He said he was going to steal a yacht and sail to the Philippines. Interestingly, about 25 years earlier, after the Wooreen kidnapping, Eastwood let slip he had another plan that required a yacht and weapons.

Police said that while being interviewed in 1977 he boasted that in his 'next' kidnapping attempt he would take a yacht and start dumping his hostages overboard, one by one, until the ransom was paid. Dirty Harry would not have approved.

Keith George Faure

THE Faures are underworld blue bloods, having produced three generations of gangsters. The grandfather of the present generation was Norman Leslie Bruhn, who made a living standing over cocaine dealers in the 1920s. Some things never change.

In June, 1927, Grandpa Bruhn was shot five times as he went to collect his pay-off from a drug dealer near Liverpool Street,

Sydney. The hit was allegedly ordered by Snowy Cutmore, who died with Squizzy Taylor in a shootout in Melbourne four months later.

Then there was father – Noel Ambrose Faure. He was one of Australia's best safe crackers and an influential member of the painters and dockers union during the dockies' wars of the 1960s. He was a gentleman compared with his scallywag sons Keith, Noel and Les, who are all convicted killers.

Keith George Faure was the most dangerous. A killer, armed robber and career criminal, he was first charged with breaking and entering when he was 11 and was said to have seen his first gangland murder when he was eight. He has a long history of escape, theft and violence. He gave his occupation as painter and docker, slaughterman and abalone sheller.

He was convicted of shooting Senior Constable Michael Pratt in the back during the robbery of an ANZ bank in Clifton Hill on June 4, 1976. Faure shot Pratt as the off-duty policeman tried to stop the robbery.

Pratt was awarded the George Cross for bravery, but the injuries forced him to retire from the force.

Faure was also found guilty of manslaughter over the killing of Shane Dennis Rowland, who was shot to death in a Richmond house on May 1, 1976.

The year 1976 was a big one for Keithy. He was also found guilty of a second count of manslaughter for killing fellow inmate Alan Sopulak in Pentridge. The victim was stabbed nine times with a sharpened butter knife.

Faure was lucky to avoid a third homicide trial. Within weeks of his release from prison in 1987, he was involved in the armed robbery of a Thornbury jewellery shop where the owner, Mario Sassano, was shot dead.

It was at a time when the more paranoid members of the

underworld believed the armed robbery squad was hunting down career bandits and executing them. A homicide squad detective used the rumours to his advantage. He had a short message passed on to Keith. Come to the homicide squad to be interviewed or risk having the armed robbery squad shoot you in bed. The next day at 9am a freshly-showered Faure was at the St Kilda Road Crime Department complex, and happy to help.

Four men were charged over the armed robbery and murder. According to police, Faure used his own form of plea bargaining. He gave one of his co-accused a simple choice: plead guilty or die. The man pleaded guilty.

The other three were then able to blame the guilty man for the murder. Faure was sentenced to 13 years for the armed robbery but beat the murder blue.

In jail he was a leader and headed a heavy faction inside Pentridge in the longest and bloodiest 'war' in an Australian prison. He fell out with standover man, Mark Brandon Read, who had his own crew, known as the Overcoat Gang because they wore coats to hide their home-made weapons, even in summer.

Faure had his own team, KGB (Keith George's Boys). Over the years, there were more than 100 attacks, including stabbings, bombings and bashings.

The origins of the war could be traced back to allegations that Read ate all the sausages promised to H Division prisoners for Christmas one year. But the real power battle was over Read's friend, Billy 'The Texan' Longley, who was in prison at the time.

Faure's painters and dockers wanted Longley dead and they needed to get Read first. 'Keith George Faure represented the power in Pentridge in the 1970s. Every painter and docker in jail backed Keithy. He represented the criminal version of the old school tie,' Read wrote in his best-selling first book, *Chopper: From The Inside*. But while Faure had more criminal contacts, senior prison officers backed Read. Faure had broken Governor Jimmy Quinn's nose in a B Division fight years earlier and prison officers have long memories.

Read would find cell doors left open when he wanted to launch a sneak attack. He was effectively green-lighted to attack any of Faure's team.

In 1990, Faure was stabbed twice in the chest in Pentridge. He survived. Years later, when he was released he went to Tasmania to visit Read. The war was then officially over. But Chopper continued to haunt him. In April, 2002, Faure was in court again, this time for driving without a licence.

The court was told that Faure was upset after seeing the movie *Chopper* where a jail character called 'Keithy George' was stabbed to death in the opening scene.

Faure's lawyer, big Bernie 'The Attorney' Balmer, told the court his client was so upset by the film's treatment of his life that it had affected his judgment at the time in question.

The movie won the Australian Film Industry best film award. And Faure was banned from driving for five years. Keithy's brother Noel Faure, 47, was convicted in 1990 of the manslaughter of a Rye man, Frank Truscott. The youngest brother, Leslie Peter, was the last Faure to be convicted. He pleaded guilty to the 1997 murder of Lorna Stevens, 27, whom he claimed died during a game of Russian roulette.

Les was convicted, appealed, won a retrial and then pleaded guilty. The trial judge did not believe the Russian roulette excuse and said it was murder. He was sentenced to 14 years.

Keith blamed himself for his younger brother's actions. He told ace *Herald Sun* court reporter Norrie Ross, 'It's his first time in trouble. I feel he's bearing the brunt for my mistakes in the past and I hope it doesn't continue in the (jail) system. I hope he gets a break.'

CHAPTER 10

Hard Men and Hitmen

Sandy MacRae

BALDING, slight, with a sharp wit and an engaging personality, Alistair Farquhar MacRae hardly fits the image of a cold-blooded, multiple murderer.

But, according to police, he is probably Australia's most prolific killer, having been implicated in at least 20 suspicious deaths and disappearances. He was finally jailed over four murders in two states.

He was first convicted in the Victorian Supreme Court of the murder of Albert Edwin Gerald O'Hara, whom he shot during a drug sting in Mildura.

Police are convinced MacRae has killed nine people, and suspect he could have been involved in up to 15 more deaths.

'I would have to say that he would be Australia's worst known multiple murderer and perhaps we will never know how many people he has killed,' says Paul Hollowood who, as a senior homicide squad detective, spent months investigating

MacRae's crimes. 'Sandy' MacRae made his name as a massage parlour standover man, a briber of police, an informer and last of all a killer who thought of murder as a legitimate tool of his chosen trade.

But MacRae is no crazed killer. He didn't kill for pleasure, or out of anger, or because of some deep-seated psychological trauma. He killed to maintain his position in the underworld or for cash. It was strictly business.

Police still don't know how many bodies are buried at his 10-hectare property at Merbein, near Mildura, but MacRae joked with friends that the small vineyard would never need fertiliser 'because there's plenty of blood and bone out there'.

Detectives have exhumed two bodies, and believe they missed at least one more. 'We really don't know how many people were killed on his property,' Hollowood said.

For police, the property was too big to dig up without knowing exactly where the bodies were buried.

They did find the body of Domenic Marafiote buried under the chicken coop in 1987. Police allege MacRae shot and killed Marafiote on July 18, 1985. He lured the victim to the property on the promise of a marijuana deal but there was no sale that day. Marafiote was a dead man walking. When he arrived at the property, his grave had already been dug.

A Supreme Court jury was told that MacRae then drove to Adelaide, where he killed Marafiote's parents, Carmelo, 69, and Rosa, 70. He was desperate to find the money that Marafiote was to use for the marijuana deal and believed the elderly couple controlled the purse strings.

He was right but he didn't know where to look. A large amount of cash was found sewn into Rosa's clothing after she was murdered.

Detectives say MacRae was so cold-blooded that before he

buried Domenic Marafiote he repeatedly stabbed the body 'just for practice'. He was sentenced to a minimum of 18 years for the killing, and later pleaded guilty to the Adelaide double murder.

He once told friends he had killed a woman, buried her on the property only to later exhume the remains, pulverise the bones in a concrete mixer and then pour the mix into a concrete garden roller, which has never been found. It was one of the crimes for which he will never be charged.

MacRae moved to Mildura from Melbourne in 1983. He had been the second in charge to a massage parlour boss, Geoffrey Lamb, who allegedly controlled much of the illegal sex industry with the help of a group of corrupt police.

But MacRae moved on after Lamb became addicted to heroin and began to lose control. Police say MacRae later chained the hopelessly addicted Lamb to a bungalow on the Mildura property in a bid to help his former boss beat the heroin problem.

In 1984, MacRae failed in a bid to establish a massage parlour in Mildura. He then met and befriended Albert O'Hara, who was planning to buy a houseboat-building business in the area.

MacRae convinced the 59-year-old man that he could make a quick profit from buying and selling marijuana. On December 21, 1984, O'Hara travelled to MacRae's property with $10,000 to buy drugs.

Police said MacRae shot him in the back of the head and buried him on the property. He then used oxy welding gear to cut up the dead man's car so it could be dropped, piece by piece, at the Merbein tip.

'He was like a scavenging vulture who made sure there was nothing left after a kill,' according to Hollowood. Flushed with his success after the O'Hara killing, he invited a massage parlour contact, Johnny Selim, to visit him at the property in early 1985. He put forward a proposition they form a local version of Murder Inc., luring people to the vineyard on the promise of selling them marijuana, killing them and keeping the money.

'He always said the people he killed didn't matter as they were outside the law. To him it was all business; there was no hate involved,' Hollowood said.

Selim declined the offer and, wisely, returned to Melbourne.

Police believe MacRae killed rival underworld standover man Michael Ebert, who was gunned down outside a Carlton brothel in April, 1980.

Ebert had bashed MacRae two weeks earlier and the beaten man had vowed revenge. The murder remains unsolved.

Police also suspect he killed his drug-addicted girlfriend, Deborah Joy Faher, 22, who was found dead of a drug overdose in a St Kilda motel in August, 1981. Police believe MacRae gave her near-pure heroin: a so-called 'hot shot'.

He is suspected of killing a prostitute known only as 'Little Lisa' in 1984.

In July, 1990, police found the remains of a woman buried in the backyard of a Kensington home once owned by an underworld figure's mother. Police believe the woman could be a South Australian prostitute killed by MacRae.

In the early 1980s, police became concerned at the number of unexplained deaths of drug-addicted prostitutes from overdoses. A homicide group, led by then Detective Sergeant Gary Landy, investigated about 15 of the cases. He said one of the common denominators was that they all knew MacRae.

'Certainly, some of them well could have been murders but there was not the evidence to justify charges,' says Landy. Hollowood has no doubt MacRae knows more about many murders than he was prepared to admit.

'He is clever, articulate, and you would never know he was a killer by talking to him,' he said. 'He was a conman killer who talked his victims into a position where he could move on them. He had no conscience at all.'

While MacRae was under investigation for murder he was also informing to the police anti-corruption investigation, Operation Cobra. He gave evidence that he helped pay off police to protect Lamb's brothel empire in the late 1970s and early 1980s.

One of the accused police, former Senior Sergeant Paul William Higgins, was sentenced to seven years' jail, and served five. He remains bitter that a multiple murderer was largely responsible for his conviction.

While in witness protection, MacRae made a fatal blunder. He confessed to another witness that he had killed the Marafiotes. He said that he had used a doona to muffle the gunshots. He complained that when he tried to fire one shot his revolver's hammer snapped back catching the webbing between his thumb and forefinger.

When Victorian police checked with their Adelaide counterparts, they confirmed there was a small, unexplained, spider-web blood stain. MacRae had unintentionally solved the mystery.

When MacRae was in Barwon prison in the mid-1990s his ex-wife was surprised when he telephoned her well after lock-up time. He told her his cell had been left open and he feared he was being set up to be murdered by other inmates.

The governor was most surprised when he received a call from the woman to inform him the cells were still open. It is believed prison officers found several inmates in the yard sunbaking.

MacRae was later extradited to Adelaide to stand trial on the

Marafiote double murder. Faced with overwhelming evidence, he pleaded guilty.

The prosecutor said he should die in jail and have a non-parole period of 40 to 50 years.

'This case comes into the worst category for several reasons,' said Paul Rofe, QC. 'On each occasion he has come before sentencing court, the words cold-blooded, planned and execution have been used ... the public are certainly entitled to think this man should die in prison.'

When he was about to be sentenced MacRae asked to be allowed to die in jail. 'To allow me leniency is a luxury I did not extend to my victims. The only way to show my remorse is to ask the court to show the same leniency that I showed my victims – absolutely none. I would ask the court to give me no possible chance of release before my death in custody.'

South Australian Supreme Court Judge, Justice Williams gave him two life sentences and extended his non-parole period to 36 years.

If he is very good, he could be released in 2023, aged 74.

Alan David Williams

IN mid-2001 Alan David Williams went to his old underworld contacts, looking for a gun. In the old days it would have been easy, but the times had changed, and so had Williams.

The once robust, top-grade Australian rules centreman and top-grade gangster was now just a shadow in the world of shadows.

A walking skeleton – fatally ill with a drug-related blood disease, either hepatitis or AIDS, depending on who was telling the story – he had one wish before he died. He wanted to kill former Victorian detective and long-time nemesis Brian Francis

Murphy. But the old contacts, who had always taken his money before, turned him away this time. Williams was crazy, dangerous and dying. He was on his own. Weeks later he was dead and few bothered to attend his funeral.

Years earlier, Williams was a man of influence – on both sides of the law. He was prepared to pay to kill an undercover policeman and when he turned to give Crown evidence, helped destroy the power base of the seemingly untouchable bent detective Roger Rogerson.

When Williams moved from armed robberies to drug dealing he tried to treat it as a business, but soon he was using his own product. 'I started smoking, then it was up the snozzer and then up the Warwick Farm (arm),' he told one of the authors.

'I was stoned all the time. I wasn't thinking straight.'

In 1982, Williams was the target of a drug squad operation in Melbourne and police used a NSW undercover policeman, Mick Drury, for the sting.

NSW police were interested in a criminal named Brian Hansen, but the trail led to Melbourne and Williams. Hansen needed to get his heroin from Williams or the deal with Drury would fall over.

'I knew Brian Hansen. He said he had a drug buyer down from Sydney,' Williams said years later. 'The deal was supposed to kick off at lunchtime but for about nine hours I smelled a rat.

'I didn't want to do the business. Brian, on the other hand, was insistent. He said he had counted the money and that everything was sweet.'

The deal was to supply heroin for $110,000 in cash. Hansen and Drury waited in a room at the Old Melbourne Hotel in March, 1982, for the supplier to arrive. But it was only after several phone calls that Williams finally fronted with the powder.

'I didn't go into the hotel. I waited in the car outside. Brian went into the hotel, came back with Drury and introduced him. Well, he didn't want to get into the car.

'I smelled a rat. I showed him the gear but there was something wrong.'

Earlier that day, the police team had been briefed but one officer was late. There was a sale on at Myer and he had been shopping. He missed the part about making sure they came in slowly. So, when Drury gave that the signal the deal was done, the unmarked car sped to the spot.

'They were so keen to block me in that they skidded past the car. I put it in gear and took off,' Williams said.

Police lost Williams nearby, at Melbourne University, where he used to work. They believe he slipped on a lab coat and simply walked away. About four months later, he was arrested in Adelaide and charged with heroin trafficking.

The police case was not strong because he was not caught with the heroin or the police marked notes. It was thrown out at committal but the Director of Public Prosecutions decided to directly present the case to a higher court.

Williams was convinced that only one man stood between him and a long stretch in Pentridge and that man was Michael Drury. The dealer contacted hitman Christopher Dale Flannery and said he was prepared to bribe the undercover policeman.

'I knew I needed help because the only bloke who stuck to his guns in the committal was Drury. He was unshakeable. It wasn't his efforts which fell down for the prosecution, it was the Melbourne police around him, trying too hard.

'Mick Drury said it like it was, the others painted a picture which couldn't be finished, and they ran out of paint.

'I asked him (Flannery) if he could do anything in regard to getting him (Drury) to change his evidence or slow it down. He said he would see what he could do, that he had a couple of Jacks (police) in Sydney sweet.

'He said it would cost and I said I wasn't worried about the cost side of it. I offered $30,000 at one stage, $50,000 at another stage, $100,000 and an open ticket in the end.'

But when Drury refused to accept the bribe Flannery offered to kill him for $100,000 – with half upfront as a deposit.

Drury was gunned down while he was washing dishes in the kitchen of his Chatswood home on June 6, 1984. But he lived.

The irony was that although Drury recovered to give evidence against Williams in his heroin trial, the drug dealer still beat the charges on the evidence. The dealer was the obvious suspect for the attempted murder but police gave him the perfect alibi. He had been picked up for speeding and had to produce his licence at the Greensborough police station. It proved he was in Melbourne at the time of the shooting.

But Williams was seen as the weak link by the taskforce investigating the shooting – and by the men who had arranged it.

Williams knew the group didn't take prisoners. A man charged over conspiracy to sell $700,000 of the ring's heroin, Robert 'Jumping Jack' Richardson, was murdered and his body found near King Parrot Creek, in country Victoria, in March, 1984. He had been shot once in the back of the head.

The informant who helped police infiltrate the ring died of a mysterious drug overdose in a Kings Cross hotel.

Williams was seen as the next to go. He was the only man who could identify Flannery and Roger Rogerson as being involved in the Drury shooting.

Soon there was a contract out on his life. He was to be hit when he went to his home in the Melbourne outer suburb of Lower Plenty. Williams was too smart to go home but his brother-in-law, Lindsay Simpson, was too naive to know the dangers. 'I was told I was to be knocked. I was completely paranoid and I clean forgot that Lindsay was to come to my house that night.' Waiting outside the house to kill Williams on September 18, 1984, was Roy 'Red Rat' Pollitt, another gun-for-hire, contracted to do the job by drug dealer Dennis Bruce Allen.

Pollitt saw a man pull up at the house, he produced his gun and made the victim kneel on the ground. The respectable builder kept trying to tell the gunman he had the wrong man. He was forced to the driveway and shot in the head in front of his wife and baby. His last words were, 'But my name is Simpson.'

'Lindsay was a good family man. It took him eight years to have a baby with his wife. Six years of hospital and doctors' appointments.'

Not only did the 'Red Rat' get the wrong man – he was ripped off in his payment. Allen paid Pollitt a $5000 deposit for the hit, but the notes were counterfeit.

Williams was later arrested and pleaded guilty to conspiracy to attempt to bribe Drury. Ironically, only months earlier, Rogerson had been found not guilty to similar charges.

Williams pleaded guilty to conspiracy to murder Drury. He was sentenced to 14 years' jail but, again, Rogerson was acquitted of being involved.

'I am not bitter about it. I was part of the conspiracy and I have paid the price,' Williams said later. He served four years, six months before he was released.

'Roger beat the charges. I am dirty on him, but good luck to him. I'm just happy that it's over for me,' he said.

Williams said the real victim was Drury. 'I can understand if he was bitter to the day he died. But I just hope he is remembered as a bloke who stuck to his guns and was vindicated in what he did.' After Williams was released he told one of the authors he was finished with drugs and crime.

'I feel like a new person. It's the first time I don't have to look over my shoulder.'

But it wasn't long before he was back to old habits. The drugs did what the Sydney underworld couldn't. They killed him.

Christopher Dale Flannery

DESPITE the rumours, there are few 'stone-killers' in Australia. These are the men who kill as a business. They take contracts and move on, mercenary soldiers in underworld wars. Sometimes they might even like their victims – but they like money more.

Christopher Dale Flannery was one of those men and he loved his work. Known as 'Rentakill' and urged on by his wife, 'Kiss-of-Death' Kath, Flannery never asked why – just how much.

For up to $50,000 he would kill and, as part of the service, he was usually prepared to dispose of the body, too.

He began as a bash artist, once flogging a discount book dealer in Melbourne for an alleged indiscretion. He was good-looking, charming and personable until he was crossed. Then he could turn into a raving psychopath. Even other killers feared his mood swings.

Flannery was born in February, 1949, but his parents divorced when he was 14 months old because his father beat his mother. Young Chris inherited his father's temper. There was some irony in the fact that the young Flannery was a champion swimmer who made under-age Victorian finals. Thirty years later, his swimming ability couldn't help him when his body was allegedly slipped into the sea after he was garrotted.

He went to five schools before leaving at the earliest opportunity at the age of 14. What Chris wanted to learn they didn't teach in school. His elder brother, Ed, became a successful lawyer and his sister became a school teacher. Ed died in Melbourne at a young age from cancer.

Christopher started as a car thief and was convicted of rape as a teenager. He was an armed robber and habitually carried a gun before he could vote. He had a thirst for knowledge. He taught himself the basics of the human body, not to heal but to hurt. He wanted to know about bone, muscle and vital organs and what bullets would destroy them. He had a book of pathology, which he used as a working text.

He worked as a bouncer at a St Kilda nightclub that was a notorious meeting place for gangsters and police of questionable reputations.

Subtlety was not his strong suit. He had a tattoo on his stomach, the word 'LUNCHTIME', above an arrow pointing to his groin.

In 1980 he took a contract from a white collar gangster to kill a Melbourne businessman, Roger Wilson. Flannery and another man pretended to be detectives and, using a home-made police sign, pulled over Wilson's green Porsche as he was heading home to his Nar Nar Goon property and his young family.

They handcuffed Wilson but Flannery's first shot failed to kill him. Wilson ran before tangling himself in a fence. Flannery emptied his gun into the victim before burying the body with 20 kilograms of lime.

It was never found.

Flannery was arrested months later near Geelong. He was driven to the local police station where he pretended to be ill and was taken to the toilet. He reached into his underpants and produced a dangerous weapon – a small pistol. Police grabbed him before he could shoot his way out of custody. Flannery was acquitted of Wilson's murder after Victoria's then longest murder trial. The failure to find the body damaged the prosecution case.

A key Crown witness, Debbie Boundy, disappeared from a Melbourne hotel before she could give evidence. It is believed she suffered the same fate as Wilson.

After Flannery was acquitted, he was immediately arrested for the murder of Sydney underworld figure Raymond Francis Locksley in 1979.

After two trials he was acquitted.

Flannery moved to Sydney at a time when the status quo in the Sydney underworld had been disturbed. Corrupt NSW police were under investigation and could no longer control the gangsters that had been their partners-in-crime. The old guard, under well-known criminals such as Lennie McPherson and George Freeman, was under threat. New crooks, flushed with cash from heroin deals, wanted to take over.

It seemed a perfect opportunity for a hitman to find plenty of work. Freeman didn't get to the top of the dung-heap by not being quick. He put Flannery on the payroll. He was a mad dog, but he was Freeman's mad dog.

Flannery quickly developed an eclectic group of contacts ranging from notorious Sydney detective Roger Rogerson to flamboyant doctor at large Geoffrey Edelsten.

The doctor and the hitman needed each other's skills. Flannery wanted a tattoo removed and Edelsten wanted a troublesome patient given the same treatment. Edelsten gave the hitman a medical certificate stating he was too ill to stand trial for the murder of Locksley.

The former owner of the Sydney Swans football team had a problem with a patient who was harassing him. He asked if

Flannery could help. His answer was as blunt as his solution – $50,000 for a murder and $10,000 for a bashing. The rich doctor thought the price slightly high but Flannery explained, 'Baseball bats are expensive.'

Edelsten was later recorded talking to his then wife, former model Leanne. She inquired about Flannery's occupation: 'Bashing up people, is that all he does?'

'No, he kills people … nice young fella,' the doctor replied.

Having been acquitted of two murders he had clearly committed, Flannery seemed to believe he was bullet proof. He made a living breaking the law – but then he decided to break the rules, as well. He took a contract to murder a cop.

Mick Drury, an undercover NSW drug squad detective, came to Melbourne to infiltrate a heroin syndicate in 1982. One of the targets was Alan David Williams, who met Drury at the Old Melbourne Hotel.

The $110,000 deal was done and, outside the hotel, Drury gave the signal but the police came in too fast for the arrest and skidded past. Williams, a former top footballer, was able to run. He was arrested four months later in Adelaide, but what should have been an easy case with the suspect grabbed at the scene, became a contested case.

Drury was the key. If he could be stopped, Williams would be cleared.

Williams approached Flannery. 'I knew Chris, I always found him to be a thorough gentleman, but he was also a murderer and a paid killer.' But Williams didn't plan to kill Drury' he wanted to pay him off.

'I ran into him (Flannery) in Melbourne and mentioned to him that I had been pinched by an undercover copper from Sydney … He said it would cost and I said I wasn't worried about the cost side of it.'

According to evidence given in a series of court cases, notorious Sydney detective Roger Rogerson approached Drury with a bribe offer on behalf of Williams, an offer Drury apparently refused.

Williams met Flannery and Rogerson at a Sydney restaurant where he was told the bribe offer had failed.

Flannery then broke the silence: 'Well, if it was me, I'd put him off (kill him).' Williams wasn't sure. He said, 'That's a big step,' but it didn't take long to convince him.

The deal, done in cold blood over cool beers, was for Flannery to kill Drury for $100,000 with a down payment of $50,000 and the rest to be collected after the killing.

Drury was shot while washing dishes in the kitchen of his Chatswood home on June 6, 1984. Everyone, including his colleagues, expected him to die but, despite being shot twice from point-blank range, he lived. When Flannery realised Drury was going to live, he told Williams not to bother sending the other $50,000.

The shooting, even in cynical Sydney, created outrage. Underworld heavies started to realise that a mad hitman who would kill anyone, even police, was a dangerous liability. There was no shortage of people wanting him dead.

In January, 1985, Flannery was shot in the ear and hand during a machinegun attack on his Sydney home. He moved away from his family but was still available for hire.

Even friends were not safe.

Double Bay restaurant owner and drug dealer Tony 'Spaghetti' Eustace was one of the few gangsters who actually liked Flannery. But when George Freeman wanted Eustace dead, Flannery saw no problem.

Flannery phoned Eustace in April, 1985, saying he had to leave Australia and wanted to borrow $25,000.

Eustace, 43, who had been helping Flannery hide from enemies, took the money to his 'mate' at Mascot, near Sydney airport. He was shot in the back six times soon after 7pm on April 23, 1985, in Gertrude Street, Arncliffe, 200 metres from the Airport Hilton Hotel. Flannery later confirmed he was to meet his old mate at the Hilton that night.

Eustace was found collapsed next to his Mercedes by teenagers on their way home from football training. He was taken to hospital and told two detectives to 'fuck off' before going into surgery. He died on the table.

The underworld war in Sydney had been going for a year. It was bad for business and, eventually, a peace deal was brokered. But there would be no long-term peace while Flannery was alive. He had to go.

The gangsters knew that the hitman was too cunning to be trapped by an enemy. In the underworld tradition, it would be left to a friend.

On May 9, he was last seen leaving an apartment building in Liverpool Street, where he was living. It was said he was heading to George Freeman's harbour-side home.

He was never seen again.

There were several theories as to what happened next.

In his autobiography, *Neddy*, Smith claimed: 'Rumour has it that Chris was picked up by a policeman he knew well and trusted, who offered him a lift. The car went only a short way before it stopped at a set of traffic lights, where two ex-police climbed in. The car took off and Chris was then shot several times in the head and chest as the car drove along.' A fictional version of this story also appeared in the novel *A Green Light*, written by Flannery's former jail mate, Ray Mooney.

But Victorian police believed that Flannery made it to Freeman's home and was lured to the boatshed to examine an

Israeli Uzi machinegun. That story says that he was garrotted, his body wrapped in a weighted tarpaulin and dumped in the harbour.

One inmate in a Sydney jail later declared he would give up fish because he didn't want to be accused of 'eating Chris'.

Mark Brandon Read told the inquest that Flannery was hit in the head with meat-cleaver and fed through a tree shredder. The theories vary, but they all agreed that his time was up.

Mark Brandon 'Chopper' Read

POLICE cradling shotguns stood on the roof. Others were scattered in the car park scanning loiterers for signs of trouble. Burly detectives frisked people, including one of the authors of this book, as they entered a courtroom full of police with bulges under their jackets. This was the scene at Brunswick Magistrates Court one day in late 1979.

In the court holding cells were some of the most feared men in the Australian prison system, ferried down Sydney Road from Pentridge to give – or not give, mostly – evidence about a jailhouse stabbing.

The hard men in court were inmates of the notorious H-Division, of which it was said that anybody who wasn't mad or bad when they went in soon would be. The best they could expect was breaking rocks with a sledge-hammer in solitary. The worst was savage beatings, injury and death.

Each criminal called on that humid day was well-known in police and prison circles. Spectators craned to look at them as they slouched or swaggered, deadpan, into the witness box. And the biggest freak in the freak show was Mark Brandon Read, then a 25-year-old usually described as a psychopath, and a central figure in the case. He was as big as a heavyweight boxer, muscular, heavily tattooed, with short jet-black hair above mutilated ears.

Prisons have a rigid hierarchy, in which the price of upsetting the pecking order is often death. At the top of this brutal pyramid are the few who can instil fear in the many with their propensity for violence. Of this few, none is better known than Read. Such a reputation has drawbacks. It makes him a target for other hard men, and the mad, the bad and the ugly.

This day, the outside world was getting a glimpse of life in H-Division because of a falling out among 'friends' – a prisoner called Greg 'Bluey' Brazel had, months earlier, slit open Read's belly with a 'shank', prison slang for a hand-made knife.

Read's intestines spilled through the enormous gash 'like sausages', he later remarked of the wound that came close to killing him. With a characteristic dash of twisted chivalry, he later complimented Brazel on 'a terrific sneak go', as politely as a World War I air ace might have praised a rival after a dogfight.

The day after the stabbing Read shocked hospital staff by getting out of bed and doing push-ups, bursting dozens of stitches. He told nurses he was getting fit to launch a revenge attack.

It's so awful it's funny. And that pretty well explains the rise and rise of 'Chopper' Read. Here's a man who once had his ears cut off – just to show he could get out of H-Division via hospital – and then joked about it. His is the blackest of black humour, coating bleak stories of the underworld.

CUT to February, 1998. The biggest news event in Australia is the constitution convention, and Steve Vizard – lawyer, tycoon, entertainer and republican delegate – is playing his latest 15 minutes of fame for laughs. 'It is only the Queen's Chopper

Read-like presence,' he tells the nation, 'that keeps Bill Deane from doing a runner to Majorca with our gold reserves.'

Later, as Michael Hodgman – flamboyant Tasmanian QC, politician, monarchist and Read's barrister – addresses the convention, fellow delegate Phil Cleary thumbs through the latest Chopper book, *The Singing Defective*, to find a cheeky verse about Hodgman, written in a nifty parody of Banjo Paterson's style that ends like this:

A master of the legal twist,
A shrewd and artful dodge man,
The man I swear this ditty to,
The one and only Hodgman.

Cleary is so impressed he quotes it next day in his *Sydney Morning Herald* column.

Chopper has become part of the language, a shared reference point that has spread beyond the lowbrow Australian culture. As a criminal, he is a self-confessed failure – but by some bizarre chance he is a member of that exclusive club of 'celebrities' known instantly by their first names – like Gough and Hazel, Rex and Sam, Eddie, Bert and Ita.

It's been a weird journey for a standover man with no ears who's spent all but a few months of his adult life in jail. How did it happen?

Part of the answer is that Read, like more conventional achievers, is driven by ego, and always dreamed of being a celebrity. Even in the 1970s it was well-known in jail that he wanted to go down in history like Ned Kelly and Squizzy Taylor.

His chance came in 1990 when this book's principal author John Silvester – a longtime crime reporter for the then *Sun* newspaper, now with *The Age* – wrote a story dismissing Read as a manipulative and violent thug with no redeeming features.

Silvester was surprised to get a Christmas card from Read which said, 'My idea of a perfect Christmas is to own a thousand room hotel – and find a dead reporter behind every door. I hope your Yuletide log rolls out of the fireplace and burns ya house down. Merry Christmas. Ha ha.'

Sensing another story, Silvester used contacts to set up an interview with Read in H-Division.

After two hours, he revised his opinion of Read. He still thought he was a manipulative and violent thug – but with some redeeming features.

He was funny, a natural yarn spinner, and astonishingly frank. So frank that the resulting series of stories Silvester wrote cost Read another six months inside, because the parole board was peeved by his failure to bother with the usual 'I'm reformed and need a chance to prove I can go straight' routine.

Read asked Silvester about writing a book on his life and crimes. Silvester parried, suggesting Read should sharpen a pencil and start work himself. 'Send me a letter,' he said.

Next day, there was a letter in Silvester's pigeon hole. And the day after, and the next. For weeks. 'It got that way,' recalls Silvester, 'that if there wasn't a letter waiting for me, I was rather disappointed.'

The letters were scratched on prison paper in Read's almost touchingly childish printing. The spelling was primitive, the grammar and punctuation anarchic, but the stories shone through because that's exactly what they were: stories. Some were horrific; some were sad; many were funny.

Here, 60 years after Runyon and five before Tarantino, was a voice with a little of the appeal of both – a raw talent with a 20-year inside view of Melbourne's underworld.

Read had seen and heard things most 'real' writers could only imagine – and he had the imagination to make them real on the page. Even on prison paper, toiling by the dull blue glow of a television set in a darkened cell.

Silvester thought that if he liked reading Read's raw material, so would other people. He approached his colleague, Andrew Rule, who had self-published several books. They stitched Read's erratic correspondence into chapters, then into a manuscript later titled *Chopper from the Inside*. A patient compositor cobbled the text into pages in a weekend, and it went to the printers.

Ten years and 30 reprints later, that book has sold some 150,000 copies, and there are another nine to keep it company. Total sales are around 500,000 and rising.

Chopper From The Inside, serialised around Australia, New Zealand, England and South Africa, was a cult hit. And, at the time of writing, it still is. Read's first two books have been published in hardback in Britain.

Bizarre footage of Read shooting a bottle out of the hand of a lackey and jokingly threatening an attractive reporter with a gun was replayed in America on prime-time television to an audience that has little idea where Australia is.

Test cricketers and rock bands read the book on tour. Television and radio presenters referred to it. Stand-up comics did jokes about it. An international American author, William Gibson, the man who invented the term 'cyberpunk', admits in a foreword that he based a scary Australian gangster in his best-selling novel, *Idoru*, on Chopper Read. Like rap singers in the USA, a street fighter and gunman had made the crossover from crime to celebrity.

So who is Read? Or, more intriguingly, who was he?

By any civilised view, he is – or was – a monster, a man who readily admits committing acts of extreme violence in the past.

But, though Read is (or was) in the criminal world, he is not of it. Unlike most of those he has been in jail with – and preyed on – all his adult life, he is not from a criminal family, condemned by breeding and circumstances to the cycle of crime and punishment.

His father was an outwardly law-abiding former soldier who held respectable jobs before retirement. His mother is a strict Seventh Day Adventist, the daughter of an Adventist clergyman. Her brother, Read's uncle, is a well-known doctor who gives advice on radio.

The young Read had a strange childhood. He could not play sport on Saturdays with other children in his neighbourhood in Melbourne's northern suburbs because he had to spend hours in church. The family's religion made him a loner from an early age – and led him to be bullied by school gangs who taunted Adventists as 'white Jews'.

Beneath the respectable facade there were stresses on the family that Read doesn't discuss in detail, but which caused him to be put in an orphanage for 18 months as a baby. He was sent to mental institutions as a teenager where, he says, he was given shock treatment and deep sleep therapy. His parents divorced during his teens, ending their dysfunctional marriage, but not its effects on their children.

Read's father, a war veteran, displayed classic symptoms of post-traumatic stress. He sometimes slept with a loaded gun at his side and frightened Read and his younger sister who, like their mother, is a committed Christian mortified by her brother's life. Read's father taught him to shoot and to fight with his fists, apparently feeding his adolescent fascination with firearms, military tactics and violence.

The religious upbringing has left a touch of the Old Testament in Read. He refers often to Hell and Heaven, Good and Evil. He is patriotic, far Right-wing and a fiercer proponent of capital punishment than the self-righteous armchair judges who cite him as an example of someone who should be hanged.

Unlike most criminals, he makes no excuses for himself. Apart from an occasional oblique reference to his childhood, he never portrays himself as a victim, and says he chose his bloody path himself.

He resists the temptation to go along with those who want to cast him as a sort of vigilante who cleans up the streets and doesn't hurt decent folks. Read says he robs drug dealers because they've got a lot of money and won't go to the police – not because he's waging war on evil.

He has built a mask of bravado but, sometimes, he lets it slip. In a letter that became the last chapter of his first book, he wrote: ' … in the end, I always end up in a prison cell. I know I have said I regret nothing – but the truth is I regret plenty.'

Why was he such a frightening character to other criminals who had more money, more weapons and more influence? Read made other killers hide because he didn't care.

He didn't care if he went back to jail, he didn't care about pain and, like a Kamikaze pilot, he seemingly didn't care if he died.

His great enemy, the now deceased gangster Alphonse Gangitano, was said to have squeezed through a toilet window to escape Read when the standover man walked into a nightclub with explosives wrapped to his chest many years ago. Gangitano knew that Read was probably crazy enough to light the fuse if anyone was rash enough to call his bluff.

In his time as a standover man, Read says he killed many times but was charged with murder only once, although he beat the charge on the grounds of self-defence – 'Thank God for juries,' he says. His crimes always involved serious violence, yet few resulted in serious money. He once attempted to abduct a judge, always carried a gun outside prison and any weapon he could get inside it.

For more than 20 years, Read's life consisted of a long stretch in jail, followed by six months of mad violence outside before returning to jail. Each time he would swear he was finished with violence, but inevitably he returned to it. Or was trapped by it.

Read left Pentridge after his first book was published and headed to Tasmania. After about seven months outside, he was charged with shooting a friend, bikie Sid Collins, who proved he was trouble-prone by getting himself murdered in 2002.

In a bizarre defence from a bizarre criminal, Read said the charge was an insult to his status as a professional hitman. If he had shot Collins, he argued, the injured man would never have been dropped off at hospital.

It was a cute argument anywhere else, but one doomed to fail in court.

This defence argument enabled the prosecution to raise Read's past, actually reading chunks of *Chopper From The Inside* to a gob-smacked jury. The first jury could not come to a verdict but the second one found him guilty. He may well have been the first Australian crook convicted more for being a bad author than being a wicked criminal.

He was deemed to be a dangerous offender, which meant that he could be given an indefinite sentence. A refined Tasmanian woman, Mary-Ann Hodge, visited him in jail, wooed him and they married inside jail with a bemused Michael Hodgman as the best man. Read could not even tell his new bride whether he would ever be freed, let alone when. But, after a five-year battle that used all the money he made from books, his Dangerous Offender status was revoked and he was released in February, 1998.

If Read thought he would slip out of jail quietly, he was wrong. Women he had never met wrote to him to share their sexual fantasies. One offered to pick him up in a limousine in which, she promised, she would be naked in the back seat. He declined the offer.

Every time Read was released from jail he faced a culture shock. Automatic teller machines, credit cards and the internet were science fiction to the man who had spent almost his whole adult life with nothing more high-tech than a bucket and a ballpoint pen.

He found it hard to settle. He left jail as a vegetarian and the fittest he had been for years, but it didn't last long. He was on strong sedatives which had been prescribed in prison and began binge drinking like a man determined to catch up on the fun he had missed out on for 20 years. The media loved him. He was quoted on everything from the Republic debate to the standard of Hollywood movies.

A producer working for comedian Elle McFeast had an idea to get her new late-night television show off to a controversial start with Chopper as the star guest. It meant flying Read to Sydney. At Hobart airport he had a few beers, a few more at Tullamarine, waiting for his connection, and then more on the flight.

At the ABC studios he was unwisely taken to the 'Green Room' and its open bar. The alcohol was there to 'loosen up' guests. Free beer was too much to resist. Read became so loose he could hardly stand up.

No-one would stop him drinking – or going on the show. When he finally got onto the set he was slurring and unsteady. McFeast nervously discussed crime while Read stared at her breasts. They laughed about an alleged underworld murder in which the victim kept trying to climb out of a cement mixer.

It was a late-night program with a small audience but Read's appearance created a national uproar. Politicians said they were appalled, and radio talkback parrots shrilled their disgust.

But some were to learn what criminals had known for decades: Read was no soft target, especially sober.

Channel Nine's *Midday Show* wanted to milk the controversy by using Read as a guest – but didn't want to bring him into the studio, in case it was accused of cynically exploiting the situation. Which, of course, is what it was doing.

The show's producers hatched a scheme by which Read was taken secretly to Nine's Hobart studio. It was set up that during a staged 'debate' in Sydney he would 'just happen' to telephone the show. They locked the fridge in Hobart. Read broke into a cupboard and found some warm beer – but not enough to affect his timing.

Colourful Sydney radio identity Alan 'The Parrot' Jones was in the Sydney studio venting opinions that Read should not be considered a celebrity and was an object of contempt. Read, all cued up with his 'spontaneous' telephone call, took advantage of the live-to-air conditions with a brutal counter punch: he said he had never been arrested in a public toilet, a reference to an unfortunate and unsavoury incident in London some years before that Sydney's favourite confirmed bachelor has tried to live down ever since. The indecency charges against Jones were dropped and the matter almost forgotten. Except by Read, who may not have the ears of an elephant but has the memory of one – which is not the only similarity.

The interview was hastily terminated as the bemused hostess (later sacked, oddly) tried to soothe Jones's ruffled feathers without laughing.

Soon, Read was in trouble again. It was alleged he was carrying firearms. Photographs of Read with guns, posed for use in one of his books, ended up with police. Charges were dropped when Michael Hodgman argued it could not be proved whether the guns were real or replicas.

It may well prove to be Read's most important acquittal.

'They normally give me enough rope to hang myself, but this time it was a little like a wake-up call. I knew I had to pull my head in.'

He and Mary-Ann moved to a farm and Read began to work around the district. He started a firewood-selling business, having completed a chainsaw course in Risdon Prison, and said he was content 'to be a fat farmer', but it wasn't to last.

On August 7, 2000, the long-awaited film on Read's life, *Chopper*, had been released for a week and was doing great at the box office, taking $1,258,717 in one weekend.

Read was not invited to the premiere. The actor who played him, Melbourne comic Eric Bana, produced a world-class performance that won awards and kick-started his career as a serious performer. Read says of him: 'He plays a better Chopper than me. I know how Elvis felt when he went to a Presley lookalike competition and finished third.'

It had taken the producers eight years to convince sceptical investors there was a market for a film on a violent standover man. Russell Crowe had liked the role but the money for a mainstream star was not available. It was Read who suggested Bana for the role, but it was only after a screen test that he got it.

In October, 2001, Read left his wife and young son, Charlie, named after his dead gangster mate 'Mad Charlie', to return to Melbourne. Seriously ill, he has been told that if he doesn't stop drinking he will die.

He moved in with his first love, Margaret, and at the time of writing, lives quietly in Collingwood. Police visit him at home to have pictures taken and books signed. He wrote a children's book, generating predictable publicity and sales. With the exception of a few old contacts, he keeps away from the underworld.

He says: 'I don't want to be Chopper any more. I can't believe that he actually existed. If I didn't change I would have to kill people, and end up in jail, or I would have got killed myself.'

Read says the people who marvel at his criminal past miss the point: 'I wasn't much good at it. I spent more than 20 years inside and still carry the wounds from all the violence.

'But I can say I did get away with one of the biggest unsolved crimes in Australia's history. I got away with writing all those books. When they've forgotten all the other nit-wits, they will always remember Chopper Read.'

In August, 2002, Read and former AFL footballer and serial self-promoter Mark Jackson flew to Kalgoorlie in outback WA, as part of their national sportsmen's night tour, dubbed 'The Marks Brothers'.

Read was an instant hit with the miners and outback workers, who loved his crime stories. He produced a meat cleaver and called for bids from the crowd. He sold it for $1300, autographed it and then produced an ink pad, leaving his finger-print on the blade. 'No-one can say it is a fake,' he told the buyer. 'Just take it to a police station and they can confirm it is an authentic Chopper Read.'

Read is a celebrity and making money without going to jail for it. 'The mentally-ill have rights too,' he protests, tongue firmly in cheek. 'If they wish to buy things from me, then who am I to stop them? What I'm doing might be criminal – but I'm not breaking any laws.'

Greg Brazel

OF 2500 prisoners in Victoria's jails, Gregory John 'Bluey' Brazel is probably the worst. The convicted double murderer was sentenced in effect to an extra three years in the County Court in 1994 on charges of holding a prison officer hostage.

This means that Brazel will serve at least 28 years, taking into account his murder sentences. It doesn't worry him. He would do it on his ear – if he had one.

Brazel is considered by the Office of Corrections the most dangerous man in the prison system. He held a Melbourne Remand Centre staff member hostage with a knife to his throat in November, 1991.

He threatened to kill Gunther Krohn because of a decision to transfer Brazel from the Remand Centre to Pentridge. He surrendered after a three-hour siege.

Convicted on 78 previous occasions, he has proved to be virtually uncontrollable in custody. He has a history of appearing to reform and returning to the mainstream prison population, only to attack staff or fellow inmates.

His prison record shows he has been involved in at least 25 violent incidents, including stabbing three prisoners in separate attacks, breaking the noses of two prison officers, assaulting police, setting fire to his cell, cutting off the tip of his left ear, going on a hunger strike, threatening to kill staff, pushing a governor's head through a plate-glass window and using jail phones to intimidate witnesses.

On several occasions, he has stabbed inmates who then refused to give evidence against him. In one of his brief periods of freedom since 1978, he killed two women. Police believe he knew he was under investigation for the first murder and killed his second victim purely to taunt them. He was found guilty of killing prostitutes Sharon Taylor and Roslyn Hayward, whose bodies were found in shallow graves near Colac in 1990.

In his trial over the Remand Centre kidnap, Brazel handled his own defence. His legal tactics were somewhat unorthodox.

In his final submission he read the jury a poem, then told them the story of Jack and the Beanstalk, and referred to the appearance of Judge Lewis in his wig and gown. 'I must say his Honour looks magnificent.' The flattery didn't help. He was still found guilty.

Medical tests showed that Brazel had brain damage that affected his self-control.

Brazel can be charming and friendly, but when he turns nasty he is uncontrollable. Brazel was one of Mark Brandon 'Chopper' Read's best friends until he stabbed him in 1979.

Read complimented him for the sneak attack before being taken to hospital for emergency surgery. The next day Read was found doing push-ups in the hospital with his stitches split and his intestines hanging out. He explained he was trying to get fit to get his revenge against Brazel.

Brazel had a habit of ringing police in their office for a chat and then dropping private details about the detective's family as a subtle form of intimidation.

He has a history of setting fire to his cells. At least three times he has been found with mobile phones inside jail. On one occasion police had to immobilise him when he tried to fight them in a cell. He was overpowered but lay there laughing as he was punched and kicked, urging them to do their worst.

Brazel was born in Blacktown, a western suburb of Sydney. His father was a New South Wales detective.

In 1976, while in the army medical corps, he took five privates hostage during an exercise at Healesville. He fired shots during the siege before a captain persuaded him to give up. He was dishonourably discharged from the army.

A confidential police report on Brazel said: 'He is cunning and sly and could never be trusted.'

Detective Senior Sergeant Graeme Collins, who arrested the career criminal over the Taylor murder, said Brazel simply smiled and said: 'I look forward to doing battle with the homicide squad.'

But after being convicted of the two murders Brazel was not finished. He was assaulted in jail and, in August, 2000, decided to tell police he had killed not two, but three, people.

He confessed to murdering Mildred Teresa Hanmer, 51. She was shot in the chest in her Warren Road hardware shop on September 20, 1982, and died two hours later. Her husband Richard was at home in Mount Eliza recovering from a hernia operation when his wife rang on the day of the shooting. She could only say: 'Dick, I've been robbed and I'm dying.'

She collapsed, but her husband could still hear her gasping and moaning on the open telephone line. A hairdresser who entered the shop after hearing shots found the mother of three dying.

The hardware shop was a State Bank sub-agency and the bandit stole $2569 from two safes. Both were opened with keys. Before Mrs Hanmer died, she managed to describe the gunman, telling police he had ginger hair. Brazel has always been called 'Bluey' because of his distinct ginger hair.

Mrs Hanmer was a triple certificate nurse and her husband an engineer. They had decided to open their own business and agreed that if they were ever robbed, they would co-operate and not risk their lives.

Police interviewed more than 1500 people during the original investigation.

In a video link to the Magistrates Court, Brazel said, 'The bottom line is ... that Gregory John Brazel appears before this court charged with murder, a murder he freely admits he committed, and after many years of reflecting has come forward.'

But, as always with Brazel, there was a twist. He told police he was a contract killer and murdered Hanmer for $30,000. Police investigated his claims of being paid and found no evidence to support them.

Police say that while Brazel did commit the murder, they believe he has confessed to increase his status in the prison system as a supposed hitman.

CHAPTER 11

Movers and Dealers

Gerry Maio, John Asciak, Kevin John Barlow, Brian Geoffrey Chambers

FOR an injured and depressed man who had lost his girlfriend and was surviving on workers' compensation, the offer of $6000 and an overseas holiday seemed money for old rope. Unfortunately, he was right.

But Kevin Barlow, 25, was too naive to see the dangers when he agreed to become an international drug courier for smooth-talking Perth heroin importer John Asciak.

Barlow moved into the Balcatta home of Debbie Colyer-Long in July, 1983, after seeing an advertisement in a local paper. It was through his new landlady that he met Asciak. The dealer quickly realised that Barlow was broke, lonely and ready to be exploited.

One morning, Barlow made cups of tea for the couple and took them into Colyer-Long's bedroom. It was then that Asciak persuaded Barlow to join his team. He simply suggested an easy and allegedly foolproof way to make money. Just bring back some near pure heroin from Malaysia.

Asciak was an expert, having organised a series of similar smuggling runs. He offered Barlow the holiday, plus $2000 spending money and $4000 when he returned with the product.

But Barlow would not have to do the trip on his own. He was introduced to Brian Geoffrey Chambers – one year older, but seemingly decades wiser – who would control the trip.

Chambers was certainly experienced. He had already made 10 drug runs for the syndicate, returning eight times through Perth, once through Sydney and once through Townsville.

Police believe Chambers imported heroin valued at $10 million from 1980 until 1983. His biggest run involved smuggling 2.5 kilograms of near pure 'number four' heroin. In the drug syndicate he worked under the code name Charlie.

Chambers was a user but not an addict. On one trip when he thought he might have been under investigation, he buried heroin in Penang and returned to Australia. Later he flew back to retrieve the drugs.

The syndicate used Chambers because, as a user, he was able to 'taste' the heroin in Malaysia to ensure his syndicate was not being ripped off. This time Chambers would leave from Sydney and Barlow from Perth.

But Barlow's landlady urged him to think again as she drove him to the Perth airport on October 28, 1983. 'I tried to talk him out of going and told him he had to think of what was going to happen if he got caught. He wasn't worried about it,' she later told a Perth Court.

Barlow and Chambers reunited at a coffee shop at Singapore's Changi Airport later that day. A week later, they boarded a train for Penang.

The next day, on November 9, Chambers bought an inexpensive maroon suitcase to be packed with clothes and 17 small packages filled with heroin.

Barlow was the 'mule' assigned to carry the bag through Malaysian Customs. He didn't stand a chance: local police had already been tipped off.

He walked around the X-ray machine at the Kuala Lumpur Airport and stood in the economy class check-in queue despite being a first class passenger. He hoped standing in a busier section would help make him invisible. It didn't.

His mentor, Chambers, stood in the first class queue nursing Barlow's canvas travel bag.

Assistant Superintendent Abu Shahriman was waiting and pulled them both aside. Barlow stood shaking as the policeman demanded he open the case. He said he did not know the numbers of the cheap combination lock. Chambers then stepped forward and calmly selected the numbers that would ultimately seal their fate.

Both men tried to blame each other. It would do them no good. In Malaysia the drug laws contained a mandatory death penalty for anyone caught with more than 15 grams of heroin. Barlow and Chambers were found with 179.6 grams of pure heroin.

While Barlow publicly declared his innocence, he was more candid behind closed doors. In an effort to cut a deal, he spoke to Australian Federal Police stationed in Malaysia. He told them what he knew about the Australian heroin syndicate. But, for reasons that have never been explained, no serious investigation was launched into Barlow's revelations.

Barlow's passport listed Colyer-Long's address as his home. She later told one of the authors she was amazed that no police came to interview her after Barlow's arrest.

'I expected a knock at the door.'

She said she threatened to go to the police, but Asciak threatened to harm her three children. 'But if someone had come to me, I would have told them everything I knew. I am amazed no-one ever came to me to talk. I think the police have handled this pretty poorly.'

More than two years later, the National Crime Authority's best and most senior investigator, Carl Mengler, flew to Malaysia to re-interview Barlow.

Soon, the NCA was able to confirm through Colyer-Long that Barlow had been telling the truth.

The authority launched a special investigation, code-named Home-run. Phone record checks showed that the drug couriers had rung Colyer-Long's Perth number from their Penang hotel two days before they were arrested.

'I still don't know why it all took so long,' Colyer-Long said.

The NCA was able to gather sufficient evidence to charge Asciak with conspiracy to import the 179 grams of heroin found on Barlow and Chambers. He was sentenced to 10 years jail in a Perth court in June, 1988.

In March, 1988, one of the heads of the syndicate, Gerry Maio, was sentenced to a minimum of 15 years' jail in Melbourne for heroin trafficking.

He was arrested by NCA officers with two kilograms of heroin valued at between $3 million and $9 million.

Police found that Maio supervised the syndicate and often strapped heroin to the body of his 'mules' in Penang hotels and then travelled on the same planes back to Australia. If they were at risk of arrest he would simply walk away. Records show that Maio was often in Malaysia at the same time as Chambers.

Maio was considered invaluable because he had Chinese, Australian and Italian crime connections. At one time he was offered a chance to buy 30 kilograms of heroin that had already been imported into Australia by a Chinese syndicate for the bargain price of $6 million but he couldn't raise the cash.

Barlow and Chambers, meanwhile, didn't get to see their former bosses jailed. They were hanged in Kuala Lumpur's Pudu prison on July 7, 1986. They were the first westerners to be executed for drug trafficking in Malaysia.

John William Samuel Higgs

IT WAS supposed to be a straightforward armed robbery when John William Samuel Higgs and his three mates bailed up a West Meadows chicken farmer called Vincent Dugan.

The gang surprised the farmer outside his home around 9.50pm on the first day of autumn and marched him into the hallway of his house. Why one of them panicked and shot Dugan dead with a .22 rifle will never be known, but at that moment young Higgs graduated from robber to killer.

In the eyes of the law, although he did not fire the fatal shot, Higgs was guilty of manslaughter. He was sentenced to 12 years with a minimum of 10. That was in 1970.

Higgs was born in November, 1946. Like many youngsters who become heavy criminals, he was in constant trouble with the police as a teenager, with his first conviction recorded at the age of 13, about the time he left school. He has convictions for theft, stealing cars, assaults, manslaughter, assaulting police, resisting arrest, possession of cannabis and firearms. He was also charged with illegal possession of a stuffed possum.

The string of juvenile offences was an apprenticeship for the budding gangster. Drugs was the growth industry in his line of work. Higgs was a founding member of the Black Uhlans motorcycle gang, declared by police to be heavily involved in amphetamine distribution for many years. Police reports show that Higgs gave the gang its Melbourne clubhouse and that he was rewarded with life membership. He was released from prison in 1978 after serving more than eight years of his manslaughter sentence and began to live with his girlfriend, Karen McLennan. They had two children.

He became close to her brother, David McLennan, who became his right hand man in the drug business and company director of the legitimate arm of the syndicate.

In 1984, police started to receive intelligence that Higgs was becoming a big player in drugs. They were told he was involved in producing amphetamines and the importation of heroin, cocaine and hashish. Like a generation of other Melbourne crooks who had moved from street offences to robbery to drugs, he was cunning. He learned counter surveillance tactics, rarely trusted telephones, spoke in code and tried to deal only with fellow crims he had known for years.

Many made a good living from drugs, but Higgs was to make a fortune. He was to become Australia's biggest amphetamine producer, dealing in tonnes while others thought of kilograms. He would stockpile truckloads of chemicals for huge speed cooks in clandestine labs.

Police say they believe Higgs had the dash and the natural flair to have made good money if he had gone straight. But it was not to be.

The Higgs group was a loose cartel, with individuals coming together to work and then splitting into different groups. They had a network of corrupt, outwardly legitimate experts to advise them on how to stay ahead of investigators.

For police, the difference between knowing and proving his crimes would turn out to be a 15-year battle. The National Crime Authority, Federal and Victorian police tried to gather evidence on Higgs but after eight separate taskforce operations, he was still the biggest amphetamine producer in the country. By 1991, police had not established the identity of Higgs's cook, where he produced his amphetamines, where he got his chemicals or the structure of the organisation.

There can be little doubt that Higgs stayed in front of the posse with the help of inside information. On August 20, 1993, he delayed an amphetamine 'cook' for more than two weeks after he was warned police were about to launch a blitz on the five biggest speed gangs in Victoria.

Police received information that Higgs took out an $80,000 contract on one Daniel Hacking who, he claimed, owed him $100,000. Hacking fell from a boat in Caloundra, in Queensland, and drowned in mysterious circumstances in 1992.

Late in 1991, Higgs called in contractors to work on homes owned by him and David McLennan. He paid cash and bragged to the workers he needed to 'get rid' of $100,000. Police say he also bought harness horses to disguise his income.

Police found the Higgs group was a collective that would deal in anything the market wanted. Cocaine was imported from America, cannabis from New Guinea, guns from the Philippines and amphetamines from Victoria. It was one-stop shopping when you dealt with Higgs.

Frustrated drug squad detectives wrote in one report, 'Evidence has been extremely difficult to obtain regarding Higgs. He has insulated himself through a number of companies and apparent legal businesses and controls a large number of other criminals in his illegal dealings.'

Police established that $1,773,491 went through Higgs's hands from 1982 to 1993. He bought a fish-processing plant and retail outlet in Geelong and an ocean-going trawler in Eden, NSW.

He used a retired town planner to set up an excavating

business which helped remove soil for the construction of Crown casino. Police claim corrupt local officials were used to obtain building permits for the company, run by a former member of the Black Uhlans.

Higgs tried unsuccessfully to organise a huge rock concert just outside Melbourne for Easter, 1994. One fellow investor was former AFL star Jimmy Krakouer, who lost his money.

In 1993, Higgs became a director of a business set up to export powdered milk to Vietnam and horse feed to Malaysia. On February 14 that year, he flew to Asia for a month, visiting Malaysia, Vietnam and Thailand.

According to police, Higgs was going to set up a fake company in order to get Federal Government grants and a subsidy to export to Asia and at the same time use the business to import massive amounts of heroin.

Police say one of the group approached a police informer and asked whether he could launder $200,000 every three days through Hong Kong companies.

According to police, Higgs was heavily involved in fixing harness races, including a failed bid to rig the Geelong Cup in 1992. David McLennan was rubbed out as a driver for pulling up a horse that year. In February, 1992, Higgs and four of his team booked into the Sheraton Hotel in Darwin and were noted as big spenders. Northern Territory drug detectives followed the five men to a remote seafood business, where they stayed for days. After they left, the owner of the business was seen to be spending large amounts of money.

According to police, one of Higgs's team later delivered two hovercrafts to the business. Police believe the hovercrafts were to be used to import cannabis from Papua New Guinea. Higgs was known to be able to supply hundreds of kilograms of New Guinea cannabis on demand.

Police had information that Higgs moved $600,000 overseas through a corrupt lawyer's trust account. They were also told, though it could not be confirmed, that he had invested $18 million in city real estate – and land in Queensland valued at $10 million.

Police accept they will never know how much he made nor have any real chance of finding his hidden wealth.

In 1992, police intelligence claimed Higgs completed one 'cook' of amphetamines that had a street value of $48 million and a wholesale value of $7.5 million.

It took years for police to finally get enough evidence to charge Higgs. Their big break came from cultivating an informer, code-named E292. The businessman was able to infiltrate the syndicate and provide the key evidence against its boss.

Higgs pleaded guilty to one charge of conspiracy to traffic methyl amphetamine between January 1, 1993, and June 30, 1996. Judge David Jones sentenced him to six years with a minimum of four.

Graphic proof that Higgs was Australia's dominant ampheta-mines producer was that the quality of 'speed' around Australia dropped substantially when he was jailed.

Jimmy Krakouer

IT WASN'T too hard for drug squad detectives working on an Australia-wide amphetamines syndicate to establish the identity of the dark, fit-looking man who regularly visited 'speed' king John Higgs at a farm outside Melbourne.

In a football-mad state like Victoria, teenagers who have played a handful of AFL games become celebrities – so, after a decade of displaying exquisite football skills, Jimmy Krakouer was hardly anonymous.

Krakouer was one of the most exciting players in the history of the game and had been well paid for his efforts. In his 134-game career with North Melbourne he earned $870,000 over eight years – yet just three years after he retired after a brief stint with St Kilda, the father of four was broke, with no career prospects.

For most football players, the AFL opens doors. They get the chance to meet industry leaders and politicians who want to rub shoulders with star athletes. Smart young men use the chance to develop contacts that will last long after their ball skills fade.

Krakouer was young but, off the field, not smart. He couldn't see that age would eventually rob him of the ability to weave through packs and find space to create goals. For nearly 10 years, he was often offered chances by employers who wanted a star player on their books. But he shunned them, preferring the races, the two-up school and the company of criminals to the regimented lifestyle of a steady job.

It was rumoured that a Melbourne armed robber with international drug contacts paid Krakouer's gambling debts in the 1980s and he started spending time with some of the most dangerous men in Melbourne. Among them were drug dealers and so, inevitably, the footballer became of interest to Victorian detectives working on a complex investigation, code-named Phalanx. During the course of the investigation, Krakouer was identified as an amphetamine trafficker and close associate of John William Samuel Higgs.

Higgs liked Krakouer and gave him the chance to make a legal dollar. Higgs was going to invest in a huge rock concert with major international acts set for 1994. Police found investors had ploughed $400,000 into the project and Higgs had invested $600,000. Krakouer was persuaded to invest his last $130,000 from his football career.

The concert went belly up and so did Krakouer's hopes of a financial comeback. But Higgs had a sure-fire way to make money – drugs – and he offered Krakouer a slice of the action.

Amphetamines produced by the Higgs syndicate in Melbourne were packed into the front door cavities of a Nissan Bluebird and transported to West Australia. But police from Operation Phalanx were able to tip off their WA counterparts.

In January, 1994, police followed the delivery and burst into a Perth garage to find Krakouer and another man unloading 5.3 kilograms of amphetamines packed into 12 freezer bags. He was sentenced to 16 years' jail, won a retrial but received the same term in February, 1999, after again being found guilty. Ironically, the 'speed' Krakouer was caught with was only five per cent pure, having already been cut by Higgs's distributors from 80 per cent. Despite this, and the fact he was only a tadpole compared with the big fish in the Higgs pool, he suffered the most severe penalty by far. Even police who worked on the case felt Krakouer was dealt with harshly.

The police informer who set him up felt the sentence was a 'disgrace'.

Krakouer was 'a naive young bloke who got caught up in something too big for him to understand,' the informer, code-named E292, told one of the authors. On the field, Jimmy Krakouer had rarely been caught in possession. Off it, he came crashing to earth.

Bruce Alexander Wilson

HIS nickname was 'Willie', but it was Bruce Alexander Wilson's big brain that was his distinguishing feature. He used it to make a fortune. He could make more money with chemicals than any bank robber could with a gun.

When bikie gangs in Australia began to produce amphetamines, they used 'recipes' given to them by affiliated gangs in America, but they soon found that cooking amphetamines is harder than baking scones. The chemicals used are notoriously unstable and mistakes during the three-day process can result, at best, in the batch being ruined. And, at worst, in fatal explosions.

Amphetamine cooks tend to be people who have learned by their mistakes, but 'speed' king, John Higgs, didn't have time for enthusiastic amateurs. He had a trained chemist as his personal chef, a man who could produce 80 per cent pure speed in a long weekend.

Bruce Alexander Wilson was a New Zealander who had walked out of the third year of an industrial chemistry course at the Auckland Technical Institute after a clash with the head of the faculty. He moved to Sydney and worked in the chemical industry until he began a motorcycle business. It was through that business he began to associate with bikie gangs and began to use their drug of choice – amphetamines.

Wilson's risk-taking behaviour wasn't restricted to producing and consuming illicit chemicals. He was nearly killed in 1990 in a skydiving accident when he landed on a rock and fractured his back. He was in hospital for three months and a body cast for a further 10 weeks. He couldn't ride a motorbike for almost two years, but he could still speed.

Wilson showed little obvious sign of wealth, but Higgs told a police informer he had personally paid him $6 million to manufacture amphetamines over the years.

Wilson's defence lawyer was to tell the County Court his client increasingly used amphetamines to deal with his constant back pain from the skydiving accident. It would have been an unusual way to deal with pain. Speed is a stimulant that gives the user a heightened sense of awareness – not a sedative. But, of course, lawyers are not chemists.

Judge Peter Rendit demonstrated his faith in human nature by sentencing Wilson to 12 months' jail, partially suspended, because he believed Wilson had reformed and had refused offers to continue making amphetamines.

Dragon 'Machine Gun Charlie' Arnautovic

MELBOURNE'S western suburbs have produced some of Australia's most prolific drug dealers and there were few busier than Dragon Arnautovic – better known as 'Machinegun Charlie'. He was given the name not because of his love for guns but for his ability as a champion kick boxer. In the ring he was known for delivering quick combination kicks. Fans thought he was like a machinegun. It stuck and was later adopted by the underworld, who couldn't spell Arnautovic anyway.

Police had been chasing him for years and he was the key target of a drug squad investigation, code-named Hamadan.

Arnautovic was a prodigious heroin seller who had been caught several times. But each time he was caught, he would learn from his mistakes and he had become one of the most cunning figures in the heroin world.

Machinegun Charlie trusted few people, tried to work alone and kept a savage dog for security. Police found that he would take his bull mastiff, Gus, in his van when he went to deal drugs. While he talked to a buyer or supplier the dog would continue to bark savagely from inside the van. The message was clear. Don't try to rip off Machinegun Charlie.

He had a secret compartment in the van where he would hide

his heroin. Detectives said he would buy about 500 grams of high-grade heroin and then cut the drugs into one-ounce lots. He would hide his heroin around the western suburbs in parks and public buildings. His logic was simple and effective. He did not want to be caught with large amounts of heroin and by distributing the drugs widely he was less likely to be ripped off and lose his stockpile.

One of his hiding spots was at the end of a dead-end street in Sunshine. Police observed him retrieve drugs at the spot 15 times. They also saw him go to the Altona North Baseball Centre eight times to collect his heroin. Police later found about 25 ounces hidden in Berocca containers stuffed in the gaps in the corrugated iron walls at the centre.

As the special operations group moved in on him during an undercover buy at the Altona North Baseball Complex, he let his attack dog loose. It was a bad move. Gus tried to protect his boss. The SOG shot the bull mastiff dead. Police found a further 560 grams of heroin at the centre. Arnautovic was finally sentenced to 12 years with a minimum of nine for heroin trafficking.

When he was in jail, fellow inmates tried to find out where he had his remaining heroin hidden. Arnautovic let it slip that his supply was hidden in a Footscray soccer ground. One dark and stormy night two criminal groups went to the soccer ground and began digging. They found nothing but left the pitch looking like a wombat sanctuary.

Bruce Richard Cornwell

BRUCE Richard Cornwell didn't look like a drug boss. But, balding and with a moustache to hide his hare lip, the man they called 'Snapper' was to make millions before he was eventually jailed.

He had once tried his hand as an illegal bookmaker but, by the age of 20, he knew his future lay in the lucrative drug industry.

In 1974, Cornwell began importing South-East Asian buddha sticks, high-grade cannabis, into Sydney. Two years later, he was heavily involved in importing heroin.

He used stunning-looking croupiers from illegal Sydney casinos to smuggle the drugs into NSW. The logic was simple. Customs officers would be looking at the girls rather than their luggage. It worked.

Police raided his luxury Kirribilli apartment in 1976 and found drugs and $19,000 cash but their man, as slippery as the fish he was named after, was not home.

Cornwell typified the problems of law enforcement in the 1970s and 80s. For nearly a decade police knew Cornwell was one of the major players in the drug industry but seemed unable, or unwilling, to prosecute him.

He made them look stupid. While they couldn't find the evidence, Cornwell was getting richer and made no effort to hide his affluence. He owned a $780,000 Sydney home when that was a lot of money, a Queensland goldmine, a 10-metre pleasure-cruiser, investment properties on the Gold Coast and luxury Mercedes and Jaguar cars.

Even though he was a well-known drug dealer he was able to move in and out of Australia undetected. His one drug arrest was over a minor cannabis deal in September, 1974. He was fined $600, in default four months' jail.

Royal Commissioner Frank Costigan, QC, found Cornwell was involved in drug smuggling, violence, corruption, money laundering and passport rackets.

Costigan said members of Cornwell's ring were suspected of being involved in contract killings, particularly the unsolved murders of Terry and Sue Basham at Murwillumbah in 1982.

Terry Basham was one of Cornwell's drug distributors. Eight days after the murders, Cornwell left Australia for a year. Police found that $36,000 was withdrawn from one of Cornwall's bank accounts two weeks before the murders and more money three days after the killings.

When the National Crime Authority was formed in 1984, its first two targets were Robert Trimbole and Cornwell.

Cornwell was finally arrested outside a house in West Hampstead, London, in 1987 and extradited to NSW.

He was flown back to Sydney in the Prime Minister's jet. He would tell a court that he kept up to $500,000 in cash at his home. His total estimated fortune was $2.3 million.

He had more than $900,000 deposited in a Swiss bank account from cannabis sales alone. In 20 months a total of $459,000 was withdrawn from one of his accounts in Sydney.

When he was about to be jailed he told the judge his one regret was that he would be too old to have children when he was released.

But the Snapper was being unduly pessimistic.

Life in jail was not unduly severe. While still serving his sentence he managed to attend Sydney's Gay and Lesbian Mardi Gras. He had been partying in Oxford Street while he was on a work release scheme.

He was sentenced to 23 years for conspiring to import two tonnes of cannabis, worth $12 million. But he was to serve only six years and was released in December 1993.

A few months later, he married former *Penthouse* Pet Donna Turner at the exclusive Prunier's Restaurant in Sydney before about 100 guests ... and the happy couple's baby daughter.

He is often seen sipping coffee in a fashionable bar in Darlinghurst frequented by colourful racing, legal and literary identities.

CHAPTER 12

Bikies
and Bandits

Michael 'Chaos' Kulakowski

MANY Australian leaders have dreamed of international power
and respect. But one of the few who had real power was the
charismatic president of the Bandidos motorcycle gang, Michael
Kulakowski.

The power and influence of Kulakowski was undisputed. He
was internationally respected in the bikie world, so much that he
flew to the United States in July, 1996, to take part in peace
negotiations to stop a war between the Hells Angels and the
Bandidos in Europe that had claimed 11 lives.

Like the best executives, he brought life experience to the job.
Unlike a lot of bikies, who come from the urban underclass that
produces most criminals, Kulakowski was raised on a country
property in NSW and had been a showjump rider, rodeo bull
rider, soldier and a car salesman before becoming a Bandido.

'Mick K' or 'Chaos' as he was known by his bikie mates,
opted out of mainstream society at 40, but he still enjoyed the

trappings of success. As a bikie, he made more money than he ever did in a dusty rodeo ring or on a tired used car lot. As Bandidos president he drove a Mercedes, owned a $300,000 home and kept an immaculate Harley Davidson.

According to police, he was a major organised crime figure, with an army of followers who would kill for him. Literally.

The Bandidos already had a strong grip on the amphetamines market and a lucrative sideline in marijuana. But, like any astute businessman, Kulakowski looked to the future and new investment opportunities.

He saw the drug market was changing and foresaw the rising demand for party drugs such as ecstasy and LSD. Kulakowski wanted the Bandidos to be the major suppliers.

According to police, the Bandidos needed distribution points to move into the new wave drugs and began to set up 'Techno Discos' where they could cultivate thousands of new clients.

The profits were massive. The Bandidos bragged that their courier was walking through Sydney airport with a bundle of LSD sheets 25 centimetres thick on every smuggling run, and each sheet contained 200 'tabs' of LSD.

Bandidos were selling LSD with the Sydney Olympic logo, a smiley design, love hearts, and Beavis and Butthead stamps. According to Melbourne undercover police, the Victorian Bandidos planned to follow Kulakowski's lead and began to move into the party drug scene.

Senior Victorian Bandidos went to Sydney to discuss the way to open techno discos in Ballarat and Geelong as fronts to sell the party drugs.

The Bandidos, under the guidance of 'Chaos', had constructed an Australia-wide expansion policy. They planned to bully or persuade smaller clubs to become part of the new empire or retire. Unfriendly and friendly take-overs were all the same to them. Few would even consider a turf war with Kulakowski's soldiers. In early 1996 the target was Wangaratta and that meant an attack on the local club, the Tramps. In February, 1996, the Tramps' president received a letter saying that all Tramps' members, their friends and children would be in danger if the gang did not disband and leave town.

The power of the Bandidos lies in all-consuming loyalty. A member of the Griffith chapter, Dean Francis Corbury, declared a member of the Tramps looked the wrong way at him at Wangaratta on October 3, 1997. He summoned 60 members from Geelong, Ballarat and Griffith to come to Wangaratta for battle.

According to the Bandidos code, members were expected to just walk out of their jobs and drive. When a brother needs help, whether he is right or wrong, you must support him. But police were tipped off by an undercover officer and when the bikies turned up, they were pulled over and checked. The Tramps were also warned and hid.

Just to show their strength, the Bandidos started their 1997 National Run in Wangaratta on October 23, with more than 250 bikers from Australia and around the world. To make matters worse for a country town with limited police resources, it was the break-up day for VCE students. The town would be filled with drunken bikies and drunken teenage girls. It was every parent's nightmare.

Police had a meeting with Kulakowski and explained the situation. He agreed and said there would be no trouble. 'Chaos' sent out the message to his troops: 'Any trouble and you have to deal with me.' There was not one incident. 'That was his power,' a senior policeman said.

Kulakowski could make peace, or war, on a whim.

The 250 bikies moved on to Geelong and, according to police, went to a popular local nightclub. The owner set up a special room for them, but they wanted the run of the nightclub and the manager baulked. Kulakowski gave the nod and they trashed the place and bashed the bouncers.

No official complaint was ever lodged.

On October 24, 1997, some of the gang, including a few international Bandidos, went out to test fire their illegal firearms. One of the overseas visitors had to be dissuaded from opening fire on a passing Geelong-Melbourne train.

The National Run was the highlight of Kulakowski's reign.

But charisma and power won't stop a bullet. On November 9, Kulakowski, Sergeant-at-Arms Bruce Harrison and fellow member Rick De Stoop were shot dead in the basement of a Sydney dance club. Another Bandido was shot in the head but survived.

Bandidos from around Australia, including two undercover Victorian police, drove to Sydney for the funeral. More than 200 bikies, including members of the Lone Wolves, Outlaws, Black Uhlans, Highway 61, Finks, Life and Death, Outcasts, Nomad and God Squad motorbike clubs filed past for a brief moment to be with their dead leader.

One of the undercover cops bent to kiss the dead man and whispered into the casket: 'I'm a copper, you know'.

Dead men tell no tales.

The bikies were grieving, but business is business. The undercover police bought 1000 LSD tabs from one of the Sydney Bandido leaders straight after the funeral.

Fearing revenge killings for the death of the three Bandidos, police carried a series of raids on the bikies.

On December 11, more than 100 police in four states did co-ordinated raids, arresting 19 people and seizing drugs with a street value of more than $1 million. They also found enough chemicals to make amphetamines worth $6 million. Police also

Hit man Christopher Dale 'Rentakill' Flannery (right) being led to court by colourful detective Peter Spence.

Veteran homicide squad detective Rowland Legg pokes his tongue out while leading Flannery into court.

Alan David Williams (left) … tried to have NSW detective Mick Drury murdered.

Bluey and
Sandy …
killers
Gregory John
Brazel (above)
and Alistair
Farquhar
MacRae.

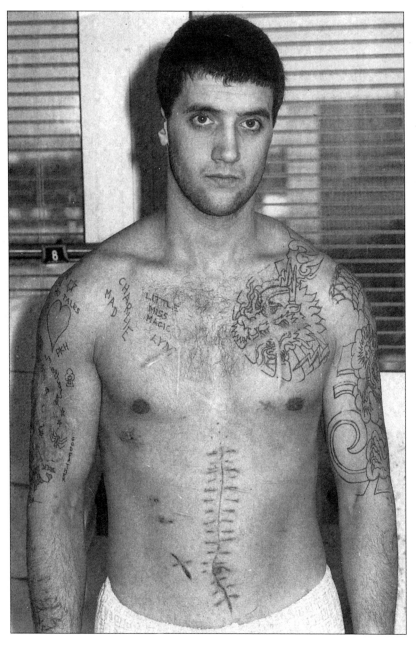

Mark Brandon Read. From standover man …

... to standup comic.

Kevin John
Barlow (above)
and Brian
Geoffrey 'Charlie'
Chambers ...
executed in
Malaysia.

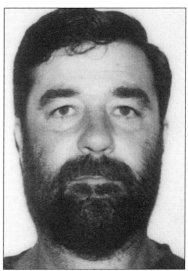

Jimmy Krakouer … a much better footballer than drug smuggler.
John William Samuel Higgs (above right) … major drug dealer.

Amphetamines chef
Bruce Alexander
Wilson … made
more speed than
Ayrton Senna.

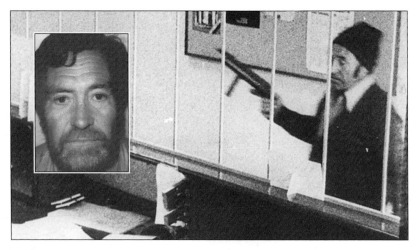

Aubrey Maurice 'Grandpa Harry' Broughill.

Hugo Alistair Rich.

After Dark
Bandit Peter
Kay Morgan
… Detective
Graham Creece
should have got
six months for
the tie.

Twin bandit …
Douglas Kay
Morgan.

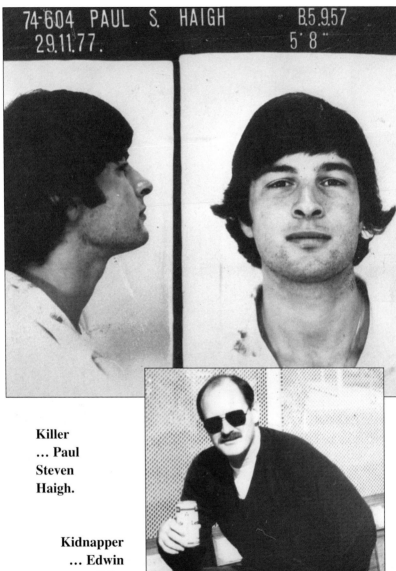

74-604 PAUL S. HAIGH B.5.9.57
29.11.77. 5' 8"

Killer
… Paul
Steven
Haigh.

Kidnapper
… Edwin
John
Eastwood.

Barry
Robert
Quinn …
killed by
Alex
Tsakmakis
(left).

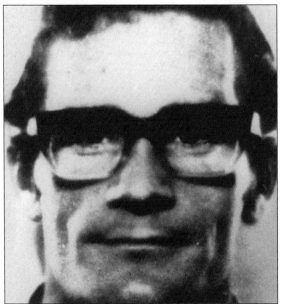

Russell 'Mad Dog' Cox and (top) police shotgun blasts in his car from when he was recaptured.

Jockey Smith
… he fought
the law and
the law won.

John Reginald
Killick escaped in a
helicopter with the
help of Lucy
Dudko.

Christopher Dean
'Badness' Binse.

**Lord Anthony Patrick
Andrew Cairnes
Berkeley Moynihan.
Bent Peer … is there
any other kind?**

**David Peter McMillan.
Private schoolboy
turned drug dealer.**

Postcard bandit Brenden James Abbott on the road and enjoying a scotch on the rocks (below). Now he's just breaking them.

seized firearms, including an AK 47 assault rifle and pen pistols. Former Rebels biker Bruce Malcolm Harrison, 39, and club member Constantine Georgiou, 33, were later charged and convicted of murdering Kulakowski, 41, and the other two Bandidos.

They were sentenced to a minimum of 28 years' jail.

James Paton Brandes

EVEN big tough Hells Angels have mothers and a Victorian detective owes his life to one. Bob Armstrong had worked on the bikie group for years and he was used to threats – most of them idle. But when his phone rang with a message from the mother of one of his targets, saying a hitman had been sent from the United States to kill him, he knew it was serious.

The man with the job was James Paton 'Jim-Jim' Brandes – a senior member of the Oakland, California, chapter.

The Oakland chapter was in debt to the Melbourne bikies and so owed a big favour. The locals had been providing the Americans with a key chemical in the production of amphetamines. The Americans could not get the ingredient but their Melbourne connection was able to smuggle the drug to California hidden inside large Golden Circle pineapple tins.

So when the Melbourne Angels wanted an outside expert to come in and do some dirty work, Oakland sent 'Jim Jim' Brandes, officially listed by the FBI as an enforcer and murderer.

When he flew to Melbourne on Qantas flight QF4 from California on August 26, 1982, police from the Angels taskforce, Omega, were there to meet him. Brandes was well-known in bikie circles, but he still brought his CV with him, in the form of newspaper clippings of his attempted murder of US policeman Bill Zerby. Zerby, like Armstrong, was a constant threat to the

Angels. On January 30, 1978, Brandes planted a bomb outside Zerby's home. Zerby routinely checked under his car for a bomb, but Brandes planted the bomb in a flower bed a few metres away. As Zerby leant to look under his vehicle, Brandes detonated the bomb by remote control.

It left Zerby deaf in one ear and with 75 per cent hearing loss in the other. It destroyed his career.

According to US records, Brandes was alleged to have killed a former Angel and two drug dealers as well as planning the attempted murder of two policemen.

When Brandes arrived in Melbourne, police found he had come well prepared. His luggage contained thumb-cuffs, a de-bugging device, instructions on how to tap telephones and a confidential copy of the US Treasury's forensic handbook. The book had special sections marked on explosives and a computer code index that could be used to tap into secret US files on outlaw motorcycle gang investigations.

Police grabbed Brandes as soon as he landed at Melbourne Airport and he was thrown into a holding cell. There can be little doubt that the Melbourne Angels had already sent details and pictures of his next target.

Bob Armstrong is a pleasant-looking man who looks like the late British comedian Benny Hill. When Armstrong looked into the cell to see the man sent to kill him, Brandes just looked over the top of his dark glasses and said, 'God-damn, you do look like Benny Hill.'

But it was the policeman who got the last laugh. Brandes was expelled within 24 hours. He committed suicide in an American prison nearly 20 years later.

Aubrey Maurice Broughill

WHEN police waited to ambush a gang wanted for a crime wave covering a thousand kilometres they knew at least one of the suspects would not do anything silly. With a criminal record spanning seven decades, Aubrey Maurice Broughill always knew when the game was up.

As 13 police ran towards the white Holden panel van in the outer Melbourne suburb of Keilor Downs, Broughill sat quietly in the passenger seat with a resigned look on his face.

He knew police would not have to hunt far for incriminating evidence – in the van was a stolen lawn mower from South Australia. With diabetes, high blood pressure and a bad heart, he knew there was no point making a run for it. To make matters worse, it was his birthday. He had just turned 73.

The arresting officer, Senior Detective John McIllree, of the stolen motor vehicle squad, said Broughill was polite and calm. 'He knew what it was all about. He'd been through it all so many times I don't think he was worried.'

He had first felt handcuffs in September, 1938, when he was charged with housebreaking and larceny at just 12 years old.

But even after being caught red-handed 61 years later, Aubrey Broughill remains under investigation – this time as a victim rather than a perpetrator. Unfortunately, he hasn't been able to help police in this matter. Not since his body was found in a flooded Wodonga quarry in February, 1999.

It was the end of the road for a career criminal who had kept a relatively low profile until 1961, when he stole a £4000 payroll from the Camberwell Town Hall and was sentenced to eight years. After his release in the mid-1960s he remained clear of the law. His jobs included working as a boundary rider in the outback and in the kitchen of an exclusive Sydney girls' school, he once told the authors.

He eventually returned to Melbourne and settled in Geelong with his much younger de facto wife, mother of his young daughter. Unemployed and in debt, he returned in 1978 to armed robbery. He was 52, and looked older.

He became known as the 'Beanie Bandit' when he robbed seven banks. He wore a beanie or cap and made no real attempts to disguise his identity. He always was a little careless in matters of concealment, having previously been convicted in 1951 of wilful exposure.

Even though police had excellent security pictures of the 'Beanie Bandit' they had no idea of his name until he robbed a State Bank in North Blackburn in March, 1979.

An off-duty constable saw him leave the bank and jotted down the registration number of the getaway car. Sadly, for Aubrey, he had decided to drive his own car, breaking one of the first rules of the robber's handbook.

The car registration showed his home address in Corio and members of the armed robbery squad actually beat him home that day. The old boundary rider wasn't one for speeding, especially when armed.

'He was an obliging old soul,' Senior Detective Graham Creece was to recall later. 'If there was such a thing as a gentleman bandit it was Aubrey. I felt quite sorry for him really, but you have to remember, he was still doing stick-ups that left victims traumatised.' He was sentenced to 15 years with a minimum of 12 when he pleaded guilty to all seven charges but, as a model prisoner, he received full remissions and was released after seven years in November, 1986.

He could not find a job. They was no great demand for a 60-year-old diesel fitter with a long criminal record covering most of the 20th century. Within two weeks he bought a giant .44 handgun for $1000 and was back in the bank business, robbing the Wantirna National branch of $11,000. 'I couldn't find work. I kept getting knocked back so I decided to get a gun and do a stick-up,' he was to explain.

At an age when many look at retirement, Aubrey felt he was in his prime. He flew to Brisbane for one job but found the pickings better in the south, robbing seven banks and two building societies in Melbourne over three months, escaping with more than $50,000. His biggest haul was $15,597 from a bank in Heathmont on December 17, his worst $410.50c in coins from a credit co-op on January 14, 1987.

Security pictures at the first bank identified the gunman as Broughill. Detectives believed he would hide out around Geelong. His career-long carelessness about disguises continued. During one robbery on the National Australia Bank in Seville he walked up to the accountant and produced his giant handgun. The accountant said, 'That's not funny, put it away.'

Broughill responded, 'No, that's not funny. This is the real thing.' But the veteran armed robber had got the normal bandit routine out of order. He was menacing the victim before putting on his disguise. While trying to persuade the sceptical accountant it was a real stick-up he put on his balaclava.

At least Aubrey had learned one trick. He decided to live near Traralgon, 200 kilometres east of where police were looking for him. Nicknamed 'Grandpa Harry' due to his age and because he used the same sort of gun as Clint Eastwood's *Dirty Harry* character, he set up a flat, but he knew not to take a long lease.

Police were warned through underworld contacts that Broughill had vowed to stay out of jail and was prepared to 'shoot it out.' But when they raided his flat in February, 1987, with guns drawn he did not resist. 'Geez, you gave me a scare before. I was expecting you sooner or later, I knew that I had to be caught … Yeah mate, I'll come quiet, I'll be no trouble.'

This time he was sentenced to 16 years with a minimum of 12. In February, 1994, he was given day release from Castlemaine prison to prepare for life on the outside, but when he got to Melbourne he had a few beers in a pub and missed the train back to jail.

He stayed on the run – or, more accurately, on the stroll – for two weeks before he was spotted by an off-duty prison officer and arrested. His barrister, Brendan Wilkinson, said Aubrey was one of his favourite clients. 'Inside jail he was king of the kids.' Wilkinson said Broughill kept blow-up photographs on his cell wall of security pictures from his armed robberies.

'He was always friendly. I suspect even judges liked him.'

When he was released from prison on November 27, 1995, he moved in with his younger sister. 'When he was with me he was never in trouble,' she said. 'What he did was wrong and he paid for it, but he was never a violent gangster type.'

But that December he left – 'He was always a roamer' – and headed off with a gang of younger criminals. Police now think the gang included at least two killers.

Police allege he was involved in a number of crimes, including car thefts and computer thefts.

After his arrest on January 12, 1999, police recovered two .45 calibre pistols that may have been used in other unsolved crimes in Victoria and South Australia.

He was charged with two counts of car theft and six of burglary and bailed on the condition he report twice a week to police. But, never one for the subtleties of the criminal justice system, Aubrey turned up just once before he disappeared again.

His body was found face down in a water-filled quarry in

Wodonga on February 17, 1999. Police believe he had been in the water a week.

Why he was there and how he died remain mysteries that may never be solved. The man who found his body, Reg Golding, said many locals didn't know of the disused quarry. It is not near a walking track and 30 metres from a rarely-used dirt road that runs off the Hume Freeway.

No car, possessions or campsite were found in the area. Why he was in the district or how he got there is a mystery. Wounds on the body fed suspicions of foul play. There were virtually no major injuries to the body except one – his testicles were missing. One theory was that they were eaten by eastern snake neck tortoises that live in the flooded quarry.

But some police believe he was tortured and killed by some of the South Australian criminals arrested with him. South Australian police ran an investigation into two of the gang, a father-son team, believing they murdered four men between 1992 and 1999.

Could Aubrey have been killed because he fell out with his former partners or did he go to the quarry – for no apparent reason – without a car or camping gear, fall in a flooded quarry and then have his testicles eaten by native animals?

The inquest into his death was inconclusive. Coroner John Murphy concluded: 'I am unable to say if any person or persons contributed to the death of the deceased or if his death was caused by natural causes.'

The case was handed back to local police because there were no obvious signs of foul play.

Murder, suicide or natural causes? None can be discounted, but Aubrey never seemed the type to go to so much trouble to kill himself.

Peter and Douglas Morgan

SOMETIMES it might be in the breeding. On December 15, 1949, when a man called Kay Morgan tried to rob the Eltham Commercial bank, he fired three shots at a bank officer who promptly used his branch handgun to return fire. Morgan tried to escape but crashed his getaway car into a ditch.

Morgan was arrested a month later and served nearly three years jail.

The interesting thing is that his twin sons, Peter Kay and Douglas Kay Morgan, were to become prodigious armed robbers – the ones known as the 'After Dark Bandits'.

They learned law-breaking from their father, who used the twins when they were 10 to act as lookouts while he carried out burglaries.

The brothers were to outdo their dad in crime. They were both building contractors and when the industry became depressed in 1977 they turned to armed robberies. They committed 24 raids on country and outer suburban TABs and banks in the next 23 months.

Police spent two years trying to identify what they thought was a single offender, but the two used such unusual tactics they were almost untraceable.

They used pushbikes and motorbikes or simply walked up to 50 kilometres through the scrub to escape from their robberies.

When Peter robbed the TAB in bayside Edithvale, he paddled four kilometres in a canoe in Port Phillip Bay and into the mouth of the Patterson River. Later, the home-made canoe was stolen. He was angry. You can't trust anyone.

Doug once had to cross a flooded river near Heyfield in Gippsland while escaping after a robbery. 'I lost my grip and was swept into the middle of the river. I nearly drowned,' he later told police.

The twins developed a policy of double hits – one raiding a country TAB, then the second hitting another branch in a nearby town about 20 minutes later. They would wear identical clothes to add to the confusion.

Police believed the one suspect was responsible and they would move their road blocks to the second town. Meanwhile the brothers would be hiking through the bush to safety.

The brothers tended to stop their robberies during daylight-saving months, leading police to the logical conclusion the 'bandit' preferred to strike near closing time, knowing darkness would cover his escape.

The truth was that the latter day bushrangers had another reason for not striking in summer: Peter Morgan was frightened of snakes.

On April 27, 1979, Peter Morgan was set to rob the CBC bank in Heathcote. He had robbed the bank twice previously, but this time he was confronted by the local policeman, Senior Constable Ray Koch.

Morgan shot the policeman twice, then forced him into the bank and robbed it of $11,000. He was arrested the following day by Senior Constable Rick Hasty in Bendigo. It was only then that police became aware there were two bandits.

Doctors needed to give Ray Koch about 15 litres of blood as they removed his spleen and repaired 17 punctures in his stomach and intestines.

But they were only able to recover one bullet, despite finding two entry holes. It was 10 days later when they discovered the second bullet was lodged in his heart, having moved there through a blood vessel. He survived the second round of surgery.

Douglas was sentenced to 20 years with a minimum of 17. Peter was sentenced to 21 years with a minimum or 18.

In April, 1983, Peter Morgan escaped from Pentridge but was recaptured a few days later. Douglas tried to escape in November, 1984, but stopped when a tower guard fired a warning shot.

They were eventually released and found work in the building industry.

Hugo Alistair Rich

HUGO Rich seemed to be a sharp operator in the stockmarket. He had the trappings of success, such as the South Yarra luxury apartment and a gold BMW, and he was a big spender.

Rich was a client adviser on share purchases, a computer expert developing a lucrative software package for the stockmarket and an importer of expensive amino acids for the fitness industry. He was also one of Australia's most prolific armed robbers.

In October, 1995, after a legal battle lasting nearly four years, Rich was finally convicted in the County Court of three armed robberies, including a raid on two Armaguard employees that netted $118,000, and three counts of stealing cars. Police claim he did eight armed robberies between April and December in 1991 that netted around $500,000.

Hugo Rich had invented himself in 1990. Before that he was Olaf Dietrich, a former associate of neo-Nazis and a man who had served five years for importing heroin after swallowing condoms filled with the drug.

Rich was a pest in court, an accused who could throw a tantrum if he felt matters were not going his way, but he helped refine the system to make it fairer for all. He made legal history when he fought his drug conviction all the way to the High Court.

He argued that he was denied natural justice because his case was allowed to continue when he was not legally represented. Ultimately, his conviction was overturned and a nationwide precedent was established that an accused must have a lawyer in major trials. It resulted in legislative changes in Victoria; all legal students are now taught the consequences of the 'Dietrich Case'.

When Dietrich was released on parole in April, 1990, he wanted to leave his past behind … and he did it with a stroke of a pen. He simply changed his name to Hugo Rich and his criminal record effectively vanished.

Rich had left school at 14 but he was a self-taught expert in the sharemarket, and managed to talk his way into a job with one of Victoria's most prestigious stockmarket firms, Vinton Smith Dougall.

The company made checks to ensure their new whiz-kid had no criminal record. It came back as a clean sheet.

A former colleague said no-one suspected Rich was leading a double life. 'He was quite a good broker, actually. He had a broad view of the world, which made him a reasonable adviser to clients. He was extremely easy to get along with and was a lot of fun. He said he had previously been involved in the real estate industry.'

Charismatic and confident, Rich impressed colleagues and clients alike. What he lacked in qualifications he made up for with a retentive memory and natural intelligence.

Young Dietrich had learned the hard way. Born in a refugee camp in Germany in 1952, he had come to Australia with his parents when he was nine. He left school at 14 to work in a grocery store, then a clothing shop, and became a window dresser. He married at 18 and had a baby daughter. He then became a successful insurance salesman but, after business turned bad, he had debts of $1.4 million and was later declared bankrupt, owing $360,000.

If he had used his ability as a salesman without crossing the criminal line he could have been wealthy ... and free. With a new identity and his natural talents he had the chance of a fresh start that many crooks claim to crave.

He joined the stockbroking firm as a trainee adviser in July, 1990, and was promoted the following month. He worked with the company until March, 1991, as a client adviser. According to police, he set up company accounts under names of his friends and bought and sold shares on credit. The company became suspicious when his purchasers did not relate to his client base. He left the office one night owing $33,000 and simply didn't return. The company hired a private investigator, who established that Rich was really Dietrich, a convicted criminal. The company immediately cut its losses and its relationship with the plausible confidence trickster.

Rich set up a new company, 3B Corporation, to establish a software program for the stockmarket. Police claim it stood for Bullshit Baffles Brains.

He loved his expensive lifestyle. He owned $2000 suits and a German bed that cost $6000. His BMW lease was $1500 a month, as was the rent on his apartment. He even had the mandatory socialite girlfriend. But, in the deep end of the financial pool, Rich's three Bs were not enough. He needed Backing, Brokers and Bucks.

Around the time that Rich began to suffer liquidity problems, police noticed a pattern in a series of armed robberies. In each, the getaway car was a 1988 or 1989 Ford Fairmont sedan stolen from the long-term car park at Melbourne airport.

Eventually, 18 cars had been stolen. Each theft involved removing the rear passenger side door lock, a method unique in Australia. The Fairmont gang did eight armed robberies from April 8 until December 2, with takings of $499,000.

Every time Rich's debts became pressing, he would swap his suit for his armed robbery kit – which contained guns, masks, radio scanners and ear pieces – and pull an armed robbery. Always fashion conscious, Rich insisted on wearing an Italian Trussardi jacket and a German silk ski mask, similar to those worn by Formula One drivers, during the stick-ups.

Most robbers would use the sleeve of a jumper or a football beanie as a balaclava but Rich wanted the best. The head of the armed robbery investigation, Graham Kent, said: 'He demanded the upmarket Fairmont and wouldn't steal the basic Falcon model because he felt it was beneath him.'

But the money wasn't just used to pay debts. Hours after robbing an Armaguard crew at Waverley Gardens of $98,000, he wandered into the exclusive jewellers Kozminsky and bought himself a present, a diamond ring valued at $17,000.

He then popped $150 into the prison account of his old friend, Russell Street bomber Craig 'Slim' Minogue and dropped off a computer for the convicted murderer.

He wasn't as generous with his fellow robbers. After the Waverley Gardens heist, he gave his partner Kevin Patrick Parker $20,000, claiming it was half the proceeds. Rich pocketed $78,000 as his 'half'.

In seven months, Rich spent $113,562, yet he had no known legitimate income. He made two payments of $10,000 each for computer software as part of his plan to develop a stockmarket program. Each payment was made within two days of a major hold-up.

The end came when police put the airport car park under

surveillance. They saw Rich and Parker stealing a Ford in the tell-tale manner. Rich and one of his partners, Claudio Crupi, were arrested after the robbery of two Armaguard guards at The Glen shopping centre of $118,000 on December 2. Detectives recovered $63,000 in cash.

Rich promised a legal battle that would drag on for years – a war of attrition that would bury police and prosecutors in paper. He tried hard, prolonging the case into a 51-day committal before a County Court trial that began in January, 1995. Twice juries had to decide whether he was fit to stand trial.

Psychiatrist Dr Norman Lewis examined Rich for the defence. He wrote: 'His confidence is nil. He cries frequently. He has compulsive thoughts. He is sad. Overall Hugo feels very frustrated.'

'My suggestion would be that this man should have a break of six months. He should be persuaded to do one case at a time. I believe that he should be persuaded to have help as much as possible in his case.'

'Ideally, I would agree with Mr Bernard Healey that the client should be allowed to be on bail away from jail to be able to settle down and then be able to defend his case properly. At the moment Hugo is too tense, persecuted and depressed to be able to think clearly.'

Rich had to be removed from the court when he abused Judge Geoff Byrne. At one point he yelled: 'I don't give a rat's arse. I'll drag it out a bloody year, I don't give a shit.'

During the proceedings he sacked his barrister and then called the judge 'you silly bastard', among other insults.

After being refused permission to leave court, he yelled: 'I'm telling you now, I want to leave now, you are not going to do this, rat, I'm telling you, all right? I will throw every c... in here, you ain't going to fucking do it, all right? You are driving me over the fucking hill, you hear that? You understand that? You want to shaft me at a time like this, wake up to yourself, you silly old dog. There will be no fucking jury, I want to leave. I don't want to fight nobody, but if you force me, that's what will happen. Now get out of here, before I lose it completely, get out of here. I'm telling you, get me out of here. There'll be no fucking arraignment, rat, I'm telling you. Now, please let me go before I lose it completely, I plead with you, please let me go. I'll get on my hands and knees, please let me leave here, before I lose it completely, I plead with you, let me out of here. I don't want to get into any more trouble, I can't handle the pressure, you understand that? Can't you see that? Are you blind as well as deaf?'

Rich delayed the trial any way he could. From his arrest until his conviction, there were 67 separate legal processes before the trial could be completed.

While giving evidence one bank teller was asked how he could be so sure that four years after the robbery he could identify Rich as the gunman.

He replied: 'I still see that face every night.'

The court was told that on August 9, 1995, while waiting for Judge Byrne to enter the court, Rich turned to Crown Prosecutor (later County Court Judge) Carolyn Douglas and said: 'One chance – one fucking chance. Watch your back. Every time you turn the car on of yours where you're living at the moment, I'm telling you, okay. I don't care how long it takes, 25 years, bitch. I'll have a go at you. One go, that's all I want.'

Alexander Robert MacDonald

HE was a Vietnam veteran, a bomber, prolific armed robber and escapee and he was used to getting his own way – even if he had to kill to get it.

MacDonald was serving 23 years for armed robbery and escape when he escaped from the Borallon Correctional Centre, near Ipswich in Queensland, in September, 1995.

In the next two years MacDonald robbed seven banks in three states and got away with a total of $320,800. He robbed country banks, taking hostages to try to prevent bank staff from activating security alarms, and then used his bush skills to camp out until police road blocks were removed days later.

MacDonald would hike hundreds of kilometres and drive thousands to rob banks in NSW, Queensland and Western Australia.

But his bush skills were not enough. He believed he needed a new identity and, two months after he escaped, he developed a cold-blooded plan to get one.

On January 26, 1996, he ran an advertisement in the *Herald Sun* for a man to join him on a mining expedition to Western Australia. He wanted a loner with no family so he could kill him and take over the victim's identity.

Ron Williams answered the ad. He happily provided his new 'boss' with documentation such as a driver's licence, deed poll papers and a birth certificate.

MacDonald used them to set up two accounts, one in a bank and the second in a credit union, which he used to hide his armed robbery funds.

He went to the Registry of Births, Deaths and Marriages to get a copy of the birth certificate he would later claim was his. He was to end up with a passport, driver's licence, five credit cards, a Myer card, ambulance subscription and private health insurance under Ron Williams' name. MacDonald was only three months older than Williams and they had uncannily similar faces and builds, although the escapee was slightly taller.

In February, they left Melbourne and drove across the country. They stopped to fish at Cheyne Beach, near Albany.

As they chatted, MacDonald undid his knapsack and quietly took out a 10-shot, sawn-off, semi-automatic .22 rifle. He shot Williams twice in the head and buried the body near the beach.

The former soldier had first seen the inside of a police cell when he appeared at the Brisbane Magistrates' Court in 1967, charged with theft. He was fined $100 and given a two-year suspended sentence. A month later he joined the army, and in April 1968, he trained as a gunner. He had two tours of duty in Vietnam, the second at his own request.

Police believe he learnt about explosives in Vietnam. His army experience made him self-sufficient in the bush and proficient with firearms.

In 1972, he was charged with 'unlawfully killing cattle', fined $50 and ordered to pay $80 restitution at the Caboolture Magistrates' Court in Queensland. Later that year he went absent without leave and was discharged a year later.

In March, 1978, the licensee of the Crown Hotel in Collie, Western Australia, found a plastic lunch box at the rear of the hotel with a note addressed to him. It said the box contained a gelignite bomb that had not been primed. It was a warning.

MacDonald demanded $5000 from each hotel in the district, threatening to bomb them if publicans didn't pay. He kept his word. Three months later a bomb exploded at the Crown, badly damaging the hotel, and it was only luck that stopped MacDonald being a cop-killer. A local policeman handled and examined the package only two minutes before it exploded.

MacDonald was arrested after he made an extortion demand for $60,000 from the hotels. He had built a bomb with four sticks of gelignite and had another 16 sticks hidden in the bush.

He was sentenced to seven years but served far less. Released in September, 1981, he headed to Queensland.

A year later, MacDonald was a wanted man. Between November, 1982, and March, 1983, he robbed several banks and service stations in Queensland.

During this time he began to take hostages. In three bank robberies he took a staff member with him to ensure police were not immediately called.

In February, 1983, he robbed the National Australia Bank at Mossman of almost $10,000. He took a staff member to the edge of a cane field and then vanished into the cane on foot.

Police believe he used a CB radio to contact a partner to pick him up.

In July, 1983, MacDonald was arrested in the Northern Territory as he was about to return to Perth. Later that month, he escaped from the Berrimah Jail while awaiting extradition.

In the escape he broke his ankle but still managed to travel four painful kilometres. He was forced to surrender after 12 hours on the hop.

He was sentenced to 17 years jail. In 1984 he was given another six months for attempting to escape from Townsville's Stuart Prison. Not to be deterred he tried to escape again, this time bashing a prison officer and trying to take a nurse hostage. He got another five years for his efforts.

He had served 12 of his 23-year sentence when he escaped while on gardening duty at the Borallon Correctional Centre, near Ipswich. On September 12, 1995, he simply walked off and camped in the bush near Gympie for about three weeks.

In October, 1995, he robbed a bank in Cooroy, near Noosa,

escaping on a pushbike with $15,000. He camped out for two nights to beat the road blocks. He used the money to get camping gear he planned to use for more robberies.

He robbed the Westpac bank at Airlie Beach in December, 1995. He got there by walking and hitchhiking and then camped in the scrub before escaping with $83,000.

After murdering Ron Williams, he used the same method to commit five more bank robberies in Queensland, NSW and Western Australia.

He was a disciplined, cool loner who went to great pains to cover his tracks. He lived quietly in Victoria as Ron Williams and would never pull a robbery there, instead travelling big distances interstate. He wanted police to believe that one of Australia's most wanted men was half-hermit, living in a tropical rainforest, coming out only to rob banks. No-one, he believed, would look near Melbourne for the Queensland bushranger.

He even had a fresh tattoo, a parrot with the name Megan, put on his left arm, covering an older tattoo that was recorded on his police record.

On June 2, 1996, he turned up at a Somerville boat yard near Melbourne, saying he wanted to buy an old cabin cruiser advertised in a magazine for $23,000. He didn't haggle. Three weeks earlier he had robbed the Yepoon Commonwealth Bank of $107,000.

He produced a $500 deposit to settle the deal on the cabin cruiser. He returned 10 days later with a briefcase. He opened it and took out $10,000 in cash. Three days later he was back with the same briefcase and another $12,500.

He was going through a messy divorce, he explained, and didn't want his ex-wife to know about the money, so he carried it in the briefcase. It seemed reasonable to the salesmen.

He was to spend $80,000 on the boat, *Sea Venture*, fitting satellite navigation gear and reconditioned motors. He paid $1200 cash to moor the boat at Yaringa and began to live on board. He told locals he was a builder and renovator who dabbled in prospecting.

In June, 1997, MacDonald told his friends he was short of cash and needed $10,000 before he could finish the boat and sail to the Solomon Islands where, he said, he was going to hook up with a friend.

He said he would head north on June 27. Police believe he was going back to Queensland for one more armed robbery before sailing out of Australia to freedom. He loaded up his Toyota with camping gear and provisions, then drove to the Hume Motor Inn in Fawkner and booked in to room eight.

While he was preparing to head north, the television program, *Australia's Most Wanted* screened a segment on the escapee-bandit. Police received a call to look for a Toyota four-wheel-drive in Melbourne's north. Within hours they found the car, registered to Ron Williams. A police check confirmed that Williams was a reported missing person.

A detective walked into the restaurant where MacDonald was sitting and immediately knew he was the wanted man. He was arrested by members of the Melbourne armed robbery squad outside the motel at 5.15pm on Thursday, June 26, with his brother. He was extradited to Perth, pleaded guilty to murder and sentenced to life in prison.

When police went through his papers, they found documents from the Christian Children's Fund. Here was an armed robber who could kill a harmless stranger and steal his identity without compunction, and yet sponsor a poverty-stricken child in South America.

You work it out.

CHAPTER 13

Bombers and Bad Men

The Russell Street Bombers

IT was the day before Good Friday, 1986, when a stolen car loaded with about 60 sticks of gelignite exploded outside Russell Street police station a few seconds past 1pm.

The famous Russell Street building was no longer the headquarters of the Victoria Police but it was still its heart. The serious crime squads and the D24 communications centre were still housed in the old centre, built in the style of Manhattan's Empire State Building.

The blast hurled debris more than 100 metres; some was later recovered from the roof of the Queen Victoria Hospital three blocks away.

The timing was designed to create the maximum carnage with the busy Magistrates Courts across the road breaking for lunch and Russell Street at its busiest.

The bomb injured 21 people, including Angela Taylor, the dux of her police academy class, who died 24 days later.

A taskforce of 30 police was assembled. The taskforce ran down hundreds of leads before receiving a call from a Gippsland woman with information about a man who had been building a bomb to blow up a police station.

Impressed by what she had to say, the investigators, on further inquiry, found that the man, Claudio Crupi, had been building a bomb on a kitchen table the day before the bombing. He had previously fired shots at police.

On the day of the bombing he left his Broadmeadows home about midday and returned an hour after the explosion.

He was interviewed by two members of the taskforce, Gary Ayres and Gordon Davie. Crupi admitted he had built a bomb but said it was a fake, designed to frighten Flemington police. Answering the second last question on the formal record of interview, he agreed that he hated police. The last question was where the police he hated worked. He replied: 'Russell Street.'

'I was satisfied he had done it,' Davie would later recall.

'I was instructed to charge him but I refused. I really believed he had done it but I didn't have a nexus between him and the bomb car.'

During the investigation, an experienced detective with the stolen car squad, Sergeant Arthur Adams, noticed that the bomb car and a second one used in a bank robbery in Donvale on the day of the explosion both had the chassis numbers drilled off. It was a technique known to be favoured by a prolific car thief called Peter Reed.

When police raided Reed's Kallista house on Anzac Day, 1986, they thought they were after the man who had supplied the car to Crupi.

They were wrong.

The man they were about to approach had a pathological hatred of all police. 'He blamed police for his mother going insane,' a member of the taskforce said later. During the raid Reed fired shots, hitting one of the detectives, Mark Wylie. Reed was also shot.

Police found evidence at the scene linking Reed and a Craig Minogue – a huge man with an appetite for family pizzas and violence – to the bombing. It was then that police realised Crupi was the wrong man.

'He (Crupi) is probably one of the luckiest buggers alive,' Davie said. 'If we had charged him, I believe there would have been sufficient evidence against him to gain a conviction.'

Police investigations then found that Stan Taylor, a career criminal and bit-part actor, had helped turn his younger accomplices from a group of car thieves and street criminals into a professional armed robbery gang.

Taylor was smart and ruthless. He combined the charm of a conman with the violence of a psychopathic gangster. Masquerading as a reformed man, he had recruited brothers Craig and Rodney Minogue and the dangerous Peter Reed. He was the puppet-master. His plan was to use the young hoods to commit armed robberies, but cut them loose if they were caught.

Later, police found that Reed was the most violent and vicious of the gang and that during armed robberies he had tried to humiliate female victims sexually.

One of the police who interviewed Reed was the urbane and charming Detective Senior Sergeant Ray Watson, from the armed robbery squad. 'It was like dealing with a rattlesnake, he would just hiss and spit and would not talk at all,' said Watson, a man used to persuading people to chat.

Taylor, desperate to cut a deal, admitted his involvement in all the armed robberies and implicated his former gang members in the bombing, but has always maintained he was not involved in the attack on Russell Street.

He said he knew they were going to commit the crime and was driving up the Calder Highway when he heard of the bombing on the car radio.

He claimed he returned to see Craig Minogue and Reed and confront them over what they had done. Yet he confessed that only hours after the bombing he committed an armed robbery on a Donvale bank with the two men, as if to capitalise on the confusion in the police force. According to Watson, Taylor couldn't wait to implicate the others in the bombing.

Police believed he had freely admitted to all the robberies so that he could claim he had made a full confession. This would later make his denial of involvement in the bombing more believable. It didn't work.

Another snake-oil merchant, Paul Hetzel, had already dumped on the group, and became the jewel in the Crown case.

Stanley Brian Taylor

CONVICTED of the murder of policewoman Angela Taylor and a series of armed robberies. Has always maintained his innocence and has said that, while he was involved in the robberies, he had nothing to do with the planting of the car bomb outside Russell Street.

Police believe he made the bomb and knew he had the expertise. He had previously made a smaller bomb inside Pentridge using a similar detonating device.

He was sentenced to life by Justice Frank Vincent. A prison source says a close family member won Tattslotto when he was inside. But his number has already come up. Sentenced to life with no minimum, he expected to never be released.

Craig William 'Slim' Minogue

SENTENCED to life for the murder of Angela Taylor. Given a minimum of 28 years. Sentenced to 14 years for armed robberies and 27 years for killing murderer Alex Tsakmakis in Pentridge's H Division.

The obese bomber launched into a fitness-and-diet campaign while inside. The once grossly fat enforcer now runs every day and has lost 45 kilograms. When he was in Pentridge he was given a ladder to complete unaccompanied building work inside the jail. It was later confiscated when authorities feared he might use it to escape. The new slender Minogue complained to prison authorities that a female prison officer would watch him during strip searches. He has also officially complained about the standard of prison food. Because of his weight loss he was given the nickname 'Jenny' Craig Minogue.

Release date listed as November 23, 2016.

Peter Michael Reed

WAS acquitted of the bombing, although police maintained it was his idea to bomb Russell Street. 'Reed was the baddest and the maddest of the lot,' one detective said. Police gathered evidence that in one armed robbery he wanted to throw a bound female victim into a swimming pool to drown her, until an accomplice dissuaded him. Reed shot and seriously wounded armed robbery squad detective Mark Wylie during a raid on Anzac Day, 1986. Police returned fire and wounded him. Reed was acquitted of the attempted murder of the policeman he shot but, ironically, convicted of the attempted murder of the police-man standing next to Wylie during the raid. He was also convicted over armed robbery and false imprisonment charges. He was sentenced to 13 years, with a minimum of 11, over the attempted murder of police and 12 years, with a minimum of eight, for the armed robberies.

Rodney Patrick Minogue

CRAIG'S 'little brother'. A follower who got caught up in the plans of the gang. Convicted of being an accessory to the bombing, he was later acquitted on appeal. He was sentenced to eight years, with a minimum of six, over armed robberies. Released from Beechworth on August 24, 1990. Believed to be living near Albury.

Paul Kurt Hetzel

A LONG-TIME criminal associate of Taylor's who gave key evidence for the prosecution against his former friends. Convicted of armed robbery charges but bailed and put into witness protection on February 11, 1987. Paroled on May 25, 1990. Moved to Western Australia but returned to country Victoria against police advice. Was given a new identity, including tax file number. Charged in Seymour and extradited to WA in 1993 over charges relating to the theft of gold valued at more than $100,000. Acquitted of charges and now believed to be living in the WA goldfields with his de facto wife, whose grand-daughter, Prudence Ann Bird, 13, disappeared from her Glenroy home in 1992. Police now believe she was murdered by an old mate of Hetzel's, who had been molesting the girl, and was concerned she might report him to police. Hetzel, who was prepared to inform on Taylor and his team, has remained silent about the murder of the teenager.

Maurice John Marion

HE remains the prime suspect for the murder of Prue Bird, whose body has never been found. Like his contemporaries, Stan Taylor and Paul Hetzel, Marion is a good crook but an evil man. And the closest thing Hetzel has to a best friend.

Marion's crime 'form' goes back to 1959, but in the 1970s he was the armed robber known as 'Bank Enemy Number One'. He later switched to less dramatic areas of crime, particularly gold-stealing. But there is a sinister side to the smooth-talking crook who, like Hetzel and Taylor, pretended to be rehabilitated and enthusiastically learned acting and make-up with a Pentridge theatre group, the Mess Hall Players. Marion was to land bit parts in television serials such as *Matlock Police*, *Bellbird* and *The Box* — and, later, *Blue Heelers*.

He liked acting but his real passion was sex with violence. He was convicted of rape and associated offences in 1975, and later also charged with 11 counts of abduction, two of indecent assault and of using a firearm to resist arrest. The abduction charges arose because in each robbery, he took a female hostage. One bank security photograph shows him standing over a cowering girl, pointing a pistol at her head.

He once raped a woman in her Sunshine home while her young children were in the house. He sexually assaulted a woman in East Keilor, then locked her in a cupboard, but left a fingerprint that led to his arrest. A prison psychiatrist described him as a 'Walter Mitty' type who indulged in vicious sexual fantasies.

A decade in jail cemented Marion's friendship with Hetzel, but it didn't curb his deviance. In 1986, he was charged with a bizarre assault following a car accident in which he coerced the other driver to a secluded spot near Geelong and tried to rape her. The terrified woman was saved by an off-duty police officer. When police searched Marion, they found a balaclava.

James Richard Finch

IN the early 1970s, some of the biggest names in the Sydney underworld decided to expand their lucrative nightclub protection racket into Brisbane.

On March 8, 1973, someone placed two drums of petrol at the foot of the stairwell into the Whisky Au Go Go nightclub and lit the fuse.

A fireball went up the stairs, creating a cloud of carbon monoxide that killed 10 men and five women on the dance floor. Another 20 people sitting at tables survived by smashing windows and escaping.

Sydney crime boss Lennie McPherson denied he was trying to move in on the nightclub, but two men connected with him, John Andrew Stuart and James Richard Finch, were later arrested and charged with the murders.

Stuart had once shot at an enemy of McPherson and James Richard Finch served seven years for shooting at Sydney hitman Johnny Regan. They were considered loyal soldiers who would do what they were told.

Both Stuart and Finch were to maintain their innocence, claiming they were framed by NSW and Queensland police who fabricated evidence to get a conviction.

There was little objective evidence in the case. Stuart said he was told by the Sydney criminal group to front the takeover bid on the nightclub scene. He said if he had refused he would have been killed. Finch claimed he was at home in bed at the time of the fire.

A jury would not believe them. Finch claimed that an unsigned confession he was supposed to have made was written by police.

He said the confession was slipped into his top pocket while he was handcuffed by a detective who said 'cop that'. He claimed he grabbed it with his teeth and spat it out.

One of the police who was present when the alleged confession was made and typed was a rising star from the NSW police force who flew from Sydney to help the investigation.

He was a man with a reputation for getting results. His name was Roger Rogerson, later sacked and found to have an uncomfortably close relationship with Sydney crime figures, including Lennie McPherson.

Both Finch and Stuart swallowed nails and sharp objects during their trial in protest. They got publicity, and indigestion, but the jury remained unimpressed.

Finch went on a 35-day hunger strike. At another time he was found in his cell holding a finger he had chewed off his hand. He held prison officers at bay for four hours during a protest on the roof of the Boggo Road jail with a metre-high sign claiming he was innocent.

In 1984, the Reverend Andrew Morton, an international expert in stylometry – the scientific examination of speech patterns – concluded there was only a one in 236,472 chance that the wording in the confession was Finch's original words. A key piece of evidence was the statement by fellow prisoner Arthur Murdoch that Finch had confessed to him. He received part of the $50,000 reward, but later retracted his statement in a sworn affidavit.

Stuart died in his cell on January 1, 1979, from inflammation of the heart. Before the Whisky Au Go Go massacre he had warned police and Brisbane crime journalist Brian 'The Eagle'

Bolton, that a firebombing was imminent but his message was ignored.

By the 1980s the conviction of Finch, based largely on the controversial unsigned confession, became an Australia-wide cause, taken up by Friends of Finch, the National Freedom Council and Lindy and Michael Chamberlain.

The ABC current affairs program *Four Corners* won a Walkley Award for a story exposing inconsistencies with the prosecution. Defence barrister, Jeffrey Spender, maintained his concerns about the conviction when he was appointed a Federal Court Judge.

In 1983, Finch married a terminally-ill woman, Cheryle Cole, who continued to fight for his release.

He kept birds and became known as 'The Birdman of Boggo Road'. He became a model prisoner and a fitness fanatic. Tired of a diet of nails and fingers, he became a vegetarian.

He spent 15 years in jail before he was finally released and deported to his native Britain in 1988.

There, he admitted that he was guilty and that his freedom campaign was based on lies. He said it was 'time to end all the bullshit.'

He maintained the unsigned confession was fabricated but added, 'I would have done the same if I was a copper.'

CHAPTER 14

Kath's Crew

Kath 'Granny Evil' Pettingill

IF Kath Pettingill had been barren, one of Australia's most prolific and notorious crime dynasties would never have been established. 'Kath', as she is universally known, had six sons and a daughter. All had criminal records and three of her sons were to die young – though not necessarily prematurely.

The eldest was Dennis Bruce Allen, known as Mr Death, who was a suspect in 11 murders, and managed to keep out of jail by becoming a valued police informer. And a valuable one ... it was suspected that, as added insurance, he also paid a corrupt cell of detectives for protection.

Not content with her own six sons, Kath virtually adopted another young man. It was a bad move for Gregory Vivian Pasche, who was stabbed to death and whose body was dumped in Olinda, in the Dandenong Ranges east of Melbourne, in 1983. Police believe he was murdered in a drug dispute involving Dennis.

But Kath did not need to live off the reflected 'glory' of her offspring. She was the most influential woman in Melbourne's underworld in her own right. She even released her own book, appropriately titled, *The Matriach*. But, to police, she was always known as Granny Evil.

Few could read the currents of the underworld like Kath. She had worked as a madam, a drug dealer and had provided aid and comfort to many of Australia's heaviest gunmen.

She was a target of a police undercover sting operation that revealed that while she made at least $4000 from one deal, she still was using Salvation Army emergency petrol coupons to fill the car she used to run her drug trafficking business.

Even though she was making good money from bad drugs, old habits die hard and she remained an active shoplifter. Once, she told friends, she stole a toy dinosaur for one of her grandchildren. She slipped it under her clothes, next to her armpit. As she tried to pay for other items at the checkout, the stolen toy began to slip and Kath had to squeeze to make sure it didn't fall. The pressure made the soft toy let out a growl. Kath pretended she had a bad case of wind and was making the growling noise herself. It worked. No store detective was prepared to confront an elderly woman making noises like an extra from *Jurassic Park*.

Another shoplifting trip resulted in a haul of cosmetics and lingerie later sold at a discount through a suburban massage parlour. The grandmother took to wearing a see-through crochet white top in what she thought was a bold fashion statement.

In her younger days Kath had a string of lovers including – it was rumoured – a police sergeant whose sexual antics were recorded on a listening device. Rumour also had it he wasn't the only policeman to succumb to Kath's seductive ways. It's just that the others weren't taped on the job.

Kath's survival instinct meant she was nearly always on

guard. She was taped patting down an undercover detective she thought was a drug dealer. 'Dennis never trusted me 100 per cent and I never trusted him 100 per cent, and he's my son,' she once admitted. She had one eye shot out by a woman in October, 1978. Police with a knowledge of ancient mythology and a black sense of humour later named an investigation into Kath's criminal empire Operation Cyclops.

Dennis and another of her sons, Jamie Pettingill, who was then just a teenager, committed an armed robbery at the United Kingdom Hotel in Clifton Hill. During the raid a barman was shot and later died from a blood clot.

Police threatened Pettingill with a murder charge unless he talked. Jamie told them he knew they were bluffing because he had read a story in the paper that the evidence would not sustain a homicide prosecution.

In May, 1985, he bombed the Coroner's Court as a warning to prospective witnesses in an inquest that could have implicated Dennis in the murder of a prostitute called Helga Wagnegg. A few days later, Jamie died of a drug overdose.

Two other sons, Victor George Peirce and Trevor Pettingill, were charged and acquitted with two other men of murdering two police, Steven Tynan and Damian Eyre in Walsh Street, South Yarra, on October 12, 1988.

The star witness against the four suspects was Jason Ryan – Kath's grandson. Kath would turn up at court often wearing a T-shirt that read, 'Life's A Bitch. Then You Die.'

Dennis Bruce 'Mr Death' Allen

DENNIS Bruce Allen was a suspect in 11 killings yet he was never convicted of murder. The man they called Mr Death managed to buy freedom.

He fed police information to stay out of jail and, it was often said, gave more than 'mail' to some detectives. Allen's mail came in brown paper bags. He was prepared to pay friendly police cash to be warned about any investigations into his empire. Unfriendly ones got even more.

It was, from a criminal viewpoint, money well spent. Allen made between $70,000 and $100,000 a week from drugs and was on bail for 60 different offences in the early 1980s. The sureties alone were $225,000, then the price of several inner suburban houses, which were another of Allen's hobbies. He had more houses in Richmond than he had coppers on the take.

It was in one of these houses that Mr Death killed a Hells Angels associate, Anton Kenny, on November 8, 1985. He took the body into the garage and used a chainsaw to amputate the legs before stuffing the remains in a 44-gallon drum. He stopped in the middle of the job to have a beer because, he would later claim, dismembering bodies was surprisingly hot work.

The drum was dumped in the nearby Yarra River. Allen was later to tell homicide squad detectives where the body was, but blamed others for the murder.

A police taskforce believed he was the prime suspect in a fatal shooting, three suspicious drug overdoses, two missing persons cases and five confirmed homicides.

He was connected with the mistaken identity murder of Lindsay Simpson, who was killed on September 18, 1984, in Lower Plenty. Allen and Roy 'Red Rat' Pollitt, were supposed to kill a drug dealer called Alan Williams but shot Williams' innocent brother-in-law instead.

Many in the underworld claimed that Allen was a specialist at 'hot-shots' – giving drug addicts pure heroin so they would overdose. At one stage his heroin ring supplied nearly 100 people a day though an inner-city massage parlour.

After 19 years in crime Allen was raking it in. As well as the houses, bank records showed he was depositing $7000 a week in his bank accounts. He once bragged that he paid $15,000 to two top police to leak him information on a police investigation into his operations. With inside mail he was able to launch a counter-attack. He fired 10 shots into supposedly secret police surveillance posts that had been set up to monitor his activities near his home in the back streets of Richmond.

Shots were also fired at a policeman sitting in the Prahran police station. Investigators had no doubt who fired the shots – the policeman was involved in the investigation into Allen.

When Allen feared he would be killed because he was a police informant, two detectives gave him a bullet-proof flak jacket.

Although he had the social skills of a feral goat, Mr Death was sometimes seen in the company of the upwardly mobile. His seemingly endless supply of drugs allowed him to overcome his social inadequacies.

He used a small local hotel as his business headquarters, once chaining an enemy from a rafter in the ladies' lounge. He drank in the bar and every time he walked past he would beat the man hanging from the beam.

Others generously offered to help him with the beatings but, on this occasion, Allen refused to delegate.

Allen was charged with the murder of one Wayne Patrick Stanhope, although a body was never recovered.

In August 1984, Stanhope and Allen were drinking in his home when Allen produced a silver pistol and emptied it into his guest's head. The reason for the murder was never clear, although Dennis often didn't need a reason. One suggestion was that Stanhope changed a record without asking – another was that Allen had earlier seen a photo of Stanhope wearing a policeman's hat. Believing Stanhope was a police informer, he shot him.

Allen was not a sensitive new age husband. He once cut the throat of his wife, Sissy, and dumped her in the boot of a car. She survived, but must have regretted it. Allen used to chain her to the washing machine at night. She later committed suicide.

Allen, aged only 35, developed a rare heart disease and died in hospital on April 13, 1987.

In ancient Rome, wise men looked to the entrails of freshly killed animals to foresee the future or divine the truth. In Melbourne, when gangsters meet their maker, wise men look at the newspaper death notices, for the truth is often hidden among them. One of the many death notices for Dennis Allen read:

'Dennis the Menace with a heart so big. Sorry you're gone, you were such a good gig.'

'Gig' is underworld slang for police infomer.

Victor George Peirce

FOR more than 13 years, Kath Pettingill waited for the call she always knew would come – the call telling her that one of her sons had been shot dead.

It finally came at 9.45pm on Wednesday, May 1, 2002. Victor Peirce was dead – shot less than 30 minutes earlier in Bay Street, Port Melbourne, in what police suspect was a drug-related killing. It was a reasonable assumption, given that much of Peirce's life was drug-related.

Not that police were shedding any tears over the dead man. Peirce, his half-brother Trevor Pettingill and two family friends, Peter McEvoy and Anthony Farrell, had been charged and acquitted over the 1988 murders of two young policemen in South Yarra.

Constables Steven Tynan and Damian Eyre were ambushed

when they went to make a routine check on a car dumped in Walsh Street on October 12.

Investigators maintain the four suspects killed the police as a random revenge attack after Peirce's best friend, Graeme Jensen, was shot by armed robbery squad detectives in Narre Warren just 13 hours earlier.

The detectives said a group of criminals had formed a pact to murder two police in an ambush attack if police killed one of them. Any two would do; they would die because of the uniform they wore.

Ever since, Kath Pettingill has known how it would all end. 'Without a word of a lie, every day since Walsh Street I have expected this to happen to Victor or Trevor,' she said later.

She is no stranger to crime, violence or grief, now having lost three sons of her seven children.

But Kath was and is a realist. She knew that crime was a matter of life and death.

The day after Victor was murdered she said: 'I'm not asking for public sympathy; we'll shed our own tears. I'm going to bury him in peace.'

She said that although retired from crime she would be checking with old contacts to see who had killed Peirce. 'There is an old saying, You can run, but you can't hide.'

Like an old lioness losing her teeth, she was no longer capable of protecting her brood but she continued to growl. She said Victor had given up crime and had worked on the docks for four years to support his family.

'If this had happened to Dennis (his late elder brother) – well, fair enough, but not Victor. If I had been there I would have taken a bullet for him. He's got kids and grandkids.'

Following the Walsh Street murders, Peirce became the man police loved to hate.

After his Supreme Court acquittal D24 broadcast a message, 'All units are warned, keep yourself in control.'

On many station noticeboards was a cartoon. It showed a policeman face down being kicked by a group of so-called enemies, including the Government, media and judges. One of the figures was labelled 'Victor Peirce'. All of which explains why his mother feared he would one day die at police hands – and why she said so after his death. But, sometimes, reason prevails. Granny Evil now accepts that her boy was murdered by fellow gangsters.

One of the key witnesses against the Walsh Street suspects was Victor's wife, Wendy 'The Witch' Peirce, who was to give key evidence against her husband. But, before the trial, she changed sides and refused to implicate Peirce.

She was later jailed for perjury.

The Peirces were reunited after he was acquitted. The youngest of their four children, Vinnie, was named after the Walsh Street trial judge, Justice Frank Vincent. He was born in prison while his mother was still serving her perjury sentence.

The couple had an interesting marriage. Dennis Allen once offered to shoot Wendy in the leg to assist Victor win a bail application on compassionate grounds.

The odd thing was not that Dennis suggested it, but that Wendy considered going through with it. 'If I wasn't pregnant it would have been all right,' she explained. 'Dennis would have known how to do it without doing too much damage.'

When Victor was arrested for drug trafficking in 1985 he naturally wanted bail. Wendy, heavily pregnant at the time, deliberately urinated in court, announcing to the stunned judge that her waters had broken and she was having a baby. Bail was granted. The baby was born quite some time later.

At one point Victor and one of his brothers ran a profitable drug syndicate providing inmates with drugs. Victor was the outside man while the brother was inside with his captive audience of customers.

When Peirce was released from prison in 1998 after serving six years for drug trafficking, Wendy said she was confident he had finally reformed.

'He is not a monster. When he gets out we just want to be left alone. The public have the wrong idea of Victor. He is a family man with family values.

'He is one of the best fathers you could see. No one has anything to fear from us,' she said.

'He has had six years to think about it. He has a job lined up. I know that he is finished with crime. He just wants to live quietly with his family.

'We are going to make a new start. We are going to grow old together and live happily ever after.'

Her fairy tale hopes ended in Bay Street.

Pierce, 43, was shot in the chest and left to die in his 1993 maroon Commodore about 9.15 pm.

There are several reasons police believe the murder was planned and executed by an experienced team of two hitmen.

Although the killing was carried out in a busy street the pair did it quickly, without drawing attention to themselves.

The gunman appeared confident and calm. He stepped from the passenger side door of a light-coloured mid-1980s model Commodore and fired several shots into Peirce.

The killer then hopped back into the car and the driver took off towards Beaconsfield Parade, staying within the speed limit and obeying all road rules.

Police say the car was stolen and, as usual with getaway cars used by experienced criminals, picked because it was plain and unremarkable. No fat tyres, hot motors or garish stripes –

nothing a witness could remember. The suspect car was later found burnt out in St Albans.

Peirce had earlier had a coffee with his wife, Wendy, and their teenage daughter. The two had walked home just before Peirce was shot.

Port Melbourne was once the toughest suburb in Melbourne, the centre of activities for the notorious Painters and Dockers Union, which meant that much of Australia's semi-organised crime was run out of a few pubs in the area. But in recent years it has become a trendy location favoured by the new rich and white-collar workers who had migrated there to be close to the city and the fashionable inner-suburban scene.

But a new address does not always bring health and happiness. Peirce, his wife and children, had moved from a drab house in a plain street in Rowville to a more upmarket home in Port Melbourne. He had a job as a crane operator on the docks and wanted to be closer to work, where he often started on the pre-dawn shift.

The area has also become a favourite spot for major-league drug dealers. One was renting a bay-view apartment for $800 a week. Two others moved into the area in the previous 16 months.

In 2001 a group of police, football and media figures out for a long lunch chose a small hotel in the area with a reputation for top quality food and an impressive wine list. They were surprised to see Peirce enjoying the same establishment.

He liked the good life but always remained close to crime. He became a bodyguard for Italian crime figure and market identity Frank Benvenuto, who was shot dead in 2000.

Police have been told that Peirce took a contract to kill a man connected to the Melbourne cocaine industry. The man has alleged that Peirce fire-bombed his car.

He was also alleged to have been behind a car bombing at the docks.

He had wide gangland contacts which included Mark Militano, Frank Valastro, Jedd Houghton, Graeme Jensen and Gary Abdallah, all of whom were killed by police.

Detectives believe Peirce had moved into the pill and powder market – amphetamines, cocaine and ecstasy. The drug squad had seized a pill press used to make amphetamine-based fake ecstasy. The squad had been told that Victor Peirce had owned the press.

Shortly before he died, Peirce claimed that a man connected to the drug scene owed him $75,000. He left a message on the man's mobile phone – 'Ring the man with the glasses'. The man refused and was later spotted in a Melbourne strip club by two of Peirce's associates, who tried to abduct him.

They were about to stuff him in the boot of their car but they released him when they realised they had been seen.

One theory police are investigating is that Peirce was in Bay Street to collect money from a cocaine deal and was killed in an underworld rip-off.

While police claim Peirce was active in crime, financial checks completed after his death did not show him as being wealthy. Homicide squad detectives suggested to Wendy Peirce that she could apply for up to $50,000 in crimes compensation for her children for the loss of her husband.

Retired standover man turned author and celebrity speaker Mark Brandon 'Chopper' Read expressed little surprise at Peirce's death.

'I knew him since he was 14. I had nothing against him but he thought selling drugs was a legal occupation. These blokes have never worked out that there is no place for middle-aged gangsters.

'That's why I got out of it and got into the book caper. As we all know, the pen is mightier than the sword.'

Former undercover policeman Lachlan McCulloch, who infiltrated the Pettingill-Peirce clan, says they were a dangerous and unpredictable lot.

In the operation, code-named 'Earthquake', McCulloch bought amphetamines, cannabis and heroin worth more $130,000 from the group.

As a result, 15 people were arrested, including Trevor and Kath Pettingill. 'They were not smart people. Victor was a real low-life.'

McCulloch was also to arrest Victor Peirce for his smallest known crime – shoplifting a jar of instant coffee valued at $1.66.

'It was at an Asian grocers in North Melbourne,' McCulloch recalled. 'When we got there we found 10 Asians sitting on top of him. He wasn't going anywhere. I found him to be a dill. If he was organised crime, Melbourne's pretty safe.'

One detective close to the Walsh Street case said of Peirce's death, 'What goes around, comes around.'

Whoever killed Victor Peirce selected a light-coloured Holden Commodore for the job – the same type of vehicle used to lure Steven Tynan and Damian Eyre to Walsh Street, where the car was left with its bonnet up in the middle of the road.

Peirce was rushed to the Alfred Hospital, where desperate surgeons could do nothing to save him – just as they could not help Constable Tynan when he was taken to the same emergency room almost 14 years earlier.

In what has become a Melbourne tradition, the *Herald Sun* death columns are flooded with messages when a gangster is murdered. Some are sincere, others not so.

In the days after Peirce's murder, pages were filled with

notices from killers, armed robbers, cleanskins and the clearly deluded. Many referred to the deceased as a 'gentleman', which came close to false advertising.

One notice placed under the name of 'Chopper' Read was complete with a dig about 'keeping an eye out' for Kath – a none-too-subtle reference to her having an eye shot out years earlier. Read said he did not place the notice and was offended by suggestions that he would.

Another notice was from Vicki Brooks, Peirce's sister who gave evidence against him in the Walsh Street trial. Even Kath's fellow bingo players at Venus Bay put in their condolences.

In her notice, Kath said, 'You made me proud to be your mother. You were the perfect son.'

One death notice was supposedly placed by surveillance branch police, known as 'the dogs', who had followed and photographed him for years. It read: 'Victor. We were behind you day and night. All that are left are the photos to make us laugh. The K9 Boys.'

Graeme Russell Jensen

AS a criminal, Graeme Russell Jensen was far more influential dead than alive. His death was at least partially responsible for police changing their tactics in dealing with dangerous suspects. This was because he was shot dead by armed robbery squad detectives in controversial circumstances.

At the time of his death Jensen was unemployed, single and 33 years old. Born in Carlton on May 7, 1955, he was the youngest of five children. He lived with his parents until they separated when he was seven. He moved with his mother to Tongala, where he went to school for two years.

He was shunted around, living at different times with his

sister, mother and father. He went to the Cambridge Street State School in Collingwood until sixth grade and was 11 when he was charged with stealing from taxis.

He was charged with eight counts of gross indecency, but was a victim rather than an offender – the person involved was an 18-year-old male friend of the family.

A policeman who dealt with Jensen in the early years wrote: 'He is inclined to be smart and is apparently a show-off.' At his Children's Court hearing, a welfare officer gave evidence that he was an outstanding athlete and a good student. He was given two years' probation.

He went to Prahran High School, South Melbourne Technical School and Tally Ho Boys School until he was 14. He was made a ward of the state in April, 1969.

Jensen left school in third form. One of his few legitimate jobs was at the Excelsior broom factory; it lasted only two weeks. It didn't worry him greatly because, even as a teenager, he saw his long-term career in crime.

At 14, he and four others used coat hangers to pull six fur coats, valued at the then considerable sum of $2468, through a letter slot in the door of a Melbourne shop. History does not record whether it was a large slot or whether the fur coats were particularly small.

The arresting officer noted: 'Offender is a ward of the state and at this early age shows every indication of becoming a hardened criminal.'

At the age of 15, Jensen became one of Australia's youngest bank robbers when, armed with a rifle, he raided the National Bank in Fitzroy of $1363. The arresting officer this time left a cryptic note: 'This lad, in my opinion, will in the future become a very active criminal. He requires firm handling.'

After a minor burglary when Jensen was a teenager, police

said: 'Will always be in trouble and will never tell the truth. Will become a very dangerous criminal.'

At the age of 18, Jensen was involved in a brawl at a Carlton hotel. That wasn't unusual in itself. But, later, he and another man returned and threw a hand grenade at the pub door, injuring three men. Police claim the victims survived because the explosive power of the grenade had deteriorated with age. Jensen was charged and convicted, but the conviction was later overturned on appeal.

A year later he was in another pub brawl, which spilled on to the street. The passenger of a car was hit with a bottle and his injuries kept him off work for eight weeks. Jensen was convicted and sentenced to 14 days' jail. The arresting officer made a series of scathing observations. 'He has nothing in the world in the way of assets. Is a complete no-hoper who does as he likes, whenever he likes. If a prediction has to made about him, then one day he will kill someone or finish up being killed. He will always be in trouble for violence and he is an arrogant bash merchant after a bout of drinking. Will always come under notice.'

In 1977, Jensen was arrested in Canberra over three armed robberies totalling $70,000. The arresting officer, the respected John Weel, observed prophetically: 'Offender a very dangerous type who, according to his girlfriends and other persons, always slept with his shotgun loaded under his bed. When arrested also had the weapon fully loaded in his possession. Warning, will finish shooting a policeman or some other person he has a dislike to if given an opportunity. Treat with caution.'

Jensen was sentenced to 10 years and six months with a minimum of eight for the armed robberies. He was also jailed after he attacked another man with a cricket bat.

He told Weel he would be the model prisoner when he was inside so that he would eventually be placed in a low-security prison from which he could plan his escape. He brashly told the policeman he would send him a card when he bolted. He was as good as his word. When he escaped he dropped a note to Weel that simply said. 'I told you so – Graeme.'

He later robbed the National Bank in Essendon with two other criminals, getting away with $9000 before being caught and sentenced to nine years. He was released in May 1987.

Despite his reputation for violence Jensen was popular in the underworld. One of his best friends was Frankie Valastro, an armed robber and drug dealer. Valastro was shot dead by special operations group police only four weeks after Jensen was released from prison.

According to underworld figure Lindsay Rountree, Jensen and his friend Victor Peirce were convinced police were systematically killing bandits. This view might have been because of paranoia caused by amphetamine use, combined with an unusually high number of shoot-first, ask-questions-later killings at the hands of the Victoria Police.

Rountree claimed the two decided to fight back, planning to kill two police every time a known criminal was killed by lawmen. Perhaps Peirce would not have been so staunch if he had known that his wife, Wendy, had been having an affair with the handsome Jensen.

Jensen was the prime suspect in a number of armed robberies. He became the target of an armed robbery investigation and there was little doubt he was involved in planning a series of bank jobs. He was photographed by surveillance police checking out several banks as potential targets.

But when police went to arrest him he was an innocent man. He was to be arrested over the armed robbery of a Brunswick supermarket on July 11, 1988, in which security guard Dominic Hefti was shot dead. One of the robbers was also shot. Police were confident the blood at the scene would prove a match to Jensen's. They were wrong.

On October 11 an arrest team of eight armed robbery squad detectives gathered to grab Jensen. They believed he would be armed and dangerous.

Jensen was living at the time with Sandra Faure, the wife of well-known armed robber and killer, Keith Faure, in a nondescript home in Narre Warren. When out of jail, Jensen was a late riser. On his last day he had breakfast in bed, read the newspaper and then watched the midday movie *The Postman Always Rings Twice*.

But even gangsters have chores and this day Jensen needed to pick up a new spark plug for his lawn mower.

The armed robbery squad team was waiting for him to move and planned a 'box' intercept using three police cars, the idea being that two cars would pin each side and the third would block the rear. They were to rely on the five Ss – surveillance, speed, surprise, superiority of numbers and safety.

The police were waiting in nearby streets when they got the word. The target was on the move. It was 3.20 pm.

It took Jensen only three minutes to drive 2.4 kilometres to the shop – Mower City. Two surveillance police wandered into the shop to confirm the target was Jensen.

When Jensen hopped back into his blue Commodore station wagon, two of the three police cars barrelled in, but the third was slowed by passing traffic and was a few seconds late. It was to prove a fatal delay. Jensen had a second or two to gun the motor and hit reverse. Police, armed with handguns and shotguns, later gave sworn evidence that they saw Jensen had a firearm on his lap.

They yelled at him to stop. He clipped a car as he reversed out of the Webb Street shopping strip, then flung the automatic into forward. This meant he had to pass the police again as he sped off. He didn't make it and was shot dead.

The gun later found in his car was a sawn-off, bolt-action .22 calibre rifle. It was not loaded and the magazine was upside down so that it could not function. Some people later claimed that a known gunman like Jensen would not be armed with such a poor weapon.

One of the detectives had gone to the boot of a police car after the shooting and taken out a towel which he gave to another detective. He said later he got the towel to cover Jensen's head after he had been shot.

It was later claimed the towel was used to hide the gun taken from the police car to plant in Jensen's station wagon. The detectives denied this.

Unfortunately, the towel was later destroyed without being tested for gunshot residue. The coroner dismissed the planted gun theory saying, 'There is no evidence to support this suggestion.'

Regardless of the truth about the circumstances of Jensen's death, it was to have tragic consequences. The next day two young uniformed police, Steven Tynan and Damian Eyre, were gunned down in Walsh Street, South Yarra, in what detectives maintain was a payback for Jensen's death.

The eight detectives involved in the Narre Warren raid were later controversially charged with murder. Eventually, the charges against seven of them were dropped. The detective who fired the fatal shots was finally acquitted in the Supreme Court on August 9, 1995. It was 2494 days after Graeme Jensen had left home to buy a spark plug.

Police training procedures were later reviewed and Operation Beacon was launched to try to prevent fatal confrontations with police.

CHAPTER 15

Al's Pals

Alphonse John Gangitano

ALPHONSE John Gangitano was a private schoolboy from a respectable family, but he always wanted to be a gangster. He had some of the prerequisites for the job, but discretion wasn't one of them.

Whereas clever crooks do their best work in the shadows, Gangitano was always drawn to the bright lights of Melbourne's Italian precinct, Lygon Street.

Just as Lygon Street draws tourists by selling itself as the real thing, so did Alphonse. Glamorous, well-dressed, charming and violent, he played the role of an underworld identity as if he had learnt it from a Hollywood script.

The sycophants would call him the Robert De Niro of Lygon Street, but his enemies – and there were many – called him the 'Plastic Godfather'. Gangitano was charged with offensive behaviour when he was 19 and, over the next five years, he graduated from street offences to serious violence.

A confidential police report warned of the growing danger posed by Gangitano and his followers, known as the Carlton Crew. 'They approach (police) members and assault them for no apparent reason. They are all extremely anti-police and are known to be ex-boxers. They often frequent in a group numbering approximately 15. They single out up to three off-duty police and assault them, generally by punching and kicking them. On most occasions in the past, members have been hospitalised due to injuries received from these persons.' Gangitano was described as 'extremely violent and dangerous.'

He was charged with hindering police, assault by kicking, assaulting police (three counts), resisting arrest, and other crimes of violence. Each time, the charges were thrown out.

His ability to beat charges, no matter how seemingly airtight, helped build his reputation. Some suggested he had influence inside the police force.

Before long, he started to take on the trappings of a crime boss. He wore expensive clothes, read biographies of Al Capone and watched videos such as *The Godfather*.

He bought into a profitable baccarat school in Lygon Street and some say he either part-owned or ran protection on Melbourne's lucrative two-up school.

Police intelligence reports listed him as a big punter and suspected race-fixer in Victoria and Western Australia. He was alleged to have regularly sold guns inside an old Brunswick nightclub.

In the early 1990s, many police were confused about Gangitano. Their informer network reported he was a major player in the underworld, yet several investigations found he was more style than substance.

He was seen with experienced and respected criminals. In the underworld you can never have too many contacts. One of his new friends was Australia's best safe-breaker, who shared Gangitano's interest in punting on racehorses. He also grew close to three brothers who controlled much of Lygon Street and had links with colourful Perth identities.

It perplexed police. Why did the big names of crime tolerate the dangerous and unpredictable new boy?

Gangitano regularly attracted publicity and headlines that made senior police demand reports from their organised crime experts. It was not good for business. In the underworld, fame rarely brings fortune.

Gangitano was handsome, could be charming, and liked to think he was well-read. He was a regular at concerts and became involved in managing fighters. He was regularly photographed and tried to court Melbourne celebrities.

But a heavy group of criminals, headed by Mark Brandon 'Chopper' Read, was unimpressed. Read, who had not yet put down the gun in favour of the pen, planned to use landmines to kill Gangitano at his eastern suburbs house but scrapped the plot because of the likelihood of others being killed.

Shortly before Read was released from prison in 1991, an associate of Gangitano's went to Pentridge with a peace offer. But police say Gangitano had a back-up plan: he had also placed a $30,000 contract on Read's head.

When Read was released in 1991, Gangitano took his family to Italy for a long holiday. In fact, he did not return until January, 1993, when Read was back in custody on another shooting charge.

On February 6, 1995, Gangitano was at a wake in Wando Grove, East St Kilda. At 4.40am, standover man Gregory John Workman and an agitated Gangitano went outside to continue an argument. Workman was shot seven times in the back and once in the chest. Two sisters at the wake made statements implicating Gangitano and were put into witness protection. It should have been a huge breakthrough but police failed to see they would lose their key witnesses by not taking good care of them. They were shunted into a small cabin in a Warrnambool caravan park and left alone with their thoughts.

Isolated and frightened, they rang one of Gangitano's closest associates, Jason Moran, who arranged to meet them in Melbourne next day. It was exactly two months after the murder.

According to police, Moran advised one of the women that if she gave evidence she and her family would be killed. He then took the sisters to his solicitor, Andrew Fraser, and to another lawyer's office where the witnesses made an audio tape recanting their original police statements.

Gangitano paid for them to fly out of Australia on May 20 to England. The murder case collapsed. Eventually, Gangitano's lawyer billed police $69,975.35 over the failed prosecution.

Police couldn't get Gangitano on the 'big pinch', so they decided to embark on a campaign of death by a thousand cuts. His Eaglemont house was raided. Police said he suffered nasty head injuries in the raid because he resisted arrest.

Over a period of months, he was charged with assault, refusing a breath test and illegal possession of firearms. He spent time in jail and was bailed on a night curfew. The myth that he was untouchable began to fade.

When reporting for bail, he saw an unflattering police Polaroid picture on his file. He paid for a professional shot and took it to the police station to upgrade the mug shot.

It was 9pm on January 16, 1998, when Big Al rose from a cat-nap. Earlier that day he had been to court for the preliminaries over assault charges arising from a billiard cue attack on the patrons of a King Street bar. He and Jason Moran were facing charges from the assault on December 19, 1995, which left 13 people injured. Sometime after 10pm his old friend and mentor Graham Allan Kinniburgh turned up for a chat at Gangitano's pleasant home in the outer suburb of Templestowe.

Gangitano was downstairs at a kitchen table. His de facto wife and two children were visiting relatives. From where he sat, he could see down the hallway to the front door, which was open to let in the cool night breeze. He could see out through the mesh of the second security door but no-one could see in.

It was still 18 degrees at 11pm and Gangitano hadn't bothered to get dressed in street clothes. He was wearing only a pair of shorts when a second visitor arrived – another well-known associate of Gangitano. What wasn't well-known was that the visitor was carrying a concealed handgun.

Detectives believe Gangitano would have grabbed a robe or dressed if he was about to have a business meeting. They say the man at the door was either a close friend or a subordinate – someone he didn't feel was worth impressing.

Kinniburgh told police Gangitano was on the phone when he arrived. He claimed that Al said he was about to have a meeting and had asked Kinniburgh to come back in 30 minutes.

He said when he returned from getting a packet of cigarettes at a nearby store Alphonse was on the floor, bleeding to death from gunshot wounds.

Police say Kinniburgh was lying and was present when Alphonse was shot. They believe the second visitor and Gangitano argued and that the man pulled a gun and shot him three times. They think Kinniburgh, shocked, ran to the closed front security door and tried to burst through, cutting his hand on the strong mesh. They say he calmed down enough to slip upstairs to check the security video system – and found it was turned off. Blood matching Kinniburgh's was found on the upstairs banister.

Police are convinced the second visitor was Al's once loyal lieutenant, Jason Moran.

The fact and fantasies of Gangitano's life and death will never be separated. He gave the impression of wealth, but he had serious debts. He appeared unworried by constant police investigations and court appearances, yet his autopsy showed traces of the prescribed anti-anxiety drug Diazapam.

He owed his lawyer George Defteros $100,000 and had about $2000 in a bank account. He was a paper millionaire, with assets valued at just over $1.1 million, but with debts of more than $300,000. His biggest asset was a property in Lygon Street his parents had left to him and his sister. In other words, he owned half a shop, and hadn't paid off his mortgage. That hardly makes him Al Capone – apart from the manner of their respective deaths.

There were more than 200 death notices for Gangitano in the underworld's newspaper of record, the *Herald Sun*. As has become a gangster tradition, hundreds packed St Mary's by the Sea Catholic Church in West Melbourne for the funeral.

Gangitano referred to himself as a property developer, although the occupation listed in his will was 'Gentleman'.

His murder remains unsolved. No-one is holding their breath.

Graham Allan Kinniburgh

FOR a man who is an expert in at least two demanding professions, Graham Allan Kinniburgh is a modest man. He has much influence in the Australian underworld but has always been shy about acknowledging his status.

Kinniburgh is what could be called a safe man. He is reputedly highly skilled at opening other people's safes if they lose their keys or forget their combinations. And he is also a safe punter, gossip has it, one of the few regular bettors who stays ahead of the game.

Not that he would ever talk publicly about his prowess in either area. Never one for flashy suits or cars, Kinniburgh would prefer never to see his name in headlines. Like members of the other old Melbourne establishment, he considers publicity vulgar and doesn't want it.

He has always preferred to conduct his business in private, though what that business is few really know. His criminal record understates his influence of the crime world. It lists offences of dishonesty, bribery, possession of firearms, escape, resisting arrest and assaulting police. But criminal records list only an offender's arrest history – his failures. One definition of a successful criminal is one that tends not to get caught.

Police became convinced that Kinniburgh, known as 'The Munster', was close to the infamous magnetic drill gang, responsible for many of Australia's biggest safe break-ins.

While Kinniburgh could afford imported suits, he mostly prefers the casual clothes of an off-duty dock worker, but in middle age he has acquired some expensive tastes and is a regular at the exquisitely expensive Flower Drum restaurant in Melbourne's Chinatown.

Kinniburgh now lives in a large, tasteful house in a quiet street in one of the better blocks of the prestigious Melbourne suburb of Kew, the natural haunt of doctors, lawyers and stockbrokers.

In 1994, his son married a girl from a well-to-do Melbourne family. After the wedding, it was just a short walk from St Peter's Anglican Church to the reception in Melbourne's grand old establishment hotel, The Windsor.

During the stroll, an alert observer might have noticed photographers taking pictures not of the wedding party but of the guests. They were intelligence police looking to upgrade their files. As is the case in many weddings, the groom's friends and family had little in common with the bride's group.

One friend of the bride was mildly startled when introduced to Kinniburgh, not so much by the man himself as by the four who were standing around him.

'They were all wearing "Ray-bans" and it was 10 at night,' she said later.

Dressed in a dinner suit, Kinniburgh welcomed his 100 guests with a speech that left an impression. One guest, who didn't know The Munster's colourful background, later said: 'He reminded me of Marlon Brando.'

Weddings are emotional times and this one was no different. A guest of the bride, a millionaire property developer, was dancing with a woman invited from the groom's side.

A friend of the groom, released from prison days earlier after completing his sentence for biting a man's ear from his head, told the friend of the bride that he would be shot if he didn't immediately exit the dance floor, stage right.

The property developer immediately lost interest in the music and retired to the bar. It was that sort of night.

Kinniburgh became a close friend of Alphonse Gangitano – a relationship senior police found hard to understand. Kinniburgh was wealthy but tried to hide it – Gangitano was struggling but deliberately cultivated an image of affluence. Kinniburgh kept a low profile, preferring to conduct his business in private. Gangitano loved the headlines, although his profile meant he was always the target of police investigations.

It was the relationship with Gangitano that would force the reticent Kinniburgh from the shadows. He went to visit the younger gangster on the night Alphonse was shot dead in his Templestowe home.

Police believe another man well known to both Gangitano

and Kinniburgh did the shooting, and that Kinniburgh ran to the front door, injuring his hand on the security mesh in his haste to throw it open. They say he then went upstairs to check the security video to see if there was any compromising evidence – a blood-spot from Kinniburgh was found in the area.

His occupation seems to be a mystery. When he was interviewed by police just over two weeks after Gangitano's murder, he struggled to remember how he paid the bills.

When asked by Detective Sergeant Gavan Ryan, of the homicide squad, what he did for a job, he responded: 'Occupation at the moment? It would be – I'm a – well, I'm still – I'm still – I'm still a rigger, I'm still a rigger, yeah.'

Rigging had been kind to The Munster. When police searched him outside the scene of Gangitano's murder he was carrying some change, keys, cigarettes and just over $3000 in $100 notes.

Kinniburgh told police Gangitano was on the phone when he arrived and asked him to leave while he had a meeting. The Munster said he went to get cigarettes and returned 30 minutes later to find Big Al dead.

Coroner Iain West said later: 'I do not accept Graham Kinniburgh's version of events, as I am satisfied he was present at the time the deceased was shot.'

He said Kinniburgh went to the convenience store to be filmed on the security camera 'thereby attempting to establish an alibi of being absent from the premises at the critical time.'

'… I am satisfied that both Graham Allan Kinniburgh and Jason Matthew Patrick Moran were implicated in the death.'

Jason Moran

MOST teenage boys have their heroes – footballers, basket-ballers and popular musicians – but Jason Moran had a different class of role model.

When gunman Brian Kane was shot in the bar of a Brunswick hotel in 1982, young Jason placed a respectful death notice in *The Sun,* to his 'Uncle Brian' from 'Your Little Mate.'

By the time young Jason finally graduated to the adult prison system, he was steeped in the culture and traditions of hard core crime. He knew he had to fight for his reputation and was prepared to bash anyone who got in his way.

One inmate who spent time with him remembers the new boy in the (shower) block would tell anyone who could be bothered listening that he was a force to be reckoned with. 'Do you know who the fuck I am?' he would declare.

If they didn't, they soon would.

Moran came from a crime family but he built his own reputation for violence, both inside and outside of prison. Around the inner-western Melbourne suburbs of Ascot Vale and Flemington, it was said that his father and uncle, Lewis and Tuppence Moran, considered Jason to have a psychopathic streak. The fact that he reputedly carried a handgun before he was old enough to drive might have had something to do with this view.

Regular drinkers at the Laurel Hotel in Ascot Vale were not shrinking violets, but they tended to give young Moran a wide berth when he was in one of his moods. He became a member of the so-called Carlton Crew, a group of young standover men who dreamed of being gangsters.

They dressed sharp and revelled in their gangster reputations and their connections with the Carlton Football Club, then a powerful force in football that has since fallen on hard times. Jason Moran's maternal grandfather was a legendary Carlton stalwart. Carlton is known as 'The Blues' and Moran and his crew had plenty of them, doing a fair impersonation of the ultra-violent droogs in the movie *A Clockwork Orange*.

Moran became a staunch ally of Alphonse Gangitano, the self-proclaimed De Niro of Lygon Street. The two became heavily involved in protection rackets, illegal gambling and violence.

Moran loved guns and had a vicious temper. He once followed a family friend into a pub toilet to stick a gun in his ear. He won the argument. He bashed a stranger with a wheel brace at a main street intersection because he believed the man had not used his indicator when passing.

In 1995, Gangitano was charged with the murder of another underworld identity, Greg Workman. Two sisters were the star witnesses but they changed their minds after Jason Moran persuaded them to look at things another way. He took them to a lawyer's office so they could recant their damning evidence against his associate, Gangitano. The sisters were later to leave Australia on a long holiday.

On December 19, 1995, Moran and Gangitano walked into a King Street bar and went mad. They left 13 people injured after using fists and cues to bash anyone in sight. They were both charged with serious assaults.

Moran was recorded on a police listening device saying he had to 'shower to wash the blood off' and 'to cut a long story short, I started it'. Moran and Gangitano's relationship was starting to fray. Moran was secretly taped saying of Big Al, 'He's a fucking lulu … if you smash five pool cues and an iron bar over someone's head, you're fucking lulu.'

On January 16, 1998, Gangitano was murdered in his

Templestowe home. Moran remains the prime suspect on a list of one. According to police intelligence, Moran was given a lift to Gangitano's home by a criminal associate and arrived unannounced.

Well-known gangster Graham 'The Munster' Kinniburgh was already in the house. Police believe there was an argument and that Moran pulled out a gun and fired four shots, hitting Gangitano three times.

Moran then was driven over the Westgate Bridge, the story goes, where he threw the .32 handgun into the Yarra River. It was never recovered.

When Moran was arrested over the King Street assaults, he suffered several fractures to his skull. A judge was later to comment that the police action appeared to be 'remarkably heavy-handed.'

He was jailed over the assaults and when he was released, the parole board let him fly overseas because of fears for his life.

His own lawyer, Andrew Fraser, was later arrested for cocaine use. While his offices were bugged, police heard a colleague ask Fraser who killed Gangitano.

He gave a one word reply: 'Jason'.

When Moran was interviewed by police over Gangitano's murder he feigned disinterest, yawned and refused to answer questions. He showed no signs of concern about his former friend. At the inquest into Gangitano's death, Coroner Iain West found that Moran's alibi was false and that he was in the house when Alphonse was murdered.

John Kizon

OF all the colourful characters in Australia's wild west, John Kizon is the best-known criminal figure, although he doesn't see it that way. He presents himself as just a misunderstood Perth businessman with a ponytail.

Kizon is to Perth what Alphonse Gangitano was to Melbourne and George Freeman to Sydney. Charismatic and seemingly bulletproof, they protested they were not crime bosses, yet seemed to enjoy their public notoriety.

Gangitano and Kizon even shared the same lawyer, bouncer-turned-courtroom brawler George Defteros, who graduated from working at the Croxton Park Hotel in Melbourne's tough northern suburbs, where he learned things not written in law books. Like Gangitano, Kizon a convicted heroin-trafficker, nightclub owner and entertainment promoter, claimed he was an honest man, falsely branded by courts, the media and police as a rogue.

His range of associates included the late crooked business-man, Laurie Connell, and Rose Hancock, whose daughter Joanna he once dated before she was mysteriously bashed and fled to England.

He was also close to two star West Coast players and was seen drinking with them at Crown casino. The players were advised to end the friendship but, months later, they were seen in Melbourne in the company of some of Kizon's closest friends.

One of Kizon's associates was Andrew Petrelis, a man who went into witness protection before being found dead in bizarre circumstances in Queensland.

Petrelis was given a new identity as Andrew Parker. A Perth policeman was later investigated for improper use of the police computer. Constable Kevin Davy quit after he was found to have breached security. In one instance he triggered computer traps after trying to gain access to records of 'Parker'. Davy later claimed he was an Elvis fan and checking any references to the singer's manager, Colonel Tom Parker. He did not explain why he expected the police computer would have a file on the long-dead American manager. No-one can recall Colonel Tom's Cadillac ever being picked up for speeding in the outback, mainly because he is thought never to have left the United States due to the lack of a passport.

Petrelis died of a drug overdose on September 11, 1995 – one month before he was to give evidence in a committal hearing. His body was found naked and with the needle stuck into one arm in a way that aroused speculation that he was a victim of foul play. Kizon and Michael Rippingale were later acquitted of cannabis conspiracy charges.

Kizon, originally from Fitzroy, was charged, and acquitted of punching a 15-year-old boy outside a Perth nightclub and breaking his jaw. He has maintained he has been harassed by police and that, although he has made mistakes in the past, he is now an honest businessman. In 2002 he was photographed with former US President Bill Clinton when the American was in Perth on a speaking tour. He was apparently under the impression that this would lend him some respectability.

Early on the evening of January 16, 1998, Kizon rang Gangitano from a Chinese restaurant in Perth. They talked about how the court proceedings had gone that day. Gangitano chatted easily and sounded confident. A visitor arrived in Gangitano's home during the brief conversation. It was his long-time friend, Graeme Allen Kinniburgh.

The phone call lasted less than 10 minutes. Kizon said he would ring back. He didn't get the chance. His mate was dead within the hour.

Mark Moran

THREE generations of Morans have knocked around in Melbourne criminal circles and their reputation was not earned with a pacifist philosophy.

But Mark Moran, 36, was always the apparent white sheep of the family, the one who stayed in the background and kept a low profile.

His natural father, Leslie John Cole, was ambushed and shot dead outside his Sydney home on November 10, 1982.

On June 15, 2000, Mark went the same way as his dad when he was shot dead outside his million-dollar home in the Melbourne suburb of Essendon. He was the latest victim in the underworld war that has claimed up to nine lives in Melbourne since January, 1998.

Within 24 hours of the murder, the homicide squad's Detective Inspector Brian Rix said police were receiving little help from the Morans. He then stated the obvious: that the shooting had 'all the hallmarks of an underworld slaying'.

'The indications are that he was out of his car at the time of the shooting, which means that perhaps his killers laid in wait,' Rix said.

Sometimes you can guess more from what police don't say. What Rix didn't mention was the reason why had Moran left his house for less than half an hour on the night he was killed.

He had gone to meet someone, but who?

Did the killer know Moran would go out and then come back that night?

It is fair to conclude that a killer would not sit outside a luxury house in an affluent street all night on the off chance the target would venture out. He had to have some inside knowledge.

So the real question became, who set him up?

As Rix said: 'Mark fancied himself as a bit of a heavy. I would think the underworld will talk about this to somebody, and I'm sure that will get back to us in some way.'

Moran left his home in Combermere Street, Aberfeldie, for just over 20 minutes. When he returned someone shot him as he got out of his late-model Commodore. The shotgun blast knocked him back into the car, killing him instantly.

It was no surprise when it became known that a Moran had been murdered. The surprise was that it was Mark and not his elder brother, Jason, the notorious gangster who was serving two years and six months over an assault in King Street, Melbourne.

While Jason Moran was seen as wild, violent and erratic, his younger brother was calmer and tried to keep a lower profile. 'Jason was out of control, Mark was the brains,' said one policeman who has investigated the family.

But as Jason became increasingly restrained by court action and stints in jail, his brother began to take a higher profile.

About 18 months before his death he took offence when an associate made a disparaging comment about a female relative.

'He went around to the guy's house, stuck a gun in his mouth, took him away and seriously flogged him,' a criminal source said.

In 1999, he was involved in the assault of a policeman at Flemington racecourse on Oaks Day – not a good business move.

About six months before his death the Moran brothers had a falling out with a father-son team that produced amphetamines. The dispute was over a failed speed lab. The dispute was handled with firearms. A women heard an argument in a Broadmeadows location followed by a man crying out, 'No, Jason.'

The result was that the son was shot in the stomach although he could not assist police to discover out how the bullet got there.

Detectives believe the Moran brothers claimed the father-son team owed them $400,000. They believe that Mark, not Jason, pulled the trigger.

On February 17, 2000, police noticed Mark Moran driving a luxury car. When they opened the boot of the rented vehicle, they found a high-tech handgun equipped with a silencer and a laser sight.

They also found a large number of amphetamine pills that had been stamped through a pill press to appear as ecstasy tablets.

The day after Mark's murder, police raided an associate's home, and seized another 5000 tablets similar to those found in the boot of the rental car.

Months before, Mark Moran had been ejected from the County Court after he tried to use a false name to get access to the plea hearing after his brother was found guilty over the King Street assault. AFL footballer Wayne Carey gave character evidence for Jason Moran, which was a case of history repeating itself. A high-profile Carlton footballer once gave character evidence for Moran's grandfather over a stolen property charge. Unsurprisingly, the property had been stolen and hidden at the grandfather's place by the teenage Moran boys.

Police said Moran was one of the new breed involved in drug trafficking known as the 'Bollinger Dealers', who associated with minor celebrities and the new rich.

They wore designer suits and used a pill press to stamp their amphetamine products to look like party drugs such as ecstasy.

Mark was a former professional chef and a 'gym rat' who was often seen at the Underworld fitness centre in Melbourne. He once listed his occupation as personal trainer.

But he had not worked regularly for years and police say his high-income lifestyle and expensive home could only have been supported through illegal activities. He refused to speak about business on telephones and rarely spoke with associates in his house because he feared he was being bugged by police.

He was proud of his fitness and physique and was described as 'extremely narcissistic'. He liked to be well-dressed and when he was shot, was wearing a huge diamond stud in his left ear.

Mark Moran was young, good-looking, rich and fit. But in the months leading up to his murder, he was depressed and at one point hospitalised when he told friends he was considering suicide. In the end, someone beat him to it.

The day before Moran's murder, police conducted a series of raids on a sophisticated amphetamines network and a number of criminals, including one known as 'The Penguin', were arrested.

One theory police are looking at is that someone connected with the network wrongly blamed Mark Moran for having informed on them to try to remove a competing drug syndicate.

A second underworld rumour was that the murder was a payback for Jason's alleged involvement in the death of Alphonse Gangitano and that Mark was considered an easier target because the dangerous Jason was in jail.

A third source suggested that a gangster had a personal grudge against Mark and that Moran was warned to back off. When he didn't, the gangster ordered the murder.

But the favourite early theory was it was a payback from the father-son team and certainly that was the one the Moran family seemed to believe.

However the favourites had alibis for the night. While this may have impressed the police it left associates of the Morans unconvinced. Within days of the murder there were reports of shots fired near the North Fitzroy family home of the main suspects. Some police were concerned for the welfare of a lawyer who regularly socialises with several members of the Moran family.

'It is not the right time to be taking sides,' a detective said after the funeral.

As has become an underworld tradition, the *Herald Sun* was filled with death notices to a 'lovely gentleman'. There were many from former league footballers including one from a former Carlton captain who fondly remembered them running a victory lap after a premiership in the 1980s.

There was one falsely placed under the nickname of a drug squad detective. Police suspect it was placed to give the appearance Moran was talking to police when he was killed.

The funeral was the usual procession of real friends, hangers-on and crims in black suits who refused to take off their sunglasses, even though it was a cold winter's day.

Jason Moran was allowed day leave from prison to speak at the funeral. Mourners said the brother spoke with real emotion but his death notice worried police. It read: 'This is only the beginning, it will never be the end. REMEMBER, I WILL NEVER FORGET.'

Because the funeral was going to choke local streets, a request was made for uniformed police to control traffic, but a senior policeman vetoed the plan. He didn't want media images of police holding up traffic for half of Melbourne's gangsters.

While Mark Moran had a low public profile, he had a long and violent criminal history. Career criminal Raymond John Denning once told an inquest Moran was one of three men involved in an armed robbery where a guard was shot dead.

He said the three men involved were Russell 'Mad Dog' Cox, Moran and Santo Mercuri.

The robbery occurred on July 11, 1988 in Barkly Square, Brunswick. Two armed guards were leaving a Coles warehouse with a cash tin when they were held up at gunpoint. A struggle followed and Dominic Hefti, 31, was shot in the chest and the leg. He died two days later at the Royal Melbourne Hospital.

Denning said the three men planned to kill a woman whose car Mercuri had stolen for his getaway. Denning said: 'It was decided among the three of them that they try to find her home address and knock her because she was the only one that Sam believed had identified him.'

Senior Sergeant Peter Butts, formerly of the armed robbery squad, said that when police later raided the Doncaster home of Russell Cox, they found that the page of the telephone book carrying the woman's name and address had been torn out.

The murder of Hefti sparked another spate of killings. Police wrongly believed armed robber Graeme Jensen was responsible and he was shot during an attempt to arrest him on October 11, 1988. The following day two police, Constables Steven Tynan and Damian Eyre, were murdered in Walsh Street as a payback.

Detectives on the case have also looked at another intriguing possibility. They have investigated a possible link between the murder of Mark Moran and the unsolved killing of Frank Benvenuto, who was shot dead in Beaumaris on May 8, 2000. The pair were known associates.

Benvenuto was the son of the former Godfather of Melbourne, Liborio Benvenuto, who was fortunate enough to die of natural causes on June 10, 1988.

Moran was killed with a shotgun, the preferred weapon in Italian payback killings. But he was also shot with a pistol, the weapon of choice for Australian gunmen. Either way, he's dead.

CHAPTER 16

Mystery Men

'Hop-a-long' Tom Ericksen

TOM Ericksen was a former insurance salesman with some nasty habits who knew the value of having the odds his way. That is why, as an underworld puppet-master he tried to keep hitman Christopher Flannery on his string.

Ericksen was the son of a policeman and, in the 1950s, he drifted into his father's circles selling insurance to police.

He used his easy manner to become friendly with his clients but later he left the insurance industry to become a private investigator and debt collector.

In his early years in the business, he had a contract with a major credit card firm to act as its repossession agent and he often employed young police as off-duty muscle. Years later, as the police were promoted through the ranks, he tried to use their previous loose business arrangements to his advantage.

One of his early scams, in the 1960s, was to set up a bogus attempted bombing of the Ivanhoe home of prominent defence lawyer Frank Galbally. Ericksen had been employed by Galbally to guard the house after threats were made. He exploited the situation to make headlines for himself (and Galbally) by 'scaring off' a supposed bomber who put a device under the house. What was not reported so widely a few days later was the police discovery that Ericksen had set up the whole thing.

In the 1970s, Ericksen employed another shadowy character, Gianfranco Tizzoni, in his repossession business. Tizzoni was the man who later helped organise the murder of anti-drugs campaigner Donald Mackay.

Both Ericksen and Tizzoni had letters of accreditation suggesting that they worked for the (now defunct) Federal Narcotics Bureau.

Ericksen had strong Libyan and PLO connections and claimed to have been in regular contact with Yasser Arafat.

He travelled the world, claiming to be an international diplomat. If queried he would produce a diplomatic 'passport' from the so-called 'Hutt River Province', a self-proclaimed 'nation' in Western Australia owned by an eccentric. Although neither the province nor the passport had any legal standing, the passport was questioned only once by a customs officer in Europe.

Ericksen was quietly spoken and intelligent. Many saw him as a Walter Mitty character and a pretender in the underworld. But he was a manipulator.

He was an informer for the Victoria Police bureau of criminal intelligence but his plan was always to suck out more information than he would give.

Police wanted him to inform on Flannery's activities, but Ericksen kept the hitman on the payroll.

The private investigator had to rely on brains, rat cunning and contacts to intimidate. He had one leg amputated and became known as 'Hopalong Tom'.

Ericksen always carried a gun and made sure he had ready access to killers. In 1983, he contracted Flannery to bash the then well-known discount book seller Chris Randle and his accountant at their Exhibition Street office.

He made it clear that Flannery was his pit bull and could be called on at any time. But when the hitman became fish food in 1985, Ericksen was dangerously exposed.

Ericksen had a love of electronic gadgets and he had his false leg wired to become an elaborate listening device.

He once bugged a lawyer's chambers in the hope of recording a compromising conversation with a senior policeman.

He was a first-class blackmailer and briber. He kept a so-called dirt file, where he recorded any scrap of information that could be used against police, lawyers or public officials. He attempted to establish relationships with crime reporters but, as usual, always wanted information rather than to provide any answers himself.

Hopalong Tom rarely did anything for nothing.

Shortly after he lost Flannery, he was shot at in South Yarra. It was the first sign that heavy criminals and senior police had tired of his games.

The man with one leg found it increasingly difficult to sit on the fence. Too old to change and too slow to run, he became the target of a police investigation code-named 'Viper'.

In 1988, National Crime Authority officers charged him with 195 counts of giving secret commissions (bribery) and 11 counts of making threats to kill.

On August 10 that year, he was due in court to answer the charges. He died earlier that morning, a 52-year-old blind diabetic, still protesting his innocence.

Ricky Renzella

RICKY Renzella is no Bart Cummings, but he is part of horse racing folklore, even if he has not been on a track for more than 25 years. Long before the notorious Fine Cotton scam there was the Royal School ring-in at the Casterton races in 1972.

A gambler and racehorse owner, Renzella switched the top city winner Regal Vista for a mediocre country horse, Royal School, in the Muntham Handicap. The stake money was only $325, but Renzella had taken doubles bets with Royal School and the field in the Casterton Cup. He won $33,000 – and, later, two years' jail. Others who helped with the scam were also prosecuted. It is rumoured in racing circles that many more winning TAB tickets were never cashed by people who were involved in the ring-in because they were afraid of being implicated.

Renzella was banned from race tracks for life and, when he was released from jail, it was natural that he became a used car salesman.

He was named in state parliament as being a dishonest car trader who wound back 'speedos' on cars and trucks in 1985. But an attempt to find him unfit to hold a licence in 1986 failed.

To police, Ricky was just another small-time, Runyonesque spiv, always looking for the short-cut to a big earn. Sick of tarting up rust buckets to sell, he decided it would be much more profitable to steal cars to re-sell rather than buying them.

In November, 1992, Gabrial Chase's two-year-old Toyota Landcruiser had been stolen. A week later, he noticed a used car advertisement for a car suspiciously similar to his own.

He went to a car yard in Mordialloc and saw his car, minus its number plates, for sale. He alerted the police and the stolen motor vehicles squad started an investigation. Detectives on the job wanted to code name it 'Ring-In' but were told to call it 'Cruiser.'

When they raided a workshop at the back of the car yard they found 11 Toyota Landcruisers in various states of alteration. The cars were stolen around Melbourne, the engine and chassis numbers were changed, they were given new wheels, re-registered and detailed to make them look 'as new'.

Ricky Renzella had graduated from race fixer to international car thief. Police found he had sold seven stolen vehicles, including a Mercedes and an 18-seater bus, to an agent in Nauru. In all, he had handled 57 stolen vehicles, mostly Landcruisers, with a value of around $1.5 million.

Renzella was grabbed when he returned from a trip to the Philippines. After being refused bail at the Magistrates Court, he was later freed by the Supreme Court.

In July, 1993, police received information that Renzella was back in business but a week-long surveillance operation came up with nothing.

In November, police tried again and, within four hours, they caught him red-handed after following his Mercedes to the car park at the Southland shopping centre. Police watched as he dropped off his partner, who stole a Landcruiser in less than 90 seconds.

Detectives found their factory in Highett. Inside were 25 Landcruisers being cut up and dismantled for spare parts to be sold through wrecking yards.

Ultimately, the Motor Car Traders Guarantee Fund repaid more than $500,000 to people who bought Renzella's hot cars, but many still found themselves out of pocket. Including Renzella's car thief. Renzella could not help himself. He had promised his car thief $1500 per car but ultimately refused to pay him. It was hardly a case for the Small Claims Tribunal. Renzella was a busy crook. Police found he was also growing a big hydroponic cannabis crop valued at about $1 million. The artificial lights above the crop were on rails and moved automatically, simulating the sun from dawn to dusk.

Police said Renzella and his team could turn a roadworthy Landcruiser into parts and scrap metal in less than 12 hours.

Detective Sergeant Martin O'Brien said Renzella 'would never get angry, he was very smooth. He was obviously a very good conman'.

A regular at the casino, he would normally carry between $1000 and $2000 cash. 'He likes to be seen as a high flier,' Detective Sergeant O'Brien said.

Defence barrister Nick Papas told the County Court after his client pleaded guilty to conspiracy to defraud that Renzella had been dogged for decades over the Royal School controversy.

He said Renzella found it difficult to get business loans and was constantly recognised as the organiser of the Casterton ring-in.

Judge Barnett sentenced Renzella to an extra six months on top of his jail term. His release date was set for January 1, 2001.

When Renzella was arrested, police found 13 TAB tickets in his pocket. Only one was a winner.

Some things never change.

Anthony Patrick Andrew Cairnes Berkeley Moynihan

ANTHONY Patrick Andrew Cairnes Berkeley Moynihan, the third Lord of Leeds, left England after a 'misunderstanding' over finances and fled to Australia – but he had no intention of making a new start. Moynihan was to be a mystery figure in the Australian underworld for 30 years and, even when he moved to Asia, he kept contact with major drug dealers.

He was described in 1980 by drugs Royal Commissioner, Justice Woodward, as a man with strong connections in the narcotic trafficking world.

'Lord Moynihan is a shadowy figure about whom I have learnt very little, other than he is an associate of a number of Australian drug traffickers,' Woodward wrote.

'Moynihan is, or was, in some way involved in, or assisting in, the importation of heroin from Manila.' He concluded that Moynihan must have had strong connections with some of Australia's biggest drug traffickers.

This view was supported by a NSW police investigation, which reported a roof-top meeting between the Lord and notorious Sydney crime syndicate leader and killer Arthur 'Neddy' Smith.

The dodgy peer – a former bongo player, actor, singer and journalist – fled England in 1970 after he was alleged to have bought a Rolls Royce with a rubber cheque.

Moynihan, whose mother was Australian, met Sydney crime figures when he was a drummer in the Chequers Nightclub. They were contacts he was to keep for the rest of his life.

He moved to Manila in 1980, when he suspected he was to be arrested by Australian Federal Police. In his new home, he was quick to set up a massage parlour network and a hotel with a questionable reputation. Australian criminals looking for a good time or a break from police surveillance always felt comfortable looking up 'Lord Tony'.

What they didn't know was that Moynihan was desperate to get back to England to sit in the House of Lords and he wanted to be able to pass on his peerage to his son, born in the

Philippines. He tried to cut a deal by becoming a secret informer to the US Drug Enforcement Administration. He had offered to be a National Crime Authority agent but, strangely, the approach was rejected.

He was able to help the DEA catch the world's biggest cannabis dealer, Howard Marks. The international operation resulted in the Marks network being exposed after operating for nearly 20 years.

Marks went to the Philippines on business and Moynihan tried to persuade the former Oxford University student to buy a local island to grow marijuana.

Moynihan named his best hotel suite 'The Marks Room' in honour of the drug dealer.

When Marks found that he had been betrayed by the Lord he told one of the authors from the North Dade Detention Centre in the United States that he found it impossible to hold a grudge against the man who betrayed him.

'I can't really blame Tony, actually. I'm not bitter. I blame myself for getting close to him. I am not surprised at what he did. Like a cornered rat he struck out. Who should I blame him for doing what comes naturally, or me for misjudging the situation?

'I am sure he got away scot free. He has no morals. He would do anything for money.'

Asked what he would do if he saw Moynihan, Marks said: 'I would insist that he bought the next round.'

He didn't get the chance. Moynihan died of a heart attack in November, 1991, in the Philippines. He never did get back to England.

Dennis Howard 'Mr Nice' Marks

DENNIS Howard Marks has never stepped foot in Australia, yet he has been a major influence on the local trade.

Marks was an Oxford graduate, part-time spy and the world's most famous marijuana smuggler. His charm is legendary. Even the investigators who pursued him around the world stress he was never involved in hard drugs or violence. He may have been a drug boss, but he was always a gentleman.

'Howard is an engaging, personable guy who makes people feel very comfortable with him,' according to US Drug Enforcement Administration investigator Craig Lovato, who chased Marks around the world.

The DEA once described Marks as the world's biggest cannabis dealer, and few would dispute the claim. At one stage he had links to 14 countries and had 113 known associates involved in selling marijuana on an unprecedented scale.

In a career spanning more than 20 years, he used sea-going tugs, freighters, giant rock concert speakers, ocean buoys and even US navy containers to move huge shipments of cannabis around the globe.

It all came unstuck in 1988, when he faced the prospect of spending the rest of his life in an American jail.

But fortune does seem to favour the brave, or the reckless. The audacious dope dealer was released on parole in 1995, having served just seven years. He moved to the Spanish island of Majorca and, despite his marijuana smoking, his lungs seemed to be substantially better than another well-known fugitive, Christopher Skase, who lived only a few blocks away until his death. But unlike Skase, Marks didn't run from the spotlight. He even stood for parliament on a pro-marijuana ticket in the 1997 British general elections. It all began with a few university chums who shared joints in the mid-1960s. Within a few years, they were a cartel known as 'The Enterprise', shifting mind-boggling (and mind-altering) amounts of dope across the world.

The son of a Welsh sea captain, Marks used his contacts, wit and charm to build a formidable operation. His key men were relatives or 1960s hippies. They were mostly smart, well-educated men, with no criminal records and mutual interests in dope, sex and rock and roll.

Marks was recruited by a former Oxford colleague, Hamilton McMillan, to be an agent for the MI6 intelligence agency and was used in a farcical attempt to infiltrate the Irish Republican Army.

In a classic double-cross, Marks managed to use his spy background as a cover for his lucrative drug dealings. Even when he was caught virtually red-handed in Britain in 1980 with a shipment of 15 tonnes of Colombian cannabis valued at $40 million brought across the Atlantic in an ocean-going tug, he built a bizarre and audacious defence.

He told the jury that as an MI6 agent he had been working for the Mexican intelligence service to infiltrate a drug cartel and that, far from being a big-time marijuana smuggler, he was a fearless anti-drug crusader. He even produced a dark and mysterious Mexican law enforcement agent to back his claims.

It was a ridiculous defence that even his own legal counsel said was doomed to fail. But it worked. Over his drug-dealing career he had 43 aliases. For years he was known as Albi (an anagram of bail). He planned to travel to Australia to discuss drug deals with a group of criminals but was refused entry under his real name because of a criminal conviction.

'A hundred years ago that would have guaranteed a trip to

Australia; now it was enough to prevent it,' he wrote in his highly entertaining autobiography, *Mr Nice*. By the late 1980s, Marks was ready to move to Taiwan and smuggle drugs into Australia when he was finally arrested.

At his peak he had up to 89 telephone lines and 25 companies around the world.

He had a string of boutiques, bars, recording studios and travel agencies. US police began to tap the phones and started the exhaustive process of building a case.

One of his most successful scams was to import drugs inside giant outdoor rock concert speakers from Paris to California via New York. To complete the cover Marks recruited four out of work musicians to arrive with the gear and pretend they were on a US tour. The band was given the perfect name – Laughing Grass.

Marks had connections with the IRA, the Mafia, the Japanese Yakuza, the Australian underworld, Nepalese monks, the Thai army, the Palestine Liberation Organisation, English peers, US martial arts experts and the murky world of international espionage, including the CIA.

His links included a series of big Australian drug dealers whom he met in the Philippines in the mid 1980s, in the company of one of the world's greatest rogues, former Sydney bongo player and British peer Lord Anthony Moynihan.

Marks became connected with an Australian criminal, known as 'The Boxer' who, police claim, made more than $20 million from marijuana. They dealt in tonnes, not kilograms, and both ran international travel agents as business fronts.

'The Boxer' bought a Sydney travel agency for $500,000 (and a subsidiary in Hong Kong) as a money-laundering front. The system worked easily.

The Asian connection would send false accounts to the

Sydney agency for group travel. The parent company then paid the fake bills with drug money and the transaction would appear legitimate.

Investigations into the syndicate were plagued by leaks and after the Australian connection of the world-wide syndicate was tipped off, it moved $8 million offshore in just six weeks. Investigators found that money was brought into a bank in garbage bags, cardboard boxes and backpacks.

Despite the huge profits Marks wanted to expand. According to the DEA, he paid $665,000 for a 30-metre fishing boat, the *Axel D*, to move cannabis around the world. This would enable his group to move massive amounts of marijuana to Australia, Canada, Britain, Europe and the United States. Australia was seen as a particularly soft target.

'It is a bit of a joke, really,' Marks said. 'You can take as much as you like into Australia any time you want and you have a high chance of being successful. The coast is so huge and there are no internal borders,' he told one of the authors.

As the stakes got higher Marks began to realise he was 'hot', that police were moving in. He was not addicted to the drugs he sold – but he was addicted to the rush of 'the deal'.

He had more money than he could ever use. He had boxes of it and a large number of legitimate investments. At one time he nearly collapsed with the effort of carrying $1 million in a suitcase in humid Hong Kong during a transport strike. Life can be cruel like that. Marks said police planted an electronic tracking device on the boat when it was searched in Australia. He knew he was under investigation but he didn't stop. It would cost him seven years in jail.

The *Axel D* was used to transport 30 tonnes of marijuana to a waiting market in Vancouver, Canada. A further 10 tonnes made its way to California via Mexico.

The crew dropped the tracking device in the sea of Pakistan in a floating package. It was designed to give the impression the ship was waiting to be loaded with hashish. The *Axel D* then headed to the coast of Thailand for 30 tonnes of cannabis ready to be loaded on the vessel from small fishing boats.

While Marks talked big, he didn't talk tough. He was prepared to be ripped off for millions rather than use violence. He would just move on to the next deal.

'It was just part of the business,' he said. 'You try not to take it all too seriously and keep a sense of humour.'

According to US law enforcement documents, Marks and his associates smuggled 25,000 kilograms of hashish and marijuana into New York in 24 separate deals between 1975 and 1978. They estimated the profit to be $48 million.

How much Marks made out of drug dealing is a matter of dispute. The DEA maintains he has a fortune hidden away. Marks says it has all been spent.

After years of investigation, the DEA found a huge safety deposit box in Hong Kong. A DEA agent said: 'When we opened it, there was just a jar full of dead flies. We thought that might be a message of some type.'

David McMillan, Michael Sullivan

DAVID McMillan checked out of the 'Bangkok Hilton' on a hot August night in 1996. As jailbreaks go, it was pure Hollywood.

No one had successfully broken out of Klong Prem prison in living memory, though some died trying.

McMillan, then 40, was sharing a cell with four Thais on the first floor of a two-storey block. He weakened the window bars with acid, broke them, squeezed through the tiny gap and lowered himself to the ground, using electrical flex.

He slipped past a conveniently sleeping guard, retrieved a hidden bamboo ladder, scaled the inner wall, cut barbed wire with wire cutters, crawled under razor wire and dropped to the other side. He then ran across open ground and scaled an outer wall topped with electrified cables, unharmed. Oddly, no one in the watchtowers saw him jump down, then swim across a stinking canal that forms a moat around the jail. He reached a waiting accomplice and was soon out of the country.

He was not a good advertisement for a private school education. Caulfield Grammar has produced its share of worthy old boys – lord mayors, leaders in business and bureaucracy, politics and the professions, respected members of rowing clubs, racing clubs and Rotary clubs. But even the best schools have wayward sons.

In Caulfield's case, there is the late Christopher Skase, who flew high, dreamed of being a film mogul, then fell to Earth, exposed as a flim-flam man, to die in disgrace in exile.

Then there is David Peter McMillan. AKA Westlake, Dearing, Poulter, Magilton, Rayner, Elton, Knox, Hunter and many more aliases.

Like the young Skase, McMillan was a dreamer and a schemer with an eye for the main chance, an ear for information and a head for figures. He was also a restless spirit drawn to the dark side. His undoing was that he succumbed to the worst of both impulses – the desire for fast money and the weakness for drugs.

McMillan – bright, ambitious and a heroin user – was in his early 20s when he got in on the ground floor of a growth industry as a drug trafficker. His version is that he was a harmless addict who subsidised his habit with a little gold and gemstone smuggling.

A jury almost believed him – acquitting him of all but one charge of conspiracy to import heroin – but the judge was not so sympathetic, sentencing him and two accomplices to 17 years. It was 1983. The trial of McMillan and his associates, former Olympic-standard athlete Michael Sullivan and a Thai national called Supahaus Chowdury, ran for almost six months, and it took the jury a record eight days to reach its 'little bit guilty' verdict.

It was, then, the longest and most expensive criminal trial in Victorian legal history – and, while the result must have disappointed McMillan, it didn't surprise him. Before the trial had begun, he had hatched an audacious plan to escape from Pentridge prison in a hijacked helicopter, the first leg of a plan involving disguises, an interstate truck ride, a sea-going boat and a light plane.

The police were tipped off and foiled what would have been another surreal episode in the existence of a man who lived his life as if it were a screenplay.

For someone who seemed charming, clever and generous, the young McMillan developed some bad early habits.

When he arrived at Caulfield Grammar in fourth form in 1971, the teenage McMillan didn't blend in. Born to an Australian expatriate couple who had worked in British radio and television before splitting, he had arrived in Australia as a child with his mother (and her new husband), his sister and younger half-brother, who was to become a well-known journalist.

At the end of fifth form, McMillan was told not to come back to the school. At 17, he was picked up for passing dud cheques and was already on a road leading to what a lawyer friend later wryly described as 'his *Midnight Express* life'.

McMillan devoured information he thought he could use. He was later to try forgery, disguise, fraud and smuggling but, at bottom, he was a con man. Everything else he did was based on his ability to befriend and to deceive.

When he visited Britain soon after leaving school, he served several months in Reading jail for offences involving forgery, false identities and fraud.

In 1979, McMillan, 24, was bursting with confidence. He had teamed up with Michael Sullivan, who had been a champion pole vaulter. Sullivan beat the Commonwealth medal winner when still a teenager, was the first Australian to clear 16 feet and qualified for the Mexico Olympics in 1968, but missed selection in favour of older competitors.

An ankle injury ended his career and started a depression that only heroin seemed to help. By the time he met McMillan, he was an addict dreaming of easy money.

McMillan perfected a way to beat the passport and airline ticketing system which, before computers, relied on manual filing. He applied for copies of birth certificates in the names of people who had died as children. Because there was no cross-referencing of births with deaths, these could be used to apply for passports once he had established other fake proof of identification material – student ID cards, credit cards and the like.

McMillan bought multiple sets of tickets in different names so he and his couriers, with multiple passports, could switch identities halfway through a trip.

The aim of this elaborate ruse was to present at Australian Customs at a busy time using passports with no sign of an Asian stopover of the sort that attracted attention.

Between March 1980 and April 1981, McMillan set up seven courier runs through Bangkok to Europe and back. It fell part when one of his 'mules' was a heroin addict so obviously drug-affected that he was detained and searched in Bangkok, and ended up dying in jail there.

If McMillan had retired then, he might have got away with it forever. He knew he was a marked man, but he didn't turn over a new leaf – just a new angle. At home in Melbourne, he used powerful radios and scanners to communicate secretly – and monitor police.

Meanwhile, a joint taskforce, code-named Operation Aries, was set up. Telephone taps and 'bugs' installed, and surveillance teams set loose. McMillan would brazenly double park his car in the city and wander around the streets, carrying a plastic bag full of cash, buying whatever took his fancy.

In November, a Thai courier brought in heroin hidden in ornate cutlery sets. McMillan and Sullivan knew they were being watched, but played on.

The Thai went to Mercy Maternity Hospital, with the cutlery boxes in a bag, and met McMillan in the foyer – sitting next to an undercover policeman. He knew police would be reluctant to open fire there. Suddenly, Sullivan drove into a lane near the foyer, McMillan and the Thai ran to meet him, and McMillan tossed the bag through the open car window. Sullivan sped off. McMillan walked off as police tried to chase Sullivan and the heroin.

Detectives raided McMillan's Beaumaris house at dawn on January 5, 1982. They found him and his girlfriend in bed, a packet of heroin, $8000 cash, scales, a grinder and other drug gear.

Next day, police took McMillan to a house he owned in Carlton and found a plastic bag with $69,930 sitting on a wardrobe – as much, then, as the house was worth. It helped explain why McMillan had such good information – he could buy it. Besides drugs and money, the detectives found something else – a list in McMillan's handwriting, naming every taskforce member.

While they had been watching him, he'd been watching them. A month later, McMillan's girlfriend Clelia Vigano and

Sullivan's de facto, Mary Escolar Castilo, died in a fire that Vigano and another prisoner apparently lit at Fairlea Women's Prison. But a coroner found later there was nothing to support the Vigano family's suspicions that the women were murdered.

Ten months after the Fairlea fire, police heard of the plot to spring McMillan and Sullivan from Pentridge by helicopter. Detectives traced a former British soldier who had been hired to land a helicopter on the prison tennis court, drop the escapers in a park, take them to a flat where make-up artists would disguise them, then hide them in crates to be trucked to Queensland, then go to the Philippines either by light plane or boat.

Police who re-enacted the scheme insisted it would have worked. It was based on a Charles Bronson thriller called *Break Out*. McMillan did his time easily; Sullivan didn't. Although sentenced to 17 years in 1983, McMillan got day-leave from jail by 1991 and was paroled soon after. He told family and his defence lawyer he was making plans for a fresh start. He was, but not the sort they imagined.

Just before Christmas, 1993, he was arrested in Bangkok after running from an airline clerk who questioned his passport. The passport was false, and there was half a kilogram of heroin in his luggage.

Three years later, he had made enough friends inside and outside prison to go out the window and over two walls.

Word filtered to Melbourne a few months later that he had been arrested on the Afghanistan-Pakistan border but somehow talked his way out of custody.

But not for long. All his life McMillan showed he was smart – but never smart enough to know when to quit.

On March 14, 2001, he was jailed for five years in Denmark. For drug trafficking, naturally.

Index

L

M

O

Bibliography

Alarcchi, Pino .... *Mafia Business*

Barry, Paul .... *Going for Broke*

Bottom, Bob .... *Connections*

Bottom, Bob .... *Connections 11*

Bottom, Bob .... *The Godfather in Australia*

Brown, Malcolm (Editor) .... *Australian Crime*

Dower, Alan .... *Deadline*

Eastwood, Edwin .... *Focus On Faraday and Beyond*

Freeman, George ...... *George Freeman, An Autobiography*

Goodsir, Darren .... *In The Line Of Fire*

Haldane Robert .... *The People's Force*

Haddow, Peter ..... *Jockey Smith's Last Stand. On Murder 2*
(Edited by Kerry Greenwood.)

Hickie, David .... *The Prince and the Premier*

Hickie, David .... *Chow Hayes, Gunman*

Jenkins, Bill (with Norm Lipson
and Tony Barnao) .... *As Crime Goes By*

Marks, Dennis Howard . . . . *Mr Nice – An Autobiography*
Noble, Tom . . . . *Untold Violence*
Noble, Tom . . . . *Walsh Street*
Pedley, Derek . . . . *No Fixed Address*
The Hunt For Brenden James Abbott
Moor, Keith . . . . *Crims in Grass Castles*
Smith, Arthur Stanley (with Tom Noble) . . . . *Neddy*
Silvester, John and Rule, Andrew . . . . *Underbelly*
Silvester, John and Rule, Andrew . . . . *Underbelly 2*
Silvester, John and Rule, Andrew . . . . *Underbelly 3*
Silvester, John and Rule, Andrew . . . . *Underbelly 4*
Silvester, John and Rule, Andrew . . . . *Underbelly 5*
Silvester, John and Rule, Andrew . . . . *Underbelly 6*
Silvester, John; Rule, Andrew
and Davies Owen . . . . *The Silent War*
Read, Mark Brandon . . . . *Chopper*
Read, Mark Brandon . . . . *Chopper 2*
Read, Mark Brandon . . . . *Chopper 3*
Read, Mark Brandon . . . . *Chopper 4*
Read, Mark Brandon . . . . *Chopper 9*
Read, Mark Brandon . . . . *Chopper 10½*
Richards, Mike . . . . *The Hanged Man*
Tame, Adrian . . . . *The Matriach*
Tippet Gary and Munro, Ian . . . . *Writing on Gravestones*
Wilson, David and Murdoch, Lindsay . . . . *Big Shots*
Wilson, David and Robinson, Paul . . . . *Big Shots 11*
Whitton, Evan . . . . *Can of Worms 11*